WHITEHORSE

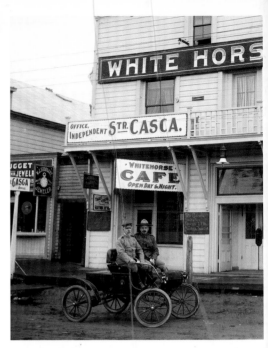

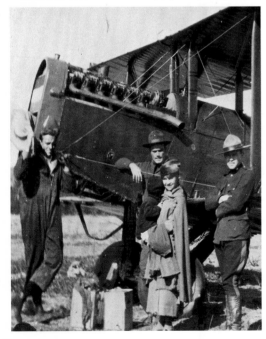

HELENE DOBROWOLSKY & LINDA JOHNSON

with

BOB CAMERON · JOHN FIRTH

MICHELE GENEST · TY HEFFNER · ROB INGRAM

MARILYN JENSEN · INGRID JOHNSON

WHITEHORSE

◄ AN ILLUSTRATED HISTORY ►

FIGURE 1 PUBLISHING *Vancouver*

Cataloguing data available from Library and Archives Canada
ISBN 978-0-9918588-6-6

Editing by Barbara Pulling
Copyediting by Peter Norman
Proofreading by Lara Smith
Jacket and text design by Peter Cocking
Front jacket photograph: Yukon Archives, E.J. Hamacher
fonds (Margaret and Rolf Hougen collection), 2002/118 #261.
Back jacket photograph: Courtesy Yukon Government.
Printed and bound in Canada by Friesens

Figure 1 Publishing Inc.
Vancouver BC Canada
www.figure1pub.com

CONTENTS

THIS PUBLICATION WAS made possible because of the leadership, support and shared memories of the hard-working volunteers who agreed to serve on the board of the Whitehorse History Book Society.

FOREWORD

A CENTURY IN THE making, forged in the rush for gold, rooted in the soil and rock that had been used by Southern Tutchone, Tagish and Tlingit peoples for thousands of years. The site was a place of plenty, a place of danger—from the black canyon walls and boiling white waters—and, once past the rapids, a place of rest. Tramways, then a railroad, steamboats, highways, more people and buildings, capital city status, incorporation: with all this colourful history and recent growth, it was time. Whitehorse was ready for its story to be written, before memories and records were lost and future generations could no longer trace the fascinating twists and turns, and all the people that created the marvellous city we see today.

In March 2011, a group of seven came together as the Whitehorse History Book Society. Art Christensen's daydream about a comprehensive History of Whitehorse gelled as an idea, and the idea moved into action: a registered charitable society that secured city, government, business, and community support. But action needed more than funding to become a reality. The gods were smiling upon us when we learned that both Linda and Helene were free to join the project as lead writers. More writers came on board to cover sports, culture, aviation, First Nations, the changing footprint of the city, the White Pass & Yukon Route and archaeology. Again, we were fortunate in finding the right people. By the nature of their craft, writers are loners, yet our lead writers used their exceptional talents to blend their own work with that of seven others into this one compelling story.

The best thing about this project was the fun and excitement each of us found in this adventure. I am very proud to have been a part of helping make Art's daydream a reality.

Through this book we offer the story of Whitehorse to younger generations and to readers everywhere. Here they may learn about the will and survival skills which were needed to exist in this faraway corner of North America, about the dreams and heartbreaks, all the successes and failures, and the many thousands of people who have walked these paths and left some small part of themselves for others to follow.

Thank you to my team, to our two lead writers, and to the subject specialists who wove different perspectives into the narrative. Thanks also to our editors and design team at Figure 1 for creating a truly magnificent book. Finally, thank you to all those who believed in us, who entrusted us with this task and generously supported us financially. Without you, there would never have been a book at all.

THE HON. IONE JEAN CHRISTENSEN, CM.
Chair, Whitehorse History Book Society

PREFACE &
ACKNOWLEDGEMENTS

WHITEHORSE IS A vibrant place with a rich history. From its earliest days as the site of ancient fishing and hunting camps, it became a busy port, the head of Yukon River navigation. Today, it is the Yukon's economic and political centre. The wilderness and its denizens are not far away, and the line between city and bush is blurry at best. Because many residents still spend much of their time on the land, the traditions of millennia continue to be part of everyday life. Whitehorse is a harmonious blending of wild and cultured, ancient and modern. Its story is one that captures the imagination.

As long-time Whitehorse citizens, proud Yukoners and historians, we were delighted when Ione Christensen enlisted us to work on the Whitehorse History Book project. We were fortunate in working with a highly qualified team of theme and topic writers. We are indebted to our hard-working and flexible contributors: Bob Cameron, John Firth, Michele Genest, Ty Heffner, Rob Ingram, Marilyn Jensen and Ingrid Johnson.

There are many to thank for their roles in the making of this book, and we've tried to list all of them in the credits section at the back. We would like to extend particular thanks to Kwanlin Dün First Nation and the Ta'an Kwäch'än Council for their generous support, including the sharing of images, Elders' memories and more. Frances Woolsey contributed eyewitness perspectives to our narrative and then did a sensitive reading of our drafts. Pat Ellis shared her experiences and research work of several decades. Yann Herry and Angélique Bernard, members of the Association franco-yukonnaise, brought our city's francophonie into focus. As was the case with many other projects, Yukon Archives was our primary resource and its staff an immense help. Jackie Pierce enthusiastically granted access to *Whitehorse Star* material at the Yukon Archives, while *Star* photographer Vince Fedoroff contributed many hours to image research, copying and identification. Our photographs came from many sources, but we are particularly indebted to early Whitehorse photographers E.J. Hamacher, James Y.C. Quong and Rolf Hougen.

We owe much to the board members of the Whitehorse History Book Society for encouragement, good advice and the wonderful stories they shared at our meetings. Ione, our fearless leader, wore many hats: fundraiser, project manager, publicist, cheerleader, host, historic resource and all-round inspiration. The team at Figure 1 Publishing—Chris Labonté, Barbara Pulling, Peter Cocking, Peter Norman and Lara Smith—were most helpful, professional and flexible. Thanks to our families, who put up with tight deadlines, marathon sessions of writing, compiling, editing and revising, and many conversations that began with: "Imagine what it would have been like living here when..."

For each of us, this often challenging project was made much more enjoyable by having a writing partner with whom to share the load, discuss ideas and identify gaps. We are happy to report that both our partnership and our friendship have survived and thrived.

HELENE DOBROWOLSKY *and* LINDA JOHNSON

PROLOGUE

RAVEN SOARS HIGH over the valley, sharp eyes trained on the sights below. Sunlight glows on cliffs of clay, foaming plumes at the rapids and jade-green canyon waters. Across what used to be wilderness, a great inflow of people, buildings, roads, farms, mines, dams and wires has spread over the past century.

Raven remembers this land when it was still covered by sheets of ice. As the glaciers melted, they left behind an immense lake that filled the valley. When the ice dam gave way, the glacial lake drained in a sudden rush. Its waters carved deep into the lake bottom, creating a bed for the turbulent new river that thundered over boulders scattered by the ice. Grasses began to grow on the land, and the caribou returned. With them came people. People were there when fish returned to the river and the nearby lakes. These early inhabitants survived eruptions of volcanic ash that drifted down from the skies for months on end, floods that changed the river's course, summer forest fires, harsh winter winds and icy cold. They persevered by harvesting the land's resources, using skills passed down through countless generations.

While Raven circles high above, Wolf pads silently through slender spruce trees to a bluff above the east riverbank. The whine of jet engines mingles with birdsong as Wolf stops near a group of grave fences and howls. Wolf recalls hunting buffalo on grassy plains in the hills above the valley. Later, trees grew to cover the hills. Moose and elk moved into the area already occupied by caribou. A century ago, Wolf used to hunt in a pack near the big river, but the noise and lights of the new town drove away big animals. Wolf watches cars roll across the bridge, signalling the start of a new day in Whitehorse.

Creatures of this land and its mythology, Raven and Wolf have populated the stories of people in this valley for thousands of years. While this bustling city is very much part of today's world, it continues to be strongly rooted in the land and its traditions. The history of Whitehorse is one of adaptation and change, of resilient and hardy people in a harsh yet beautiful land. This is the story of the place, the people and the events that created this modern city in the wilderness.

FACING The Yukon River valley at Whitehorse, looking south, 2011.

xi

WHITEHORSE IS A modern, bustling city with amenities to rival much larger places in the south. But you only have to look around at the bared rock of the mountains and the thin soils over glacial gravels to feel the immediacy of the geological forces that created this valley.

Two things in particular make Whitehorse special. The place: a beautiful valley where a convergence of geology, a mythic and powerful river, and an abundance of resources have attracted everyone from ancient peoples to recent immigrants. The people: a parade over the centuries of hunters and fishers, traders, miners, entrepreneurs, community-builders, sports icons, artists, families and that special breed of northerner, best known as "the Colourful Five Per Cent."[1]

While its geological features are plain to see, Whitehorse bears few signs today of ancient human occupation. Early trails, campsites and stone quarries date back several millennia, but the town's oldest buildings are barely a century old. The diversity of the past century is illustrated by gravesites that memorialize family members of Southern Tutchone, Tagish Kwan, Tlingit, French, Scandinavian, English, Scottish, Japanese, German and many other linguistic and national origins. All are knit together by a common thread—lives lived in this valley.

The geography of the valley and its surroundings has had a powerful influence on the animals and people who live here. As the landscape evolved, so did the creatures that populated it and the people who depended on the plants and animals. The very rocks that underlie the earth were in large part responsible for the establishment of the early fish camps and then the town.

FACING The *Whitehorse* and the *Klondike* tied up at the Whitehorse riverfront, ca. mid-1940s.

CROW BRINGS LIGHT
TO THE WORLD

Common Raven.

Fɪʀsᴛ ɴᴀᴛɪᴏɴs people have a wealth of oral traditions to explain the beginning of the world, most involving Raven as a trickster whose exploits created the land, the animals and the people. This complex series of stories has been passed on continuously since Kwädą dá ghàłan (which means "ancestors" in the Southern Tutchone language) times.[2] Many Yukon First Nations people use the English name "Crow" for the Raven when telling stories. This misnomer was probably introduced in early exchanges between Yukon aboriginal people and English-speaking newcomers.

Kàdùkikh, whose English name was Kitty Smith, was born around 1890 in the southern Yukon. Steeped in the traditions of her Tagish mother and Tlingit father, she was a fluent speaker of her ancestral languages as well as English. Smith often narrated the stories about how Crow created the world as it is today. The opening narrative of the story cycle recounts Crow's adventures in bringing light to the world. First he tricked the wealthy man who owned the sun and the moon into thinking Crow was his grandson; then he begged the old man to let him play with these treasures. Once he had them, Crow escaped through the smoke hole in the wealthy man's longhouse and flew to the river, where his friends Fox and Bear were fishing. Smith continued the story:

"I'm going to make daylight, you people.
 Just quiet now," he said.
"Aw, you got no light, you got no sun,"
    they tell him.
 He's got them now!
"What do you think I'm going to do?
 The best way, I'm going to throw it in the sky.
 It's going to stay here."
 He throws that moon the first time.
"Stay there for good," he said.
 After that, he pulled out that sun.
 He threw it, too.[3]

WARM SEAS, OOZING LAVA AND ICY LAKES

Grey Mountain.

Settled in a river valley amidst rolling hills and rounded mountains, the landscape around Whitehorse seems very old and unchanging. Geological forces that shaped the valley and nearby mountains were persistent and incremental, however, even if their sum seems a dramatic act of nature. Evidence of these forces is all around us.

To the east, Canyon Mountain (commonly called Grey Mountain) dominates the skyline. The light grey limestone formed as reefs in a warm, shallow ocean about 225 million years ago. The beds of coral exposed on Grey Mountain and Lime Peak are rare—reefs of this age are found in only a few places today. The tectonic convergence of a chain of volcanic islands closed this ocean about 170 million years ago and raised the mountain. The mountain eroded, gradually burying the reefs beneath layers of sand and gravel. These sediments turned to rock, and the later folding and shearing destroyed much of the fossil record. Much more recently, glaciation sculpted the mountain into its rounded form, and freeze-thaw cycles created surface cracks. These were enlarged by rain and groundwater dissolving the limestone and leaving crevices and shallow caves.

Eighteen kilometres (eleven miles) south of present-day downtown, the silhouette of Golden Horn Mountain resembles a conical volcano, but it actually consists of sedimentary rock. Near the base of the mountain, however, is a vent

Kwanlin, or Miles Canyon, in June 1887. This is likely the very first photograph of this site, taken by William Ogilvie when he was travelling downriver as a member of the Canadian Yukon Expedition.

from which basaltic lava seeped in pulses and flowed downhill across the valley floor between 8.4 and 6 million years ago.

Miles Canyon is six kilometres (three and a half miles) upstream from downtown Whitehorse. It was formed after the last Ice Age as the Yukon River cut through the glacial deposits and reached the ancient lava beds. While these lavas were cooling, vertical shrinkage cracks developed. As the new river flowed overtop, columnar pieces were plucked out, creating the slot-like canyon.

Downstream from Miles Canyon, the river flowed across several ledges where lava flows protruded from the riverbed. Yet farther downstream, the river boiled and swirled over a series of basalt flows and boulders left by the glaciers to form the famed Whitehorse Rapids.

Like a string of beads stretching 30 kilometres (19 miles) along the west side of the valley, a series of mineral deposits comprise the Whitehorse Copper Belt. The concentrations of iron and copper formed where magma intruded into a belt of limestone about 110 million years ago. Heated groundwater percolating through underground fissures reacted with the limestone to precipitate metallic

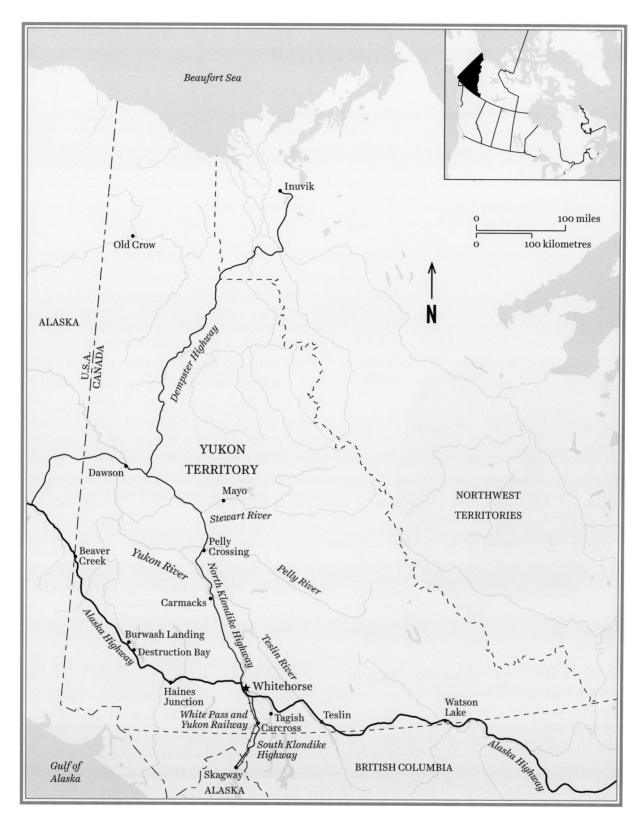

Location of Whitehorse within the Yukon Territory, Canada

As the glaciers of the last Ice Age expanded 40,000 years ago, the shallow sea between eastern Russia and Alaska disappeared. A large, ice-free area, 3,200 kilometres (2,000 miles) wide, extended from the Kolyma River in Siberia to the Mackenzie Mountains in Canada. The Beringia subcontinent, hemmed by glaciers to the west, east and south, was arid and cool, supporting tough grasses, herbs, dwarf birch and willow that fed woolly mammoth, steppe bison, horse, camel, caribou and giant beaver. The grazers in turn were food for predators like the giant short-faced bear, American lion and scimitar cat.

Bornite is a copper rich ore found in the Copper Belt. This colourful copper sulphate is known as "peacock ore."

minerals. These deposits have been exposed by erosion of ten kilometres (six miles) of overlying rock.[4]

During the Ice Ages (14,000 to two million years ago), glaciers more than one kilometre (3,300 feet) thick filled the entire Whitehorse valley so that only the tips of the tallest peaks, such as Mount Granger, east of Fish Lake, remained like islands above the ice sheet. As the ice melted (10,000 to 14,000 years ago), the meltwater formed huge lakes, dammed behind lingering ice and gravel barriers that gradually weakened.

Called pro-glacial lakes, these valley-filling expanses rose and ebbed according to the blockages and types of land, which became their outlets. One of the earliest was post-glacial Lake McIntyre, which filled the Fish Lake valley to a level 120 metres (400 feet) higher than the present lake level. Post-glacial Lake Laberge formed about the same time, flooding the upper Yukon River valley. Later it merged with post-glacial Lake M'Clintock, which inundated the valleys occupied by Marsh and Tagish Lakes today. The large lakes of the southern Yukon are vestiges of these huge post-glacial lakes, and Lake Laberge continues to shrink today from the south end (Mud Bay, Shallow Bay) as the moraine dam at its northern outlet is gradually eroded. At the site of Whitehorse, glacial-lake-bottom sediments, at a level higher than that of the present valley, formed terraces—the runways for the Erik Nielsen Airport were built on one of them. The clay cliffs rising above downtown Whitehorse resulted from the modern Yukon River cutting down through the soft lake-bottom sediments.

Looking south at T'si̇ Ma (Golden
Horn Mountain), Mount Sima ski
hill and the tailings of the former
Whitehorse Copper Mine.

A rendition of pro-glacial Lake Laberge and pro-glacial Lake M'Clintock.

After the ice had melted and the huge post-glacial lakes had partially drained away, the land around Whitehorse was dry and barren. Without trees or vegetation to hold the loose sediment, the wind scoured some areas and created large dunes in others. As the soil built up and the climate warmed, shrubby plants and grasses took root about 10,000 years ago, offering cover and food for animals. Soon trees began to grow. Caribou and bison herds moved into the new grazing territory, and people followed the herds from the ice-free lands to the north, called Beringia.

Although the glaciers are now gone, pockets of buried ice remain beneath dense forest, in shadowed valleys and on steep north facing slopes. This permafrost (ground frozen for more than two years) inhibits tree growth because their roots cannot penetrate it. In contrast, the thick, insulating vegetative mat supports plants such as Labrador tea and cotton grass that thrive on the poor drainage. Seasonal freezing and thawing cause permafrost lenses to swell and shrink, wreaking havoc on roads and house foundations.

GREAT RIVER

KWÄDĄ DÁ GHÀŁAN:
ANCESTORS

Elders today speak of their ancestors living in this region for a very long time, saying, "We have always been here."[5]

Archaeological evidence suggests that hunting cultures moved southward from the ice-free lands of Beringia, with people living in the highlands surrounding glacial Lake Laberge beginning around 8,000 to 9,000 years ago.

Later, hunters and gatherers harvested bison, caribou, moose and sheep; fished in the lakes, rivers and streams; and gathered plants and berries in season. They followed a seasonal round, moving from place to place to find needed resources, adapting to many changes in climate and landscape, and passing down their skills and knowledge to future generations over long periods of time. Archaeological research points to several different cultures inhabiting the Whitehorse valley over the millennia. Each culture had distinctive hunting technologies and tools, which help to identify adaptations to changing conditions.

The Canyon City archaeological site reveals evidence of people fishing and hunting in the area approximately 2,500 years ago. The stone tools uncovered at this site, including skin-scrapers, sharpened flakes and spear points, indicate that people regularly camped there, perhaps during salmon runs or to intercept caribou and moose crossing the river. The site would have been an ideal base camp for sheep-hunting on nearby Grey Mountain as well. The presence of obsidian from northern B.C. indicates that the people were linked to long-distance aboriginal trade networks. Archaeological findings at Fish Lake and Lake Laberge support the oral history record of long-ago occupation and use of these areas.[6]

The pre-contact inhabitants of the valley lived in the large area bounded by Marsh Lake to the south; Lake Laberge and the Yukon/Teslin River confluence to the north; Kusawa and Fox Lakes to the west; and present-day Livingstone,

THE WHITEHORSE valley is home to a large human population because of the Yukon River. In earlier times, it was a summer travel corridor and rich fishing resource. Even its name is apt: the English name Yukon, used by early Hudson's Bay traders, was adapted from the Gwich'in word for "Great River." The Ta'an Kwäch'än referred to the Yukon River at Whitehorse as Chu Nii Kwan, a Southern Tutchone name meaning "shining water."[7] Its green colour comes from the glacial silts carried in the current. The most southeasterly source of the Yukon River is an outlet stream from Llewellyn Glacier in northwest British Columbia, less than 25 kilometres (15 miles) from Pacific tidewater. This stream enters Atlin Lake, one of the five great headwater lakes. The river then flows over 3,300 kilometres (2,000 miles) through the Yukon and Alaska to the Bering Sea. Its tributaries large and small comprise the fourth-largest drainage basin in North America.

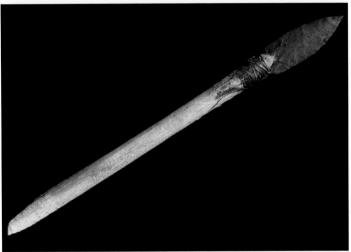

Winter Crossing and M'Clintock River to the east. The people who occupied this area around 250 years ago were the ancestors of present-day Tagish and Southern Tutchone people in the Whitehorse region. Extensive oral traditions vividly portray a way of life that persisted until recently.

This large territory provided the necessities of life throughout the annual cycle of fishing, hunting and gathering. People moved from place to place according to the seasonal availability of resources. In summer, they travelled on foot with pack dogs and navigated rivers and lakes with skin boats, canoes and rafts. In winter, they used snowshoes, dogs with packs, and moose- or caribou-skin sledges. The Whitehorse valley and surrounding lakes, rivers, hills and mountains were home to a vast array of flora and fauna. Elders refer to the land and the waters as their "pantry," a source of food, medicines and tools.

In summer, the people were surrounded by fragrant, multi-hued flowers such as wild roses, prairie crocus, lilies and the ubiquitous magenta fireweed. Bear root (*Hedysarum alpinum*), mushrooms and other plants were eaten fresh or dried. Strawberries, raspberries, soapberries, blueberries and lingonberries (commonly called lowbush cranberries) were picked fresh in season and dried or frozen for later use. Several types of moss, shrubs, sagewort grasses and sedges grew in forests, on riverbanks and on dry slopes and were harvested for medicinal and other needs.

Fish was a staple food, with burbot, grayling, inconnu, lake trout, ling cod, northern pike, and whitefish available at various lakes and creeks. In winter, people fished through the ice on the lakes; in spring, as the ice cleared, they set nets or lines and hooks. In late summer, king (Chinook) and dog (chum) salmon migrated from the Pacific Ocean up the Yukon River all the way to Marsh Lake. The salmon returned to spawn in the tens of thousands every year, providing a dependable, abundant source of protein and fat for people living through long, cold winters.

In fall and winter, men hunted sheep, moose and woodland caribou in the higher hills and mountains with spears, snares, deadfalls and bows and arrows. Other food staples included Arctic ground squirrel (commonly called gopher), snowshoe hare, porcupine, and other small game, which were snared and trapped with deadfalls or shot with bow and arrow. Animals trapped for fur included gopher, fox, beaver, marten, lynx, wolf and coyote. The lakes in the Whitehorse and Marsh-Tagish Lakes area were excellent for muskrat. Nothing from the hunt was wasted, with hide, bone and sinew fashioned into knives, scrapers, clothing, footwear and many other ingenious items.

In spring and fall, migratory birds such as ducks, geese, swans and cranes provided meat and prized feather down. Some birds were rarely eaten, enjoyed instead for their sociable chatter; these included ravens, chickadees and grey jays. In spring, songbirds such as robins and bluebirds signalled the return of longer days and warm sunshine. Bald eagles and hawks soared in the skies, while owls hooted from the trees.

Lodgepole pine was the most prevalent tree species in areas scoured by cyclical forest fires. Other species included balsam poplar, aspen, subalpine fir, birch, white and black spruce, and many varieties of willow. People used long, thin poles and roots harvested from pine, spruce and other species to construct shelters covered with hides and chinked with moss. These temporary homes were light and portable, easily assembled and quickly taken down, to move to new camps. The many species of willow were used for bows, arrows, fire sticks and building material. In fall, vast stretches of aspen, birch and poplar turned a luminous gold with the onset of cooler days and longer nights, while dwarf birch and blueberry turned the mountainsides deep red.

FACING TOP Microblades from Fish Lake. These were used like disposable razors, often attached to handles to make knives or other cutting implements. They were used from about 5,000 to 8,000 years ago.

FACING BOTTOM LEFT A multi-edged scraper found in the M'Clintock River area near Whitehorse. This tool is made of obsidian (volcanic glass) derived from Mount Edziza near Telegraph Creek in British Columbia (a distance of 375 km). It has been radiocarbon dated to 600 years ago.

FACING BOTTOM CENTRE Atlatl dart foreshaft made of birch wood with a chert point attached with sinew. This dart foreshaft was preserved in an ice patch in the Alligator Lake area near Whitehorse. It has been radiocarbon dated to 4,500 years ago.

FACING BOTTOM RIGHT Distal fragment of a chalcedony (flint-like stone) projectile point dating to the mid-Holocene period found in the McIntyre Creek area of Whitehorse. This point was likely used to arm an atlatl dart.

Elders today point to a myriad of trails used by their ancestors, many still visible and extending to locations far to the north, east, south and west. These footpaths connected seasonal harvesting areas, communities and trading groups. Whitehorse lies directly between Marsh Lake and Lake Laberge, where a long-used trail skirted the river, Miles Canyon and the rapids. The trail was used for centuries as the main transportation route for the Tagish Kwan and Southern Tutchone people, who travelled between Marsh Lake and Lake Laberge and points farther on, to trade and to visit relatives. Fish Lake was an important seasonal camping place and has been used for generations, perhaps for as long as 9,000 years.

Oral traditions suggest that no one stayed year-round on the flood plain at the base of the Whitehorse Rapids. The area was windy and much less attractive than campsites on the big lakes to the north and south, which had plentiful fish in summer and winter, along with gophers, hares and other small animals, plus caribou, moose and sheep in the surrounding hills. People visited the rapids and the canyon to fish in summer. Their ancient occupation of the area lingers in the Southern Tutchone names: Taqadji, for the fish camp used by the Tagish Kwan in the area of the canyon, which they called Kwanlín, and the name of the river itself—Chu Nii Kwan (shining water).[8]

These societies were based on oral traditions; their histories were told and preserved in their stories and songs, including celebrations, narratives of heroes, lessons for living well and accounts of the wonders of other worlds and other beings. Stories passed down to present generations tell of the creation of the earth and how Crow set the sun and moon into their cycles and places in the sky, along with explanations of many other mysteries. Spirits and spiritual essence abounded, providing connections to the ancestors and the flow of life.

WINTER CAMP AT TÀA'AN MÄN (LAKE LABERGE), 4,000 YEARS AGO

Everyone slept a little late this morning. The sky was clear but dark, the air bitterly cold. Sunrise painted the snow-covered hills in pastel pinks and blues. Camp had been set up here for two weeks, on the lee side of a low ridge set back from the windy expanse of frozen Lake Laberge: two brothers and their wives, their elderly mother and the older brother's two children. The younger couple were expecting their first child. The fire had died down overnight, and the hide-covered tent was cold compared to the warmth of their buffalo blankets. The younger women rose to stoke the central fire, then prepared a breakfast stew of meat flavoured with rosehips and cranberries picked frozen the day before. Sipping Labrador tea, they joked as they waited for the others to be enticed by the warm fire and the aroma of stew.

After breakfast, the brothers prepared for a multi-day bison hunt on the Takhini Flats to the south. In fall, they always harvested the massive bison after the rut, when the animals were less dangerous but before the herds split up. The late-summer caribou hunt had been productive in the alpine. Although they had a good supply of food, everyone was eager for something fresh after weeks of eating tough, dried meat. In winter, bison travelled in small groups, so hunting was more time-consuming. Their father had shown them a place at the edge of the forest where bison fed on grass and shrubs under light snow cover. If they could spook one or two animals into the open meadows, they could run them down in deeper snow using their long snowshoes. They said their goodbyes and headed down the trail.

After breakfast, the two younger women left to set fishnets below the lake ice in a spot they had covered to prevent it from freezing too deeply. The oldest child helped them place snares for hare and ptarmigan in the willows along the shore. Grandmother tended the fire and prepared lunch while minding the younger child. The two women returned to camp for lunch, checking their nets and snares again before dark. Hare were scarce this year, but there were ptarmigan, and the nets would yield pike and burbot. The group expected to remain in this location for another week or two before moving their camp to the other end of the lake.

High bush cranberry (*Viburnum edule*).

SUMMER FISH CAMP AT GÉIS TÓO'E' (KING SALMON/M'CLINTOCK RIVER), 800 YEARS AGO

IT WAS a cool, clear morning, with frost glittering on the grass and bushes. People had come from all directions to the mouth of Géis Tóo'e' (King Salmon, now M'Clintock River) to harvest and dry salmon for the coming winter. After the summer harvest of pine cambium and berries, people travelled here in mid-August over ancient trails or in skin boats from connecting lakes. Soon everyone within a few hundred kilometres had arrived. August was a good time of year, with the days still long and warm, and the cool nights and drier weather reducing the number of pesky mosquitoes. Summer was a time of plenty, and spirits were high as people gathered to visit and exchange news. There was work to be done, but it was collective work, and that allowed for much fun and laughter.

Salmon had been especially abundant in recent memory, and this year was no exception. The fish-drying racks were nearly full now, and only a few groups still worked the weir to trap fish in a shallow section of the river. The weir was very effective: a willow pole fence blocked the fish moving upstream and guided them into large, conical pole spruce traps. These were pulled out of the water at night, allowing fish through to spawn, ensuring a successful fishery every year. The older children tended the traps and carried fish to shore, where their sisters and mothers cleaned, cut and then hung the fish to dry. Small children shooed the jays and ravens away from the drying fish while elderly women cooked for the busy group. Between meals, they used stone scrapers to work caribou hides stretched between the trees. Once people's summer brush lean-tos became too cold, these hides would be draped over bent pole tent frames, creating comfortable winter homes.

The previous evening, migrating geese had been heard overhead. Now, as the sun set on the golden hillsides, more geese circled the lake in search of an overnight stop. Four older boys were sent out early the next morning, creeping along the shore to hunt the flock of geese before they flew away. The boys returned just before noon with three birds, along with several hare that had been caught in snares. These would be welcome additions to the evening dinner.

Several young men busily prepared for a hunting trip they would make to the mountains the following day. Two older boys assisted, eager to make this trip for the first time. They hoped to marry next year and move in with their wives' families, who expected them to be proficient hunters. Caribou clustered on alpine ice patches in late summer. The men found they could approach the animals using rock blinds or natural boulder cover and shoot almost undetected with bows and arrows. Despite dwindling caribou numbers in recent years, they expected to get enough animals to supply the camp with meat, along with hides, which were prized for making clothing.

That evening, everyone gathered around a central fire. It was time for entertainment. Children called out their favourite songs and stories; then, as the evening wore on, they fell asleep while adults discussed the events of their day and made plans for the next. The days were growing shorter—soon everyone would leave for their fall hunting camps and make preparations for the coming winter. Everyone was already looking forward to the next summer's gathering and its time of plenty.

TOP LEFT Crocus (*Anemone patens*). The harbinger of spring in Whitehorse, the crocus emerges first on dry, sunny hillsides while the snow is still deep in shaded areas.

MIDDLE LEFT Creeping Juniper (*Juniperus horizontalis*). Covering hillsides throughout the White-horse area, this fragrant shrub bears fruit that smells very much like gin.

TOP RIGHT Fireweed (*Epilobium angustifolium*). Named for the fact that it is one of the first flowering plants to come up after a forest fire, its fall foliage also looks like the fire itself.

BOTTOM Lowbush cranberry or, more properly lingonberry (*Vaccinium vitis-idaea*).

SUMMER CAMP AT ŁU ZIL MÄN (WHITEFISH LAKE), 250 YEARS AGO

IT WAS just past midsummer, and plants and berries were at the height of ripeness. The long days were marked by warm, sunny weather and an occasional shower, with only a hint of cooler days to come. High above what would later be the site for Whitehorse, a group of people were camping. They had come from several different areas to meet at Łu Zil Män (Whitefish Lake) to harvest the plentiful łu zil (whitefish). The babies, small children, older children, grown siblings and grandparents were all related by blood or marriage.

Early the previous day, several men had harvested a moose on the hillside south of the lake. Now came the work of preserving the meat and the hide. Some people headed to the kill site to begin cutting and preparing the meat to be transported across the lake in a skin boat. Others stayed at the main camp to watch over the cooking of the moose head and the fragrant stew bubbling in the moose stomach suspended above a fire. Younger children tended the fire carefully so that the stew and the moose head wouldn't burn, ensuring a feast of delicacies by day's end. The moose brains would be used to tan the moose hide.

Once the meat arrived, much of it was cut into strips and hung to dry on a frame of strong aspen poles built in a dry, breezy location near camp. A constant smoky fire underneath kept away flies and gave the meat a tasty flavour. The meat was turned frequently to ensure uniform dryness; later it would be packed away in moose stomach "storage bags" and kept for many months. The dried meat was light and easily transported for use during winter months, eaten dry or cooked in hearty soups and stews. The rest of the fresh meat was roasted on spits or tripods for immediate consumption. The cracking of large bones for their delicious marrow was left to the men with experience in harvesting this much-anticipated treat.

The moose skin had been carefully separated from the carcass of the animal. The process of readying the hide for tanning began almost immediately, with special tools used for fleshing and dehairing. Only the sharpest of bone and stone knives would work for this exacting task. Tanning the hide required many weeks, as each stage depended on plenty of clear water, special brain "soap" and overnight frosts. Once the hide was tanned and smoked, it would be made into moccasins, clothing, babiche string and rope. Other parts of the animal contributed a wealth of other necessary goods: sinew for net-making and sewing thread, bones for fleshers and scrapers, and hooves for rattles used in beaver snares.

The families camped here had been fishing for several weeks. They used sinew nets, scoop nets, fish lines and hooks to bring in the fat, succulent whitefish and trout. Being precise with the timing and location of their net-setting would ensure a successful harvest. The fish would be cooked and eaten fresh, with more fish dried to last through the long winter. Whitefish heads, eggs and stomachs all provided delicious food.

Along the hillsides to the west, women led children to the best berry-picking spots. In early summer, the raspberries along the trail provided a sweet but fleeting treat; they were often eaten as they were picked. Soapberries, cranberries and moss berries were harvested in large quantities at summer's end and "put up" to enjoy through the

Fish Lake and Bonneville Lake.

cold winter months. Mixed with rendered moose fat and stored in cool underground caches, they were perfectly preserved until needed.

In addition to the good fortune of the moose kill, the long summer days brought an abundance of other animals to harvest and preserve, including porcupine, gopher, squirrel and grouse. Hides and feathers contributed to household and clothing needs. This time at the lake also gave the men an opportunity to replace their old spear points and knives. They made new ones by knapping the shale from the stone quarry on the western shore of the lake.

As the families lived and worked together, they collectively taught the little ones how to do all the work of surviving on the land. Evenings were filled with stories of Crow, Wolf, Beaver, Porcupine and heroes of ages past. As a special treat, a drum was brought out. Much laughter accompanied stories of adventures or silly mistakes. After a full day of work, people found their beds beneath a roof of light caribou skins or woven spruce branches. Once word came that salmon had arrived in the river a few miles below, they would move camp to take advantage of the wealth of fish coming in over the month-long runs. Later in the fall they might return to Łu Zil Män to hunt moose, caribou and sheep in the surrounding hills.

But for now they slept. This summer had been a good one for the families. They had preserved a healthy surplus of food for an upcoming feast, when they would honour loved ones and share their bounty, stories and songs with more distant relatives.

Archaeologist Greg Hare speaks with Elder Julia Joe at the Canyon City archaeological dig, ca. 1994. The ancient walking trail between Marsh Lake and Lake Laberge is in the background.

PARTNERS IN TRADE

Archaeological evidence points to active trade between Coastal Tlingit people and people in the interior Yukon for many generations. Traders from communities between the Stikine and Chilkat Rivers travelled up coastal rivers, crossed glaciers through narrow passes, and descended to various headwaters of the Yukon River hundreds of miles inland every year. Separate Tlingit clans controlled the three main routes to the Yukon interior. The Chilkat people from Klukwan used the Chilkat Pass to reach Kusawa Lake, then rafted down the Takhini River to the Yukon River and Lake Laberge and on to the Pelly River, returning to the coast through Hutshi, Klukshu and Shaw'ashe (later known as Dalton Post). Chilkoot traders followed the Taiya River and then climbed the Chilkoot Pass to Tagish and Marsh Lakes and on to the upper Yukon River.

CLAN/MOIETY SYSTEM

Aᴌʟ ʏᴜᴋᴏɴ First Nation peoples organize themselves in clans as part of a moiety system (from the French word *moitié*, meaning half) to establish their identity and define their relationships with others. The Yukon system consists of Crow (the term used to designate Raven by Yukon First Nations) and Wolf (Eagle) groups, with the addition of "middle people" in northern areas. Crow and Wolf are the principal symbols.

Moieties/clans are matrilineal, with sons and daughters following their mother's lineage, acquiring its symbols, names and other possessions. Clans are exogamous, meaning that men and women are obligated to "marry out" to the opposite clan. In the past, marriages were often arranged by parents and grandparents to make the best use of resources. Penalties for breaking this tradition were severe, sometimes resulting in banishment or death for any couple who defied the law. The clan system remains important to Yukon First Nations today, with marriages between opposite clans favoured by Elders. When same-clan unions occur, community disapproval can be lessened by the couple's efforts to create a good home and upbringing for their children.

Taku people left from Auke Bay or Taku Inlet, going up the Taku River through a pass to Teslin and Atlin Lakes. These were the legendary Tlingit "grease trails," named for the eulachon oil and sea products the traders carried inland.

Based in territories with abundant resources and a mild climate, the Tlingit developed a powerful, wealthy and complex society structured around Raven and Eagle clans, with many subgroups or "houses" controlling regalia, songs, dances, trade routes and territories. The people lived in large villages, travelling extensively to trade with surrounding indigenous groups.

People in the southern Yukon were deeply influenced by their ties to the Tlingit, sharing stories, songs, dances, ideas and beliefs. Marriages cemented trade relations for generations. Moiety and clan conventions were cultural realities for interior people with Tlingit connections, especially the Tagish Kwan at Marsh Lake and Tagish with their ancestral affiliations to coastal Dakl'aweidí (Killer Whale), Deisheetaan (Split Tail Beaver), and Gaanaxteidí (Woodworm) clans. Inland knowledge was essential for Tlingit survival in the Yukon terrain and climate. The intermingling of interior and coastal peoples promoted the smooth flow of trade.[9]

A prominent family at Tàa'an Män (Lake Laberge) illustrated this interweaving of family and clan connections. Mundessa, the Tàa'an Män headman in the mid to late nineteenth century, was sometimes called "Old Man Chief Jim Boss," since he was the father of the renowned Chief Jim Boss, who would become a prominent resident of Whitehorse in later years. Mundessa was his

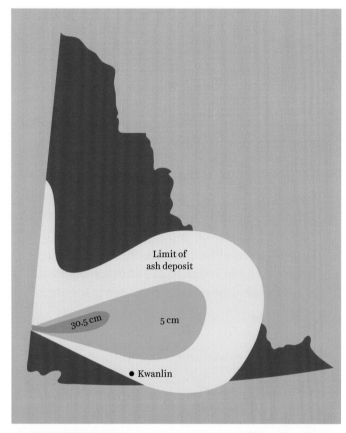

Limit of
ash deposit

30.5 cm

5 cm

● Kwanlin

TOP Area of the White River ash fall.

BOTTOM The distinctive White River ash layer in an archaeological dig. It is interesting to note how little soil has built up over the ash in over 1,200 years.

Southern Tutchone name; in Tlingit, his name was recorded as Wandasaa. Mundessa's father was from the coast; his mother was likely an inland woman. Mundessa was a Crow married to a Wolf woman from Tagish; she was identified as Het-ashat there and as Łande by Ta'an people. Łande also had family connections at Hutshi and Marsh Lake. Mundessa and Łande had four children—a son, Jim Boss (Athapaskan name Kashx̱óot or Kishwoot; Tlingit name Hundealth), and three daughters: Shuwu–teen, Tusáxal (George Dawson's mother) and Shaan Tlein (Kitty Anderson's mother). The descendants of Mundessa and Łande through their children include the Boss, Broeren and Dawson families, among many relatives in the Whitehorse valley.[10]

NAMING PLACES

Linguistics is used to study early cultures. Linguists who analyzed North American aboriginal languages in the nineteenth century assigned the term "Athapaskan" to the large group of languages spoken by people from Alaska to the Yukon, Northwest Territories, B.C., Alberta and parts of the United States. Some subcategories used to identify Yukon languages, such as Southern and Northern Tutchone, were not used by the people themselves in earlier times. More often the people identified with a particular place that was part of their seasonal round, such as the Tagish people who lived around the lake of the same aboriginal name. Linguistic evidence links speakers of the present day Southern and Northern Tutchone and Tagish languages to distant speakers of other Athapaskan languages, including Navaho and Apache people.[11]

Eight aboriginal languages are spoken in the Yukon today. Seven are closely related Athapaskan languages; Inland Tlingit is similar to Coastal Tlingit. In

THE YEAR OF
TWO WINTERS

SOMETIME AROUND 1,900 years ago, and again in the year 803, Mount Churchill in eastern Alaska erupted, spewing ash high into the air. The fallout from this explosion reached well into the Whitehorse area. Scientists speculate that the ash fall was so dense, the air would have been all but unbreathable and plants would have suffocated. First Nations people tell of the year of two winters, thought to be a result of the ash fall blocking the sun and preventing the land from warming.

These events, which must have created enormous chaos for both people and animals, likely resulted in out-migrations by survivors, perhaps to new lands far to the south and east. Today, the ash layer can be seen as a white stripe running through the ground in road cuts and riverbanks. It is locally known as "Sam McGee's ashes," after the famous poem by Robert Service.

the Whitehorse area, three key aboriginal languages—Southern Tutchone, Tagish and Inland Tlingit—were predominant over many years. Many people grew up speaking two or more languages as a result of intermarriage. For purposes of trade, cultural exchange, marriage and other social interactions, it was essential for people to be able to communicate in several languages.

The special places of this valley have been known by a number of names. Place names link present landmarks to pre-contact times, when aboriginal people were the only residents and travellers in the region. Ideas about the land and its resources, routes for travel and trade, meeting places and other details of ancient times have been preserved through oral traditions and can still be heard. With translations and interpretations by native-language speakers, plus evidence from archaeological and documentary sources, the sounds and meanings of earlier times are revealed and passed on.

People recognized many features in the valley as markers for way-finding, as locations for food and as places of beauty, inspiration and memory. Most dramatic was the mighty canyon with the river cutting through volcanic outcroppings—Kwanlin, or Unilyin, meaning "water flowing through a narrow place." Other Southern Tutchone names for waterways familiar to Whitehorse residents today include Chasàn Chùa, now known as McIntyre Creek; Ntsäw Chù (Porter Creek); and Nakhu Chù (Takhini River). T'śi Ma (Golden Horn Mountain), which translates as "ochre mountain," Naleen Dthel (Lookout or Lone Mountain) where Southern Tutchone people watched for Tlingit traders from the coast, then lit signal fires; Thay T'äw (Haeckel Hill), a landmark west of the city; and Thay Ma (Grey Mountain) which overlooks the city. [12]

Yukon beardtongue *(Penstemon gormanii)* is a glorious addition to summer flora around Whitehorse.

CITY OF IMAGINATION

The people of this area have adapted and evolved in tune with the changing environment and the availability of natural resources. They have seen the grassy hills, covered with bison and caribou, replaced by woodland, home to elk and moose. They witnessed the fish return to the rivers and lakes, and the coming and going of many cultures. Through it all, people have persisted in this place, changing as the need arose but maintaining a lifestyle pattern that lasted for 5,000 years. Then the outside world began to make itself known, and the place at the foot of the rapids was on the verge of experiencing one of the biggest changes it had seen in hundreds and hundreds of years.

Whitehorse on a winter's
evening looking toward Golden
Horn Mountain and the
Mount Sima ski hill.

Place of Many Stories

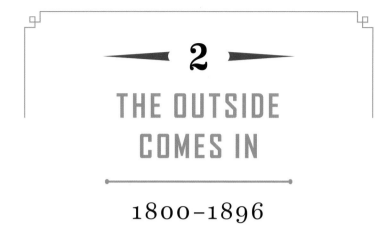

2

THE OUTSIDE COMES IN

1800–1896

Until the early nineteenth century, the Southern Tutchone and Tagish Kwan people of the Whitehorse valley lived as "part of the land and part of the water."[1] They followed the seasons, employing tools and knowledge based on kin and aboriginal trade networks. But the Yukon interior held a wealth of resources attractive to people beyond the big river. During the nineteenth century, new influences swept over the mountains and along the waterways.

Tlingit clans at Dyea and Klukwan controlled the mountain passes leading to the upper Yukon valley, delaying direct non-aboriginal access until the early 1880s. As luxurious Yukon furs, and later minerals, reached consumers in distant lands, more explorers and entrepreneurs arrived, exploiting ancient trade routes and alliances between inland Athapaskans and Coastal Tlingit. Together, aboriginal people and newcomers built social and economic connections, establishing the valley as a key corridor ahead of the great gold rush at the end of the century.[2]

Travel to the interior spawned legendary tales of hardship and losses told among both aboriginal traders and newcomers who traversed the passes. It was a challenging time for human relationships too, intensified by divergent languages, ways of life and world views. Conflicts were rare between aboriginal and newcomer, but misunderstandings arose out of profound cultural differences and economic competition. Stories told around campfires in the valley and in publications outside laid the foundation for discourse, and sometimes discord, that persisted for years. Partnerships were critical to successful co-existence, an enduring theme for people of all backgrounds.

FACING Taken at St. Michael by Swiss photographer Charles Farciot in 1885, this image shows many of the white traders on the Yukon River at the time. Back row, L-R: Arthur Harper, Al Mayo, Captain Charles Peterson, Joseph Ladue, John Franklin, François Mercier, Gregory Kokrine. Front: Dr. Willis Everette (seated on the cannon) and A.S. Frederickson.

THE COMING OF THE CLOUD PEOPLE

Russian fur traders and other Europeans sailed into Tlingit communities in their tall-masted ships with billowing white sails during the last half of the eighteenth century. A Lituya Bay Elder reported that the "cloud people" were drawn to Tlingit communities by bags of furs that fell out of canoes and floated westward "to the face of the cloud at the edge of the earth."[3] The big ships must have been an impressive sight, and the initial encounters between Tlingits and Europeans even more memorable, each with unique goods to trade for the other's desirable wares.

With generations of experience in travelling over the mountain passes and long-established aboriginal trade networks, the Coastal Tlingit became the natural conduit to the interior for goods arriving on Russian, British, French, Spanish and, later, American ships. Inland people quickly adopted new kinds of foods, cloth, metal tools and powerful weapons to ease the immense hardships of life in their cold climate.

Oral traditions and archaeological evidence document rapid changes after 1800, when Tlingit goods such as dentalium shells, smoked salmon, seaweed, walrus whiskers and woven cedar products began to be supplemented with axes, pots, guns, flour, rice, sugar, tea, glass beads, canvas and cloth. Inland people supplied superior beaver, fox, lynx and wolf furs, plus caribou, moose, goat and sheep hides, dried fish and meat, berries, copper nuggets, ochre, gopher-skin robes, moccasins, moccasin trousers and woven spruce root baskets to their Tlingit visitors for the next exchange with the "cloud people."

THE OUTSIDE APPROACHES FROM EAST AND WEST

Tlingit control of coastal mountain passes was one of many reasons for the long-delayed arrival of non-aboriginal people in the Whitehorse valley. History and geography also influenced the approach of Europeans. In need of raw materials to supply growing populations and the acquisitive interests of competing rulers and religions, European states battled for domination on land and sea. Asian spices, Chinese teas and silks, north Pacific whales, sea mammals, fish and North American furs beckoned as opportunities for commercial gain and imperial conquest.

Captain Vitus Bering sailed east across the north Pacific straits in 1741 to explore the Alaskan coast on behalf of Russian business interests. Spotting a huge mountain on his birthday, he named it St. Elias, after his patron saint. It was the first European place name to be attached to the future Yukon Territory. Names such as Malaspina, La Pérouse and Lisiansky, in southeast Alaska, document the multinational origins of explorers who followed. The British Navy's search for a Northwest Passage to China, led by James Cook, George Vancouver and John Franklin, affixed English names along the Arctic and Pacific coastlines.

Beginning in the seventeenth century, French-Canadian voyageurs spread westward across the continent, building networks with aboriginal traders and transferring to English companies after the consolidation of British North America in 1763. The American Revolution launched another colonizing force in 1783, with entrepreneurs pushing overland across the Rockies, and American sea captains starting to explore the Pacific Northwest. Hudson's Bay Company and North West Company traders raced to establish posts right across the Prairies to the Pacific and down the Mackenzie River to the Arctic.[4]

These external influences converged in the Northwest. They reached the Yukon valley indirectly at first, as new goods and stories of the strangers who had brought them were carried from the coast by Tlingit traders and from the Mackenzie valley by Athapaskan entrepreneurs. The Russian-American Company, which established settlements stretching from the Aleutians to its Sitka headquarters, was often hampered by its uneasy relations with aboriginal peoples, especially the Tlingit, who retained their cultural strength and control over interior fur supplies. Rival Hudson's Bay Company ships and plucky American captains with better goods also lured aboriginal traders and their furs away from the Russians.

Regulating competition was the focus of both the Russo-American Treaty of 1824 and the Anglo-Russian Treaty of 1825. Negotiated in a far-off city by diplomats with no first-hand knowledge of northern lands or people, the 1825 treaty designated Bering's Mount St. Elias as the anchor for a boundary that stretched north to the Arctic Ocean along the 161st meridian. Russia claimed the Alaska Panhandle plus lands to the west. Britain claimed areas to the east, including the Yukon River headwaters and the Whitehorse valley. Exploring these mysterious lands and increasing profits by eliminating aboriginal middlemen became the focus of the Russian-American and Hudson's Bay Companies, leading to the first direct contacts between newcomers and inland people.[5]

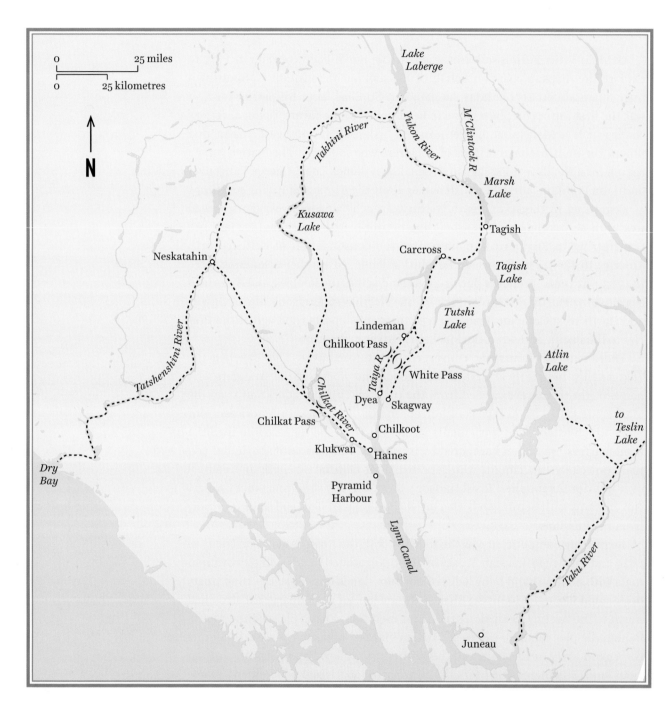

Trade routes to the interior

Russian traders explored north along the Bering Sea coast, establishing St. Michael's Redoubt in 1833, and then set off overland to locate the large river reported by aboriginal traders, which the company named the Kwikpak in 1835. Hudson's Bay Company (HBC) traders travelled from their Mackenzie River posts into the Yukon valley in the 1840s, searching for the great river that Gwich'in traders said flowed to the ocean. Alexander Hunter Murray crossed over the mountains and paddled down the Porcupine River to the Chu kon, or "Big River," as local Gwich'in called the Yukon River, establishing Fort Yukon in 1847, knowing it was likely on Russian territory. Murray encountered initial resistance from Gwich'in traders, but the HBC succeeded over time, drawing trappers and furs from the Tanana to the Klondike Rivers.

To the south, Robert Campbell travelled from the Mackenzie River up the Liard and down the Pelly to the Yukon, establishing Fort Selkirk in 1848 among Northern Tutchone people in the centre of the Tlingit economic hinterland. Campbell's initial encounters with Tlingit traders were positive. But ultimately his post was doomed, since he was trading in the same goods the Tlingit carried from the coast. In 1852, Chilkat leader Skeet-la-Ka and his son Kohklux attacked Fort Selkirk, sending Campbell fleeing to the Mackenzie and then to Montreal and London, seeking support to rebuild his post.

For their part, HBC officials decided to concentrate on Fort Yukon, where furs were more plentiful and their relationships with Gwich'in partners better. They abandoned the southern Yukon, acquiring interior furs through HBC ships on the coast. Tlingit clans continued to control the mountain passes for another three decades, dominating trade through their extended family connections on the upper Yukon.[6]

MAPS AND SCHEMES

The conflict at Fort Selkirk led to the production of the first map to show in detail the rivers, lakes and other features of the upper Yukon. Back in London, Robert Campbell began working with the famed Arrowsmith mapmakers on their 1854 *Map of British North America*, contributing his knowledge of tributaries and geographical features from the Pelly to the Porcupine. Less detail was available for the areas upriver, including a big lake and the headwaters of the

A DAY IN THE LIFE OF
A TLINGIT TRADER

ca. 1850s

IN THE early days of June, a party of ten Tlingit people arrived at the Chilkoot Pass on their long walk from tidal waters, carrying goods traded for furs with the big sailing ships anchored near their village. Their leader had made the trip inland many times, and he was now training his sister's eldest son, his eighteen-year-old nephew, to lead the expeditions when he matured.

The men carried impressive loads of cooking utensils, pots, knives, rifles and cartridges, with only a small amount of eulachon oil and smoked salmon. They had carefully assembled the array of goods, knowing that certain items were highly favoured and would bring an abundance of the premium winter furs prized by the captains on the big ships. The leader's wife would assist in bartering with the inland people; she was linked to them through an aunt married to a Tagish man. She had a full load of cloth, needles, beads and awls to trade with the women for their gopher skins, muskrat furs, goose down and sinew thread.

The elder trader had thought carefully about his nephew's future, hoping to negotiate a marriage for him. The time might be right to begin the three-to four-year process by introducing the idea to his Tagish trading partner, his wife and his daughter. The young woman was of the opposite clan from his nephew, a direct descendant of one of the Tlingit sisters who had travelled inland to marry in his grandfather's time. The elder trader felt confident. He had groomed his nephew in his social obligations and the complexities of trade.

Although the sun was warm and the days long in early June, the traders were dressed for travel through difficult trails, wearing durable moose-skin moccasin trousers and tunics along with woven

Yukon, since Campbell's only knowledge had come from his Tlingit rivals and Tutchone traders.

Fifteen years later, the Chilkat Chief Kohklux (also known by the name Shotridge) drew two comprehensive maps of the Tlingit routes to the interior, the first maps to show in detail the upper Yukon tributaries surrounding the Whitehorse valley. Kohklux drew the maps for American scientist George Davidson, who was visiting Klukwan to observe a solar eclipse. By then, Tlingit people were experiencing more upheaval. The United States had purchased Alaska from Russia in 1867, and U.S. military commanders took charge in Sitka with orders to eliminate any resistance. American traders aggressively pursued business along the coast and up the Yukon River. In 1869, they pressured their government to oust HBC traders at Fort Yukon, who were operating in territory cedar hats. For cool evenings and mornings, they had gopher-skin or woollen robes, and one wore a prized Hudson's Bay blanket. Their layers of clothing protected them from snags along the trail, as well as the mosquitoes and black flies that congregated in clouds. They also carried a mixture of grease and pine sap to protect exposed skin from stinging insects.

With the longest, most difficult part of their trip from Dyea behind them, the party rested after climbing the pass. People at Tagish and farther along the Yukon River knew the Tlingits were coming and had been expecting them for weeks. The parties would rendezvous by the lakes and proceed in skin canoes to meet other partners above the Kwanlin canyon and rapids.

The traders started a small fire to roast some whistlers (marmots) they'd caught along the trail, also making bannock to eat that night and carry with them the next day. Some greens they had collected would add delicious garnish to the meal. A mix of Labrador tea and wild mint leaves would make a relaxing tea to end the evening.

In keeping with his new responsibilities, the nephew walked up the trail the party would take

in the early morning. Once he returned to camp, he made his bed away from the others so he could spend quiet time considering his future obligations as a young leader and husband. He had gathered important medicinal objects in a pouch around his neck. He touched it before going to sleep, thinking about his deepening relationship with the powers of the universe. Soon, he would meet inland traders for the first time. Perhaps he would also glimpse the young woman his uncle had described.

Lulled to near-sleep by soft winds in the new leaves, the young man was startled by a sharp bark nearby. A small black-and-white dog wagged its tail in greeting. The Tagish traders had come a few days ahead of schedule, walking to the mountain lakes to meet their coast relatives. The young man went to wake his uncle, who spoke Tagish and would be happy to see these men. With the campfire revived and tea boiled, the young man listened and watched intently as the parties began the first exchange of news and ceremonies in preparation for formal trading. Together, the two groups would travel inland to meet Southern Tutchone partners in their homelands above and below the big canyon.

that now belonged to the United States. The HBC briefly relocated on the Porcupine and then abandoned its Yukon trade.

Among the new fur traders working for American companies were the French-Canadian brothers François-Xavier and Moïse Mercier, along with several Quebec compatriots. They extended French and Roman Catholic connections first established by HBC voyageurs along the Yukon River in the 1850s and 1860s. Sending letters and reports to friends back home, they ensured that news of the far northwest became a continuing feature in Quebec, laying the foundation to attract future generations.[7]

François-Xavier Mercier spent seventeen years altogether on the Yukon River, both witnessing and influencing profound change in the region. Small steam-powered boats were replacing canoes for commercial river transportation, and the fur trade economy waned as more prospectors moved north. English overtook both French and aboriginal languages as the language of commerce, with Americans predominant among the newcomers. Mercier was there to greet the first wave of gold-seekers, employing Leroy McQuesten, Arthur Harper and Al Mayo when they arrived in 1873. Ten years later, he was overjoyed to meet a fellow countryman, one who would stay on to play a major role in the new golden era: "Now on a beautiful day of April 9, 1883 (it was Easter day) being on a walk in front of my house, in glancing upstream on the Yukon I perceived coming toward me four people on snowshoes... the foremost gave me his hand, addressing me in French. It was Joseph Ladue, French-Canadian, native of the area of Plattsburg, N.Y."[8]

Some of the first American maps of Alaska and the Yukon included information contributed by the Merciers and by another French Canadian, Michel Laberge. Laberge had explored the Yukon from St. Michael to Fort Selkirk in 1867 on behalf of the Collins Overland Telegraph Company, which planned to link North America and Europe with a line through B.C., down the Yukon River and across the Bering Sea. The project failed when a line was laid across the Atlantic ahead of it. William Healey Dall, who had met Laberge while working on the project and later became a prominent U.S. official, attached Laberge's name to the big lake north of the Whitehorse Rapids. The new name ultimately replaced those given the lake by both the Southern Tutchone (Tàa'an Män) and the Tlingit (Kluk-tak-Sy-ee).[9]

TIMES OF CHANGE

American commanders used force to subdue several Tlingit villages, resulting in the loss of lives and property on both sides. Overwhelming military might joined with negative influences such as alcohol and epidemic diseases to weaken the Tlingit people. They made fewer expeditions to the interior as new American companies drew many former Tlingit customers downriver to posts near the Klondike and Tanana. Only the Tlingit's Tagish and Southern Tutchone partners near the coastal passes remained as viable trade contacts; even that slipped away as rumours of Yukon gold circulated among prospectors working their way north following gold rushes in B.C., Juneau and surrounding areas. Tlingit control over coastal passes forced gold-seekers to travel north to St. Michael and up the Yukon, or down the Mackenzie and over the mountains to reach new

prospects on the Stewart, White, Tanana and other tributaries. Their existence in the interior was tenuous, with prospecting limited to brief summer months, complicated by arduous travel and scarce supplies.

Dreams of gold along the Yukon River persisted, kept alive by a small group of men who arrived on the lower Yukon in the 1870s. Arthur Harper, Leroy McQuesten and Al Mayo worked as fur traders; first hired by François-Xavier Mercier for the Alaska Commercial Company, they established independent posts by the mid-1880s. They married aboriginal women, gaining advantage through the skills of their wives and of relatives who worked as hunters and guides. With a firm base and regional allies, they extended their trade network upriver to the Pelly, operating small steamboats to overcome the great distances from St. Michael. They prospected while managing their fur trade and supply business, promising golden opportunities in letters to prospectors and newspapers outside.

The pace of development quickened with each passing year as the economic focus turned irrevocably from furs to mining. American agencies generated reports and maps to stimulate interest in Alaska. A Hän man named Paul Kandik compiled the *Kandik Map* with François-Xavier Mercier. Their map was used by Ivan Petroff to prepare maps for the first Alaska census in 1880, fuelling further agitation from entrepreneurs keen to exploit northern resources. The *Kandik Map* clearly showed that the most direct route to those riches lay across the coastal passes. However, travel there was still controlled by Tlingit clans and prohibited to outsiders.[10]

OPENING THE CHILKOOT PASS

The ancient Tlingit monopoly ended in 1880 through American military persuasion, probably aided by Tlingit perceptions of new opportunities. U.S. Navy Captain Beardslee met with clan heads at Pyramid Harbor, arriving in an armed gunboat to bolster his authority. Klukwan leaders insisted on maintaining control over the Chilkat Pass, which was easier to ascend and had no menacing rapids. Dyea leaders agreed to open their Chilkoot Pass, with Beardslee accepting the condition that prospectors not trade with interior people—a prohibition no one was prepared to enforce. The selection of the Chilkoot Pass was a pivotal point, generating prosperity for Dyea Tlingit packers and steering prospectors to the Whitehorse valley as the primary corridor to emerging goldfields downriver.[11]

Within a few years, the trickle of miners increased from a few dozen to hundreds and then thousands, as prospects on the Yukon yielded more gold and even more stories of riches waiting. The Kwanlin canyon and rapids were daunting impediments for small watercraft, so both aboriginal people and prospectors usually portaged around them, following ancient trails along the canyon's steep sides. The big lakes to the south and north were familiar rendezvous points, but sudden treacherous storms blew up to mar paddling or sailing. Winter travel in the passes was not customary for Tlingit traders, but a number of non-aboriginal newcomers attempted such trips, sometimes with fatal results.

The earliest prospectors wrote few reports of their struggles, but American and Canadian government officials provided extensive details about the burgeoning frontier. In 1883, U.S. Army Lieutenant Frederick Schwatka tackled the Chilkoot Pass, and then floated on a raft through Canadian territory and Alaska all the way to the Bering Sea, later producing numerous articles and books as well as his official report.

Schwatka described his trip in glorious detail, laying claim to being the first to survey the entire river and criticizing previous cartographers for mapping areas they had not visited: "All Alaska is filled up... with rivers... that have yet to be traversed by white men... let alone [doing] topography and survey. Probably these parlour authors... think they are doing no harm... but [it is] dangerous and misleading to miners and other travellers."[12]

Schwatka assigned numerous new names on the maps he created. Marsh Lake was named to honour a Yale professor, though miners knew it as Mud Lake for its muddy shoreline. Robert Campbell had named the Yukon headwaters above the Pelly confluence the Lewes River in the 1850s, but Schwatka designated the entire river as the Yukon. He also named the great canyon above the Whitehorse Rapids after his commanding officer, General Miles.

On June 28, Schwatka remarked on a large thundershower, claiming it was "the first ever chronicled on the Yukon River."[13] He described the "great rapids of the Yukon" as:

> five miles long and extremely dangerous... [water] rushes and boils through a canyon with upright basaltic columns... the center... widening into a whirl-pool basin... then... running swiftly over shoals, bars, and drifts of water logged timber much more dangerous than the canyon itself... the river-bed again contracts... and finally rushes through a narrow cascade... so swift... and so narrow the chute that the water is forced up the banks... and pours in sheets... into the cascades below, making a perfect funnel formidable to behold... [when] the raft was "shot" July 2... the side logs were torn off in a collision with the basaltic columns of the canyon... and she was beached about a half mile below the cascades... where [we built] new decks from the fine, straight and seasoned poles found in the vicinity. Fine grayling were caught in large numbers in all the rapids near the canyon.[14]

As his guide, Schwatka had hired a Chilkat man named Ind-A-Yanek who spoke the Chinook trade language common on the coast and also communicated

Detail of Miles Canyon to Lake
Kluktassi (Laberge) from map in
Frederick Schwatka's report
on his 1883 expedition. Kluktassi
was the Tlingit name for Lake
Laberge, which was known as
Tàa'an Män by the Ta'an Kwäch'än
who lived there.

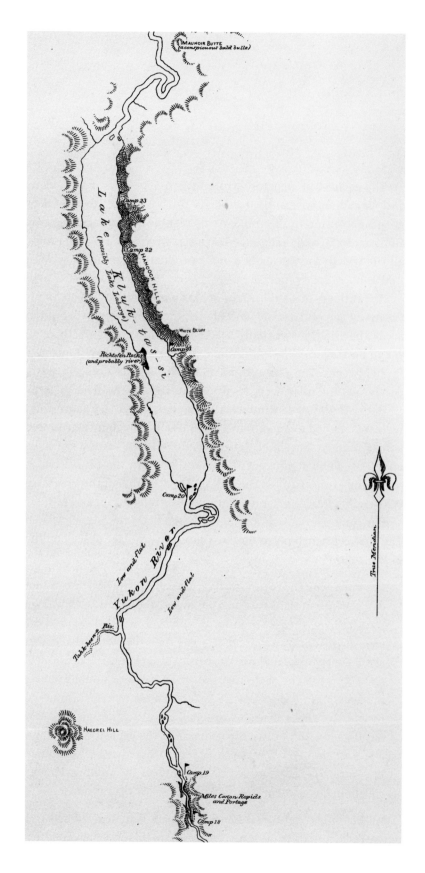

in Tagish with people as far as Fort Selkirk. Ind-A-Yanek travelled all the way to the Bering Sea with the Americans, then on to San Francisco. He returned home the following year, no doubt with many stories to tell.[15]

In 1887, Ottawa sent its own Yukon expedition, led by George Dawson, William Ogilvie and R.G. McConnell, to report on the people, resources, conditions and routes to and within the interior.[16] Dawson took issue with much of Schwatka's grand narrative, especially his naming of places: "to change the name of the Lewes which had already been on the maps for about thirty years ... [was] quite arbitrary and unjustifiable. In addition ... he ignored the names of many places well known to miners ... substituting others of his own invention."[17] Despite his irritation, Dawson retained many of those names out of deference to the eminent people Schwatka had honoured with Canadian landmarks.

Dawson's assessment of the navigational hazards at the canyon was milder than his American counterpart's, but still he cautioned future travellers to be wary.

> The portage is on the west bank and it is usual to carry both boats and cargo over it. Between the White Horse and the foot of the cañon the river is very swift, and at one place, a mile above the former and three quarters of a mile below the latter, the set of the stream is so strong round a rocky point as to render it advisable to make an additional short portage of 130 feet. A third portage of five eights of a mile is necessary at Miles Cañon. This portage is on the east bank, and at the lower end, a very steep ascent has first to be overcome. Here a sort of extemporized windlass has been set up by the miners for the purpose of hauling up their boats.... The river flows through the cañon with great velocity, but is unimpeded in its course, and it is therefore not very risky to run with a good boat. The White Horse Rapid is ... more dangerous, and though some of the miners have run through it—generally accidentally—it should not be attempted.[18]

Tlingit guide Ind-A-Yanek accompanied Frederick Schwatka on his 1883 exploration of the Yukon River, afterwards adopting the explorer's name. Here he appears in a sealskin parka and mukluks, with Southern Tutchone style snowshoes and a walking stick for crossing the coastal passes. He stands on a gopher skin robe—likely made by Southern Tutchone people—exchanged or gifted to coastal Tlingit visitors.

Ogilvie and some of his crew did run the rapids in their Peterborough canoe—a wild ride that scared their cook but left the unflappable surveyor in fine fettle:

> Seated on a pile of stuff in the bow I directed the helmsman with my arms as speech was out of the question. The passage was made in about three minutes ... at the rate of twelve and a half miles an hour. The only exciting episode was the final plunge, where there are three heavy swells, each about five feet in height.[19]

Ogilvie continued downriver to spend the winter of 1887–88 surveying the booming Forty Mile gold district and establishing the 161st meridian boundary line on the Yukon River. Despite cold weather, he was favourably impressed with the region's prospects and especially the hardy character of miners toiling on their claims. Dawson was optimistic too: "It is not likely that this great inland country will long want some easy means of connection between the coast and its ... river waters .... When this is afforded, there is every reason to believe that it will support a considerable mining population."[20]

Dawson also assessed the numbers, conditions and attitudes of local aboriginal people, since officials had heard complaints of hostile encounters from miners. He recognized the inland people he met along the Yukon as part of the large Tinne or Dene linguistic group, now called Athapaskan, extending north and south, but he was puzzled by the inland Tagish, whose vocabulary was similar to that of the Tlingit:

A YUKON PROSPECTOR'S SEASON

ca. 1885

WILLIAM PIERCE was a hardy American frontiersman who came north to Alaska in the 1870s and prospected around Juneau for many years. In the mid-1880s, he tried his luck in the interior, following reports of gold on the Yukon River. The following excerpts are from his memoir, which was later published as *Thirteen Years of Travel and Exploration in Alaska, 1877–1889*.

We were obliged to take supplies [for] six months... [and] employed Indians to pack [paying]... about twelve dollars and fifty cents for one hundred pounds. The price was too much but... we had to pay it or do our own packing... [our] tools and all were near a thousand pounds.... Those Indians... of the Chilkoot Tribe... are very saucy... and would delay us from day to day.... Then the whole gang turned out and carried all our goods over on one trip... travelling near twelve miles per day. Some of the stronger ones carried as much as two hundred pound.... As we ascended the snow became deeper [and]... it was necessary to cut a stair-case in the hard ice-like snow... the sun reflecting on the snow was almost unbearable....

[Drifting on the river] we occasionally stopped... at streams and taking out pick, shovel and gold pan would try the gravel... and found there was gold [but] as prospectors always have the feeling that it is richer ahead, we kept on... drifting until... we came to a canyon... [and carried] our stores... to the lower end... [then ran] through with the empty boat.... As we got into those tremendous boiling breakers I felt decidedly uneasy.... The water came rolling in over the sides... travelling at railway speed.... The boat was half full of water... at the lower end.... We quickly jumped out... safe once more....

[We ascended] the Stuart River... about one hundred miles... [built] rockers and went to work.... The result was twenty-five dollars per day to the man... the gold... was very fine and limited.... Nothing breaks the stillness... I cannot describe the feeling... [of] extreme loneliness.... [As summer faded we built light boats] for our return, only to find [our food caches] destroyed by... camp-fires of [those ahead].... It was eight hundred miles to the nearest supplies... up the river.... We caught some fish... but could not fish and travel.... [At] Pelly River we found... that unless we got some game we should die of starvation before reaching the coast.... Our provisions had entirely given out, with [just a] little tea and a small sack of salt.... The weather was also growing cold... in late September.... [A] miserable situation—no food, no tobacco, our clothing almost worn out....

[Four] of us... took one boat [reaching the canyon, then]... the lakes.... The wind was blowing... so hard we could not travel.... We had not eaten anything for three days.... Bringing out three fox skins that I had traded for with Indians I picked and singed the fur off.... The total value... was three hundred dollars.... Had they been worth three thousand... they must go into the pot.... We were strengthened... for a few more days... getting nearer the coast every day.... The cold wind blew fiercely through our worn and ragged clothing.... If we could reach the summit... the balance of the trip would be

down grade; only thirty five miles further and we would be safe…. We were afraid to start in our starved condition [and hunted] for one day [killing a pair of lynx]… rested and fed up for two days and then felt strong enough to climb the mountain… our pockets [filled] with cold roasted meat…. Although we suffered considerably… we got through without accident.[21]

Photographer Veazie Wilson took these images on his Yukon River trip in 1894.

TOP Camp life in a wall tent along the trail on the upper lakes, 1894.

BOTTOM Pelly River people in factory clothing, with Hudson's Bay Company blankets over canvas wall tents and meat-drying racks in the background. Fort Selkirk, 1894.

The interior Indians are collectively known on the coast as "Stick Indians"... this name is also applied to the Tagish [who have]... two rough wooden houses somewhat resembling those of the Coast Indians [on the river between Tagish and Marsh lakes where] the greater part of the tribe congregates during the winter... [but] they claim [as far as] the headwaters of the Big Salmon River.... [Until recently] dominated by the Chilkoots and Chilkats of Lynn Canal [they were]... in the position of intermediaries in trade between the Coast and the Tinne Indians, without being sufficiently strong to levy a toll.... The Tagish tribe is... about fifteen families... seventy or eighty individuals. Their snowshoes... travelling and hunting equipment... and... mode of camping, are identical with those of the Tinne.[22]

PRELUDE TO BONANZA[23]

Two people who accompanied William Ogilvie in 1887 were destined to play major roles in the evolution of the Whitehorse valley, though neither ever lived there. Keish, or "Skookum Jim," was a Tagish man who worked as a packer on the Chilkoot Pass. With relatives in Dyea, he was allowed to participate in the Chilkoots' new monopoly, paying part of his fees to clan leaders. Captain William Moore had spent decades as an entrepreneur in B.C., freighting goods for prospectors and trading with aboriginal people. In the 1880s, he and his sons travelled to Alaska, then crossed the Chilkoot, seeking opportunities on the Yukon River. Ogilvie hired both men as assistants for his expedition.

Moore persuaded the surveyor to allow him and Skookum Jim to explore another pass southeast of Dyea, which Tlingit packers described as lower in elevation but longer to cross, with more complicated valleys. William Ogilvie later named this the White Pass, in honour of the Minister of the Interior, Thomas White. Moore's son Bernard recorded details of his father's trip:

My father told me of his trip through a pass leading from a little bay called Skagway... through which... he [and] Skookum Jim picked their way through to Lake Bennett. It took them seven days... there was no trail of any kind and travelling was very hard.... My father reported [it was] about one thousand feet lower in altitude than... Chilkoot Pass... [and] hard work getting through; mosquitoes were very bad, all the streams were swollen, there was dense underbrush, and travelling over and around rocky bluffs way above the canyons; but on nearing the summit and after reaching it, the going down to Bennett was much better.[24]

Skookum Jim returned to packing on the Chilkoot, but Captain Moore continued downriver with Ogilvie's party, looking for Bernard, who was prospecting. The two met near Cassiar Bar, then returned together to the coast, where Captain Moore wanted to stake the land he had seen at Skagway Bay:

> His object was to... divert the early spring travel through this pass to the interior... which... would be easier [in]... early spring or winter travel with hand sleighs... than the Chilkoot, though a few more miles travel to reach Lake Lindeman.... Skagway Bay was accessible by large ocean steamers [year round]... and his idea was to exert all endeavours toward getting a trail... blazed through this pass... take up some land... on Skagway Bay, and... erect some kind of... small wharf.[25]

After an extremely difficult crossing over the Chilkoot, the two Moores went to Juneau to collect supplies, and then returned to stake their claim to the Skagway waterfront in October 1887. Bernard recorded his father's prophetic words at the time: "I fully expect before many years to see a pack trail through this pass, followed by a wagon road, and I would not be at all surprised to see a railroad through to the lakes."[26]

Over the next decade, father and son built docks, a sawmill and a store at Skagway Bay, extending trails up the valley, and carried mail to the growing communities along the Yukon River. Renowned for their freighting skills, their hard work and their knowledge of the routes and rigours of the region, they lobbied officials in Ottawa and Victoria to support the White Pass trail.

Sounding a familiar echo to earlier Tlingit partnerships, Bernard Moore married Tlinget-sai-yet, daughter of George Shotridge, a Klukwan clan leader and son of Kohklux. The marriage gave Moore additional influence among coastal people and their inland relatives, and his wife's family gained prestige through this link to a growing commercial enterprise that rivalled the monopoly of their ancestors. The Moore route through the White Pass to the upper lakes and on to Miles Canyon and White Horse Rapids was never the first choice of gold-seekers, since the Chilkoot Trail was faster. Yet the route the Moores forged proved to be a viable option for large-scale transportation systems, which in turn secured the future of the Whitehorse valley as the central hub of the interior.[27]

Once the coastal passes were open to non-aboriginal travellers, the Tagish and Southern Tutchone people began to encounter newcomers directly, usually during summer and early fall. These first meetings involved caution and concern on both sides, with communication proceeding using coastal trade jargon or whatever methods people could devise to bridge their cultural differences. Oral traditions related to those times include many humorous stories about the food, clothing and activities of the newcomers, together with more serious issues involving disrespect for aboriginal people, animals and the land.

Ta'an Elder Irene Adamson remembered stories told by her grandmother Maggie Broeren about the first white people her family encountered at Tàa'an Män (Lake Laberge). Maggie was about fourteen years old and still wearing skin clothing at that time, the mid-1880s. Her family was camped at the upper end of the lake when they heard people talking in a language they didn't understand. Then they saw a boat coming down the river with men dressed in unusual clothing. The people thought the strangers must be the *gu ch'an*, or cloud people, that their Tlingit trading partners had described meeting on the coast. Maggie's father, Mundessa, told the women to take the children up to a safe place in the bush while the men went to see if these newcomers were friendly. After some discussion, Mundessa brought the gu ch'an back to the camp, where the visitors offered the people pilot bread that they didn't like at first. The gu ch'an also had apples, which the people identified as big berries.

On another occasion, Irene's uncles and grandfather were hunting near T'ši Ma in August when they spotted several white tents, with a number of gu ch'an talking in their own language. Some of the Ta'an people were afraid to meet these men, but others were curious about what they were doing, so they went down to the tents. The visitors used Chinook trade language and lots of hand motions to communicate with the Ta'an men, then gave them presents of tobacco and sugar.

A Kwanlin Dün Elder, John C. Smith, heard stories his father told about first meetings with white men at the big bend on the Yukon River near the old Whitehorse dump site. One of the white men was notable for his big, bushy beard. Polly Irvine related her father Billy Lebarge's experience with a very old

COPYRIGHT 1895. BY VEAZIE WILSON

prospector downriver near Big Salmon. The prospector had no groceries, and he wanted to trade some gold for food. Billy's family had no need for gold, but they gave the man some dried salmon and other food before he went on his way. The frequency of meetings with gu ch'an in the Whitehorse valley increased dramatically through the 1890s, as tantalizing discoveries lured more and more prospectors to the Yukon River and its golden tributaries.[28]

POISED ON THE BRINK

By the end of the nineteenth century, the Whitehorse valley had transformed from a hunter-gatherer haven to an industrial hub linking the outside world and the golden interior. Almost all the old realities and relationships were swept away in the wake of change. Some aboriginal people were keen to participate in the new economy, but for most, the overwhelming impact of the newcomers had devastating effects. For visionary entrepreneurs like Joe Ladue and skilled intermediaries like Skookum Jim, Chief Jim Boss and others, exciting times were just ahead.

Tàa'an Män people meet white traders at their traditional campsite near the upper end of the lake. Dressed in a mix of aboriginal and factory-made clothing—including one woman wearing a Tlingit-style button blanket—these inland people are likely Mundessa and Łande's extended family, perhaps including a young Jim Boss.

AFT EVER CAME
LE CANYON LENGTH 130 FEET
OSE PILOT.

3

THE KLONDIKE GOLD RUSH YEARS

1896–1899

FACING One of the largest rafts to run Miles Canyon. This 132-foot craft was piloted by Al Larose.

"GOLD! GOLD! GOLD! GOLD!"

"STREAM OF GOLD FROM KLONDYKE."

This was the story that blared from countless headlines in July 1897, electrifying people all over the world.[1]

Almost overnight, news of rich gold finds focussed the globe's attention on this remote corner of Canada's far northwest. Canadian history abounds in stories of the Klondike gold rush: the overnight millionaires; the speed with which the news spread; the deluge of clerks, farmers, shopkeepers and experienced miners who risked all to make the trek north. There are also the stories of those who transported, safeguarded and occasionally fleeced the stampeders. For the region's aboriginal people, the stories passed down are about family disruptions, scars on the land left by the newcomers, game driven far from the river corridor, disease that invaded their territory and, in only some cases, new opportunities. For most outsiders, the saga is indelibly associated with Dawson City and the Klondike goldfields. In actuality, some of the most compelling stories of the rush originated near the Yukon River headwaters at the canyon and the rapids. The stampede of gold-seekers to the Klondike, more than any other factor, led to the founding of the town of Whitehorse.

Although prospectors seeking the ultimate lode were already panning and sluicing in rivers and creeks of the upper Yukon River, the big strike was not made until August 17, 1896. It involved several Tagish people from the southern Yukon. After marrying prospector George Carmack, Shaaw Tláa (better known afterwards as Kate Carmack), a woman from the Carcross area, moved downriver with her husband. Her sister had previously gone downriver with another

On Chilkoot Pass

The never-ending line of gold seekers ascending the "Golden Stairs" of the Chilkoot Pass. Note the dugouts in the snow where weary climbers could rest before resuming their journey.

white prospector. Two years later, concerned family members went to look for the two women. The party consisted of their brother Keish, known to many newcomers as the Chilkoot packer Skookum Jim, his wife, Mary, and two nephews, Ḵáa Goox (Dawson Charlie) and Patsy Henderson. After meeting up with Kate and George, the group hunted, fished and prospected. It was Skookum Jim, Dawson Charlie and George Carmack who staked the rich discovery claims on Rabbit Creek, a feeder of the Klondike River. Rabbit Creek was quickly renamed Bonanza Creek, and the three men became northern legends.[2]

The first rush to the area was made by miners and prospectors living in the Yukon River basin. Communities such as Forty Mile and Circle, Alaska, were abandoned so quickly they became instant ghost towns. It took nearly a year for the news to reach the outside world via two "treasure ships," steamships bearing early miners and their tons of gold. The *Excelsior* docked in San Francisco on July 15, 1897, and the *Portland* reached Seattle two days later. The response was immediate and overwhelming. Coming as it did during a worldwide economic depression, the news captured the imaginations of

thousands inspired by prospects of instant riches. The rush was on as clerks, farmers, factory workers and merchants dropped everything to head north. An estimated 100,000 gold-seekers set out for the Klondike, while about 30,000 actually reached Dawson City.

There were many routes north, but the most popular were the ancient trade and travel routes through the Coastal Range, over the White and Chilkoot Passes to the great headwater lakes, then down the Yukon River. During the winter of 1897–98, would-be miners packed tons of gear over the mountain passes to the shores of Lindeman and Bennett Lakes. There they encountered a new challenge: they had to build watercraft to bear them down the Yukon River to Dawson City. The vessels were as varied as the carpentry and navigation skills of their builders. Soon after the ice went out in May 1898, a vast armada of rowboats, poling boats, dories, scows and rafts set off. Many gold-seekers used tarpaulins as improvised sails to catch the prevailing winds on the headwater lakes and Lake Laberge. At one point, North-West Mounted Police Superintendent Sam Steele counted over 800 vessels on an eight-mile stretch of Lake

Two of the Klondike discoverers at Skookum Jim's house in Carcross, 1899. L–R: unknown miner, George Carmack, Mary Mason, Daisy, Skookum Jim and Patsy Henderson.

ABOVE A flotilla of stampeders on Lake Laberge, 1898.

RIGHT Grave of a victim of the Whitehorse Rapids.

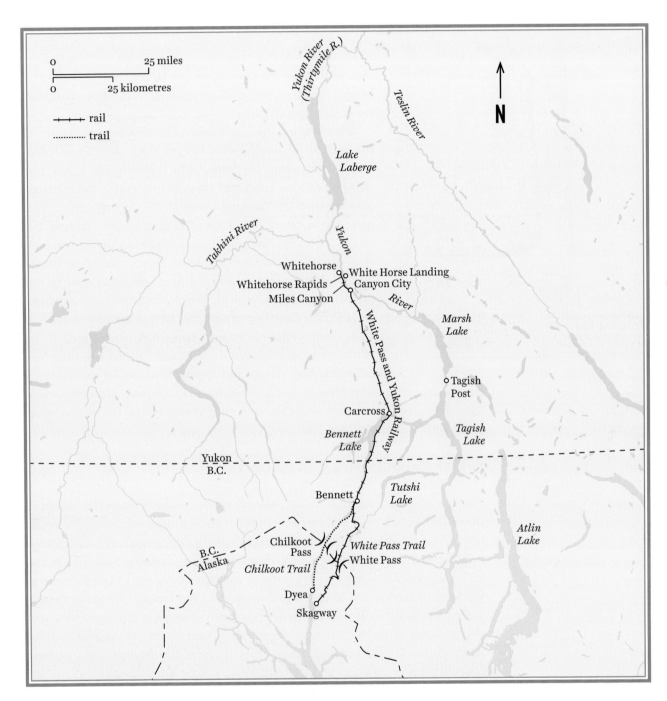

Routes into the Yukon interior from the south

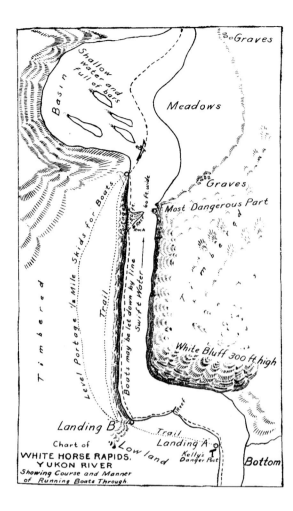

Chart of
WHITE HORSE RAPIDS,
YUKON RIVER
Showing Course and Manner
of Running Boats Through

ABOVE "Chart of White Horse Rapids and Yukon River showing Course and Manner of running boats through," published in 1897. The rapids were named by prospectors for the white spray that resembled horses' manes.

FACING TOP Klondikers drying out goods on the shore after a boat wreck at Whitehorse Rapids, Yukon Territory, 1898.

FACING BOTTOM Running Whitehorse Rapids in a scow.

Bennett, with many more on the way. Steele went on to note that while travelling 45 miles (72 kilometres) through the headwater lakes, none of the vessels were more than 200 yards (183 metres) apart.[3]

After braving the windy lakes, the travellers encountered the only major navigational hazard along the Yukon River: Miles Canyon and the tumultuous rapids below were a bottleneck, slowing the great armada to a crawl. Rather than packing their gear around the five-mile portage, many inexperienced boaters dared the churning waters, risking the loss of their supplies, their vessels and even their lives. Generations later, Southern Tutchone Elders told of an entire family—father, mother and children—who drowned in the rapids. The Elders went on to recount how their ancestors had recovered the bodies and then buried them on shore.[4]

By June 1898, about 200 boats had been wrecked, 52 outfits of supplies had been lost, and at least five men had drowned. The death and destruction would undoubtedly have been much worse were it not for two factors: Norman Macaulay's new enterprise, the Canyon and White Horse Rapids Tramway, and the intervention of the North-West Mounted Police.

THE TRAMLINES AND CANYON CITY

Norman Macaulay, a Victoria, B.C., businessman, had anticipated the needs of the northbound horde, and he came up with an ingenious way to capitalize on the perilous location. Over the winter of 1897–98, Macaulay hired a crew that included two Acadian brothers from New Brunswick, Tony and Mike Cyr, to cut and grade a right-of-way for a tramway on the east side of the Yukon River from the head of the canyon to just below the foot of the rapids. The simple track, made of eight-inch-diameter peeled logs set over cross pieces, or "sleepers," carried horse-drawn tramcarts with concave cast iron wheels, capable of hauling large loads of freight and even small boats. To avoid the deadly rapids, customers paid three cents per pound for freight and $25 for a small boat.

Within months, the ancient First Nations fish camp at the head of Miles Canyon was unrecognizable. By early summer of 1898, the site had been cleared

RIGHT A party of stampeders with their boat being hauled on a tram cart. Note the little dog atop the boat and the swathes of mosquito netting on a few of the hats.

BELOW The *Gleaner* and the *Australian* docked at Canyon City.

The original townsite at White Horse Landing, 1899. The tramcars are unloaded at the first point where boats could safely tie up to the riverbank. The log building in background is the first telegraph office.

and then filled up again with a set of docks, a large log roadhouse, stables, several cabins, many wall tents and, most critically, the head of the tramline, hewn through the forest to the base of the rapids. The site bustled with the tons of freight being offloaded from ships. A windlass constructed in the spring of 1898 hauled up the small boats to be loaded onto the horse-drawn carts. Vessels were tied up all along the shore, everything from simple rafts to small sternwheelers, awaiting their turn to go through the canyon.

Human activity was everywhere. "Freight hustlers" unloaded the watercraft, and then repacked the boxes, sacks and gear onto the tramcars. Hostlers fed, groomed and harnessed the hard-working horses. Mounties rode along the line and monitored the flood of vessels to ensure safe passage. Anxious, pack-laden gold-seekers stumbled along the trail.

Macaulay's headquarters at the upriver end of the line became known as Canyon City. There he built docks and a large log roadhouse and bar. Smaller structures followed, including crew quarters, stables and a North-West Mounted Police detachment. Another small settlement sprang up at the downriver terminus of the tramway. It became known as White Horse Landing, named after the nearby rapids. Although a few steamboats made the perilous passage through

White Horse Landing, ca. 1898.

the canyon and rapids, none went back upriver, and the humble community of White Horse Landing became the head of steam navigation on the Yukon River. Goods were transshipped between steamers on the upper lakes and sternwheelers that came upriver from the Klondike as far as White Horse.

By summer's end, however, Norman Macaulay had lost his monopoly on the cartage business. Another Victoria businessman, John Hepburn, established the Miles Canyon and Lewes River Tramway Company on the opposite side of the river. The tramway began about a half-mile upriver from Canyon City and was about six and a half miles long. Hepburn's track was built using rough-hewn four-by-six-inch timbers set three feet apart, with crosspieces at five- to twelve-foot intervals. Otherwise, his operation was the same as Macaulay's: carts with iron wheels pulled by horses.

Hepburn's tramway never attained the success of the original line across the river. Nonetheless, it was a hindrance to Macaulay and any expansion plans. After extended negotiations, Macaulay bought out the Hepburn tramway for $60,000.[5] By the summer of 1899, Macaulay was planning to replace his horses and carts with a narrow-gauge railroad. But even as he prospered from his enterprise, a much more formidable competitor was building a railway north towards the White Horse Rapids.

THE NORTH-WEST MOUNTED POLICE

The great northbound migration of thousands of would-be prospectors, most lacking experience living on the land, was a recipe for chaos. This human swarm was also a magnet for opportunists who went along to "mine the miners." While there was a respectable contingent of merchants, hoteliers and entertainers, there were also thieves, professional gamblers, confidence men and the infamous "macques," or pimps, selling the services of prostitutes. The Alaskan port of Skagway was described as "little better than a hell on earth." During the winter of 1897–98, robberies, public shootouts and murders were common events.

Shooting Miles Canyon in an empty scow at high water.

On the other side of the international boundary, however, there was amazingly little crime. This was largely due to the presence of the North-West Mounted Police. The first NWMP detachment had travelled north in 1895 to establish a detachment at Forty Mile, scene of an earlier and smaller gold rush near the Alaskan border, approximately 80 kilometres (50 miles) downstream from the Klondike River. Consequently, the Mounties were on hand for the great gold strike, and their commander, Superintendent Charles Constantine, was quick to call for reinforcements once he realized the extent of the influx. By early spring of 1898, there were over 200 Mounties in the Yukon, and a string of posts had been set up to shepherd the great flow of humanity from the mountain passes all the way to Dawson City.

The previous fall, two Mounties had been dispatched to White Horse Rapids with six months' worth of rations and orders to build a shack and assist winter travellers. The following May, Superintendent Steele sent two more men to Canyon City. Their orders were to warn stampeders of the hazards ahead and ensure there was "no overcrowding or unnecessary haste" in entering the canyon. By the time Steele inspected the site personally in June 1898, he found that the Mounties were spending most of their time rescuing unfortunates who had foundered in the rapids.

Steele immediately posted new orders for travellers, to be enforced by the Mounties. He later reported on his actions:

When I went down the river, I found that accidents were of almost daily occurrence. This was in great measure occasioned by inexperienced men running boats through the Rapids and Cañon, in the capacity of pilot, many taking through women and even children. This I immediately stopped and gave orders that, in future, only really qualified "swift water" men were to be allowed to act as pilots. Since then no lives have been lost and only a small quantity of general goods.

Once Superintendent Steele had laid down his edicts, only experienced pilots were allowed to steer vessels through the canyon and rapids. Women and children were required to walk around the rapids by the portage route. As Steele later put it, "If they are strong enough to come to the Klondyke, they can walk the five miles of grassy bank to the foot of the White Horse."[6] Nonetheless, a few daring women disregarded the order to experience the thrill of the ride. Martha Louise Black, who later became a prominent Dawson resident and Canada's second female Member of Parliament, insisted on riding through the rapids with her brothers.

Constable Edward Dixon was charged with ensuring that boats had sufficient free board, enabling them to safely ride the waves. The Mounties also posted a list of qualified pilots to be engaged in turn. The charges for piloting services were $150 for a steamer, $25 for a scow or barge and $20 for a small boat. Pilots made up to ten trips a day through the canyon, returning to Canyon City each time on horseback. For those unable to pay, Constable Dixon arranged for their vessels to be piloted free of charge.[7]

Canyon City/White Horse Landing continued as one of the busiest NWMP detachments during the gold rush. Police checked all vessels to ensure they were not overloaded or carrying contraband liquor. The Mounties answered countless queries about the trip ahead and generally assisted travellers. By the end of the 1898 navigation season, over 7,000 vessels had passed through Miles Canyon and the White Horse Rapids. After Steele's edict, there were few accidents, and no further lives were lost.[8]

THE YUKON ACT OF 1898

The federal government in Ottawa passed the Yukon Act on June 13, 1898, separating the northern Yukon District from the rest of the Northwest Territories. The idea was to maintain control over the booming new gold district, reaping revenues that would cover federal expenses for administering the area. The act established a federally appointed Commissioner and an advisory Yukon Council to assist in making decisions in the Yukon Territory, but no elected body. This lack of representative and ultimately responsible government would become an issue among Yukon residents, requiring many subsequent amendments after years of protest.

Major James Morrow Walsh, a retired NWMP officer, was appointed Chief Executive Officer and Commissioner in August 1897, when the Yukon was still a judicial district of the Northwest Territories. The political and administrative tangles of Dawson City proved too much for him, however, and Walsh was recalled to Ottawa within less than a year. His replacement, William Ogilvie, was appointed on July 4, 1898, the Yukon's first Commissioner after it became a separate territory.[9]

With Prime Minister Wilfrid Laurier in power at Ottawa, many French-Canadian Liberals and associates obtained appointments in the new Yukon administration. These influential civil servants and professionals and their families made up the largest non-anglophone group in the capital at Dawson City. Their active social life centred around St. Mary's Church and School.

CULTURAL COLLISIONS

The aboriginal people who lived here were forced to make many adjustments. With thousands of stampeders hunting and driving game from the river corridor, they had to go farther afield to make a living from the land. The entire Yukon River corridor turned smoky, due to the numerous forest fires caused by inexperienced campers and their untended cook fires. There were other hardships too. Lacking immunity to the diseases carried by the newcomers, many people sickened and even died. Some set off downriver to check out new opportunities, disrupting families and kinship ties.

Some found new ways to earn income. Many Tlingit people, including women and children, profited by packing freight over the Chilkoot Trail through the country they knew so well. The late Carcross Elder Lucy Wren told of how her mother, at age sixteen, had earned $30 for carrying a 30-pound pack from Dyea over the Chilkoot Trail to the headwater lakes. Along the route, aboriginal hunters earned money selling game meat and fish to the newcomers. Women created and then sold hide and fur clothing ideal for weathering a Yukon winter.

Many "Cheechakos"—the Chinook word for newcomers—owed their lives to the aboriginal people who assisted them along the route north. But while the newcomers benefitted from the knowledge and assistance of the aboriginal people they encountered, the original inhabitants found themselves in a strange new economy of cash and land ownership.

RAILS TO THE RIVER

No sooner had the great stream of humanity begun ascending the Chilkoot Pass than people were devising profitable ways to move it more efficiently: from chopping a set of steps into the steep, icy incline to erecting an aerial tramway to haul freight to the summit. The so-called "wagon road" over the White Pass became known as the infamous Dead Horse Trail, claiming the lives of thousands of starving and overloaded packhorses that perished on the treacherous route. Most ambitiously, a consortium of English businessmen came together to invest in a railway into the interior.

Laying track along the "Big Bend" just upriver from Whitehorse, along today's Robert Service Way, fall 1899.

Captain William Moore was an early advocate for a rail line to the Yukon River valley via the White Pass. After some persuasion, the railway syndicate allied itself with the Moores and their proposed route. Although Moore and his son Bernard had staked much of the Skagway waterfront, they had never been able to secure title to the land to get the full benefit of their strategic location and, after a prolonged legal battle with the railway owners, even had to surrender control of the Moore wharf. Both Moore and his son moved on to other ventures, convinced to the end that they had been swindled of their rights.

Once the first major wave of gold-seekers was underway, there was hot competition to gain government support from other transportation interests, including a competing proposal from three businessmen—Joseph Acklen, George Brackett and Norman Smith—to build a wagon road over the White Pass. By the spring of 1898, Brackett's toll road through the White Pass was operational and a severe hindrance to the railway planners. Eventually the railway builders bought out their competitor's right of way, and construction began in May 1898.

Weary railway labourers taking their noonday rest near the White Pass summit, May 1899.

The original intent was to extend the railway from Skagway over the White Pass all the way to Fort Selkirk, a Yukon River settlement roughly half-way between Dawson City and White Horse Rapids—a distance of about 640 kilometres (400 miles). This plan was scaled back once White Horse Landing became established as a sternwheeler stopping point and the head of steam navigation on the upper Yukon River. Even so, the new 110-mile line had many obstacles to surmount, from obtaining charters in two countries, a province and a territory to the physical challenges of laying a line through the most rugged terrain imaginable.

The railway was another intrusion into aboriginal traditional territory. John Joe, a Southern Tutchone man from the Marsh Lake area, first learned of the railway in a dramatic manner when he was drying meat at Fish Lake. Many years later he told this story: "We hear a bang. Something is blown up down there at Lewes Lake. They drain that lake so they can build the railway across it. Nobody had heard anything about it, they didn't know if the railway was coming or not, but it had come that far." [10]

The railway was built in phases between 1898 and 1900. As portions were completed, the line immediately went into operation, hauling supplies for workers farther down the line as well as taking on Dawson-bound freight. Construction began in Skagway in May 1898, and the line reached Lake Bennett on July 6, 1899. The company was now ready to start building the stretch from Carcross to Whitehorse. There was one problem, however.

As long as Norman Macaulay controlled both sides of an essential six-mile stretch of the Yukon River, he owned the logical route for the railway right-of-way into Whitehorse. Macaulay was also a strong potential competitor while his tramways linked steamer traffic above and below the canyon and rapids. The owners of the White Pass and Yukon Railway determined that the best solution was to purchase both tramways. To do this without revealing the railway's interest and possibly driving up the price, White Pass employed an intermediary to handle the transaction. C.E. Peabody, managing director of the Alaska Steamship Company, bought the two tramways for $185,000 in late summer 1899.[11]

By late May 1900, the line had progressed far enough that the railway camp could be moved to the new settlement of Whitehorse on the west side of the river. On June 8, the Carcross-to-Whitehorse section was officially opened when Frances Augusta Wood, wife of NWMP Superintendent Zachary Taylor Wood, hammered in the last spike. The completion of the entire railway was celebrated in Carcross on July 29, when the northern end of the line was linked with the last section, from Bennett to Carcross. Now it was possible to ride the rails from tidewater in Skagway to the Yukon River at Whitehorse, then steam downriver to Dawson City and beyond aboard a sternwheeler.

FOUNDING THE COMPANY TOWN

When the railway builders decided to end the line below Whitehorse Rapids, they selected a terminus site on the west side of the river, right across from White Horse Landing. The company was seeking not only a right-of-way for the tracks and grounds for the rail yards and depot, but also sufficient land for a townsite that would supplant the small community across the river.

In October 1899, company officials commissioned a survey of the entire flat on the left limit of the river. Dominion Land Surveyor H.G. Dickson staked out nineteen large lots, most about 40 acres in area, occupying just under 800 acres in total. This survey was registered in Ottawa on February 8, 1900, as Plan 8406.

Apart from two 40-acre lots north of town, the large Group Lots were purchased by the railway company, using proxies, for a total of $34,000. The

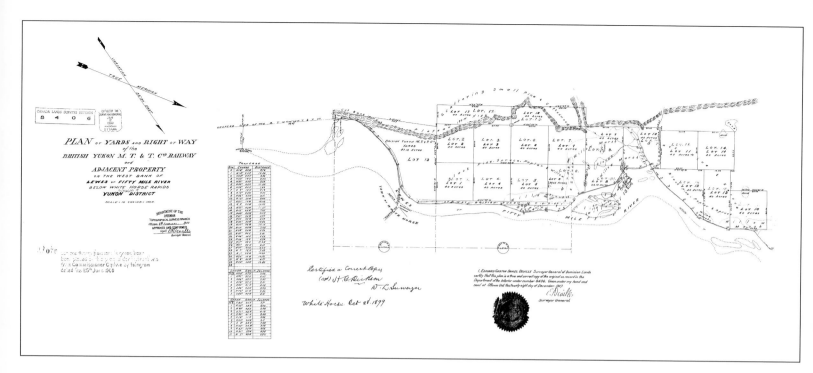

ABOVE The first survey of White-horse was made in October 1899. Earlier that year, Paul T.C. Dumais had surveyed White Horse Landing, the tramline terminus on the east side of the river, just before it was abandoned in favour of the new community.

RIGHT Shovelling snow from the grade near the summit, June 20, 1899.

original surveyed townsite occupied 160 acres, an area bounded by the river to the east, the escarpment to the west and what later became known as Hawkins Street to the south and Strickland Street to the north.

Whitehorse in 1900.

The railway company decided to name the new community Closeleigh, in tribute to Close Brothers & Company of London, major financiers of the railroad. Yukon Commissioner William Ogilvie decided otherwise. In late 1899, he requested that a post office under the name of White Horse be established at the new site, a name that was shortened to Whitehorse within a few years.[12] The townsite was barely open for business when people flooded in from all over the southern Yukon to build the new town.

Many individuals who came to the area during the gold rush stayed on to help found the community of Whitehorse. Their entrepreneurial skills and readiness to tackle a variety of endeavours contributed to the pioneer spirit and growth of the early settlement. Equally essential to the community's development were the First Nations people who assisted the stampeders and found ways to capitalize on their presence.

COMMUNITY PORTRAITS

EDWARD ALGERNON DIXON 1871–1955

Constable Edward Dixon of the North-West Mounted Police was stationed at the Miles Canyon/Whitehorse Landing detachment during the peak of the gold rush. A skilled pilot, he earned extra income by steering hundreds of vessels through the canyon—everything from rafts and small homemade boats to large steamboats. According to Superintendent Sam Steele, writing in 1898, "Constable Dixon has been of invaluable assistance to the public in running the White Horse Rapids. He is one of the best pilots on the river and with one exception has brought through safely every boat he has handled." [13]

Steele's high regard for Dixon was echoed by Professor Lowell Jackson Thomas who was quoted in the *Weekly Star* on July 14, 1916: "I would say that when it comes to good piloting, Ed Dixon is in a class by himself and I believe he could bring a train load of quaking kneed Cheechakos through Miles Canyon and Whitehorse rapids on a two-by-four plank, and not get any of them wet."

Dixon had joined the NWMP in 1893 and was stationed at Regina until he volunteered to go to the Yukon. When he left the force in August 1899, he stayed on to become a leading entrepreneur in the new town of Whitehorse. With the earnings from his piloting business, Dixon established a number of businesses, including the Hotel Pioneer, which he built and operated with his partner J.E. Smart. He owned claims in the Whitehorse Copper Belt, went on to become one of the proprietors of the Whitehorse Steam Laundry and co-owned and managed the Regina Hotel for several years. Dixon served a term as a Territorial Councillor from 1914 to 1916. He volunteered as chief of the local fire department and president of the Whitehorse Conservative Association.

In 1916, Dixon enlisted to fight in Europe. After the war, he settled in B.C. When he died in 1955, at age 84, he requested that his ashes be scattered over Miles Canyon. Fittingly, this ceremony was attended by an RCMP honour guard. [14]

Yukon Council members in Dawson City, 1915. Ed Dixon is standing fourth from the right.

NORMAN MACAULAY 1869–1919

Born in 1869 and raised in Ontario, Norman Macaulay moved to Victoria with his family at the age of nineteen. A few years later, he and J.J. Shallcross formed a partnership, working as commission merchants. The firm moved north to Dyea in 1897, and later that year Macaulay moved to the Yukon. Working with a crew of five other men, Macaulay began building the tramway he'd envisioned, and completed the line in June 1898. A year later, he bought out the competing line across the river.

After selling his tramways to the White Pass and Yukon Railway, Macaulay moved to the new town of Whitehorse, where he went into the lumber business. He built the White Horse Hotel on Front Street, the first building in town to have electric lights.

Macaulay left the Yukon in 1902 and travelled around Alaska for several years. Eventually he settled near Seattle, and he died at Port Townsend on the Olympic Peninsula at the age of 50. Two of Macaulay's cousins were also prominent early Yukon citizens. Henry Macaulay became the first Mayor of Dawson City, and Charles D. Macaulay was a territorial judge for many years.[15]

Canyon City workers with their boss Norman Macaulay who is seated and wearing a homburg, June 1900.

THE CYR FAMILY

The seeds of the French-Canadian population in Whitehorse were sown during the gold rush. Two representatives of this demographic were Max "Mike" and Antoine "Tony" Cyr, who had headed north from the logging camps of New Brunswick. When they arrived at Canyon City in June 1898, they went to work for Norman Macaulay, helping to build the tramway. Neither man ever reached Dawson, their original destination, but they made a pretty good living at Canyon City. They worked on both tramlines, building track and driving the horse-drawn carts loaded with supplies. They piloted boats through Miles Canyon and the rapids, and if they didn't think a stampeder's craft was sturdy enough, they would build a raft.

Both brothers went on to become established Yukoners. Mike Cyr built the original Montague Roadhouse on the winter road between Whitehorse and Dawson. When it was destroyed by a fire in 1915, he rebuilt the structure and worked there until the early 1920s. Tony settled in Whitehorse, where he acquired a team of horses and went into the delivery business. He also cut and hauled wood, his first woodlot being the site of the present Whitehorse Airport.

In 1918, Tony Cyr married Marie Beaudin, a widow from Quebec and mother of two children, Aline and Wilbrod. The recently bereaved Marie had been enticed north by François-Xavier Ladéroute, a family connection claiming to be a successful rancher and the Mayor of Kirkman Creek. She made the long trip with her children, only to learn that the community of Kirkman Creek was a crude cabin in the wilderness, 160 kilometres (100 miles) from Dawson. The only other inhabitants were dogs and sheep. After some months of misery, Marie made her way back to Whitehorse. There, unable to speak English, she had trouble getting a train ticket to Skagway. The stationmaster called in Tony Cyr to translate, and the rest was history. The pair married five days later and went on to have five more children: Laurent, Lomer, Gloria, Paul and Rosalie.[16]

CAPTAIN PATRICK MARTIN 1864–1940

In his unpublished memoir of 1933, Patrick Martin described the scene at one of the jumping-off points for the Klondike:

> We found Victoria filled with people fitting out for the Yukon, they were from all parts of the United States, Australia, New Zealand, Europe and Africa, from Ballarat in Australia, and the diggings of California, they were in all manner of shades and trim. Some real old men with long whiskers streaked with grey that in turn become tanned to a dirty brown with tobacco spit. Others sleek with the big mustache that gave them the appearance of cattle men from the Cow States, and again there were more that looked like they should not be allowed to travel.

Captain Patrick "Paddy" Martin took an especially long route to get to the foot of the White Horse Rapids. In 1898, the Canadian Development Company built three sternwheelers in Victoria—the *Columbian*, the *Canadian* and the *Victorian*—all destined for the Yukon River trade. The three vessels left Esquimalt, B.C., to make the perilous sea voyage up coastal B.C. and Alaska, through

Captain Patrick "Paddy" Martin seated with wife Winifred. Standing L-R: Sybil, Wilfrid, Irene and Katie.

the Aleutian Islands to St. Michael and then from the mouth of the Yukon River up to Dawson City—and, in the case of the *Canadian*, White Horse Landing.

Martin was well qualified for the voyage. He was born in Grates Cove, Newfoundland, in 1864 and made his first sailing voyage, on a sealer, at sixteen years of age. He went on to literally sail the world: freighting cod in small schooners to the Caribbean, South America and the Mediterranean; whaling near Greenland; hunting for fur seals in the north Pacific; and captaining a schooner from Nova Scotia to Victoria, B.C., around Cape Horn.

Many times, Martin derided the flat-bottomed "slab wagons" and "crates" that were never meant to travel over 2,000 miles of unpredictable ocean before steaming up the uncharted Yukon River. The hazards and setbacks of this adventurous two-month voyage took their toll. At the conclusion of his first trip to Whitehorse Rapids, he left seafaring forever.

Martin moved on to a new adventure—helping to build the town of Whitehorse. He became a well-known businessman and, together with his wife, Winifred, raised a family of four children. He operated a general store and trading post, served a term as Territorial Councillor, did some fur farming and pursued a variety of other entrepreneurial ventures.[17] His former house, relocated to LePage Park, a block from its original site, has been declared a municipal historic site.

KASHX̱ÓOT/CHIEF JIM BOSS CA. 1871–1950

One of the most influential figures in the southern Yukon was Kashx̱óot (more commonly Kishwoot), known to the newcomers as Chief Jim Boss. His descendants recall him as a large, powerful man with a strong physical presence and a distinguished lineage. Kashx̱óot was a successful entrepreneur, quick to adopt the practices of the new economy. Stories abound about his many enterprises. He charged stampeders for camping on his territory and later built a bunkhouse to house travellers. He sold fresh fish and firewood to the sternwheelers, and he even ran a fox farm on Lake Laberge.

Jim Boss was the only son of Mundessa and Łande. He had three sisters: Maggie, who married "Dutch" Henry Broeren; Susie, who married a man from Haines/Klukwan; and Jenny, who married Dawson Jim and was the mother of George Dawson. Jim Boss's mother, Łande, also known as Annie Jim, was the sister of Skookum Jim (Mason), Kate Carmack and Jennie Jim. Jim Boss married three times during his life. His first wife was Kathleen Kitty; they had one son, Fred. Jim Boss and his second wife, Maude, had four children: Alice, David, Lena and Ned. His third wife was Annie, and their children were Aggie and Sam.

Jim Boss was the recognized Chief of the Laberge people until his death in 1950. Notable during his tenure as Chief was his letter to the Superintendent General of Indian Affairs in Ottawa in 1902, written on his behalf by a lawyer. The letter is recognized today as the first approach to a land claims settlement in the Yukon. In the letter, Jim Boss stated: "tell the King very hard we want something for our Indians because they take our land and game." Jim Boss understood the responsibility of the Crown for First Nations people and their lands, and he foresaw the devastation to the local populations that the dramatic influx of miners and settlers would exact. When the land claims process was rekindled in 1973 with the Council for Yukon Indians' claim document *Together Today for Our Children Tomorrow*, Chief Jim Boss was recognized by Yukon First Nations as the forerunner of the modern land claims movement.

An early portrait of Chief Jim Boss.

Jim Boss remains a legendary figure in Yukon First Nations history. Many Elders remember him as an imposing man, someone who inspired fear and awe in them as children and then respect and admiration once they became adults. He was a hero in his attempt to take on the Canadian government and the Crown on behalf of his people and all First Nations people of the Yukon; and was an adept businessman who saw economic opportunities in a changing world, while continuing to uphold his traditional values and culture.[18]

4

THE COMING METROPOLIS OF THE GOLDEN NORTH

1900–1913

THE NEW TOWN on the west side of the Yukon River sprang into life with great energy and unbounded optimism. Scores of prospectors, miners, merchants, hotel-keepers and other entrepreneurs were quick to move to the railway terminus from short-lived gold-rush communities such as Bennett, Canyon City and the original settlement of White Horse Landing across the river. Along with them came many of the workers who were completing the railway, working in the new shipyards and labouring on nearby mineral claims. There was a staking rush in the Whitehorse Copper Belt, and expectations were high that major mines would be opening soon. The leaders of the growing community, mostly white businessmen, were quick to set up a board of trade, which immediately began advocating for all the services and institutions of a typical southern town. Within months, there were two newspapers to trumpet the brilliant future of the nascent settlement. Overlooked in newspaper reports and official records, however, were stories about the reactions and fortunes of the original inhabitants of the area. Once again, aboriginal people were forced to adapt to great changes and were displaced from many fishing and hunting camps within their homeland.

Over the winter of 1899–1900, people moved tents and even buildings across the river ice to the brand-new townsite. Sawmill operators and importers of lumber and building supplies scrambled to meet the demand for the materials needed to erect several new buildings on Front and Main Streets. By the time the first train arrived in July 1900, a bustling town-in-the-making was ready to greet it.

FACING Townsfolk gather at the shipyards to celebrate the completion of the first vessels built in Whitehorse: the *White Horse*, the *Selkirk* and the *Dawson*, 1901.

73

Whitehorse ca. early spring, 1905.

A few years later, the town's photographer, E.J. Hamacher, created a portrait of the brand-new town, looking west across the river. In the foreground were the railway station, warehouses and docks, along with a few vessels from the sternwheeler fleet—the main reasons for the town's existence. These were surrounded by substantial stores and hotels. Just out of the frame to the south were new public buildings—the fire hall and the post office, also home to other government functions, such as the customs office. Farther west was the large compound housing the North-West Mounted Police headquarters for southern Yukon. The town's religious needs were represented by the Roman Catholic church to the northwest, one of three new churches. Around the fringes of this apparently substantial community were a host of small buildings and tents seemingly set at random in clearings in the spruce trees. It seemed almost as if these edge-dwellers were waiting to see how the town developed before making a permanent commitment.

On August 10, 1900, the town received its first notable visitor: the Governor General of Canada, Gilbert John Elliot-Murray-Kynynmound, fourth Earl of Minto. Lord and Lady Minto had travelled north with a small party. The vice-regal visit took place during a strained period in government relations. Many northerners resented Ottawa's control of Yukon affairs, and there were accusations of favouritism and corruption. Nonetheless, everyone went all out to impress and entertain the Queen's representatives.

Harry Graham, aide-de-camp to Lord Minto, left an entertaining account of the party's overnight visit in Whitehorse. He described Whitehorse as "a mushroom city of wood and canvas" with 400 to 500 inhabitants. While the Board of Trade entertained the viceregal couple, who retired afterwards to their steamer, Graham and another staff member joined White Pass president Samuel Graves and two NWMP members on a tour of the local entertainment, featuring saloons, gambling, dance hall girls and great amounts of "intolerably vitriolic whiskey."[1] Despite claims to the contrary voiced by local papers, this was still very much a frontier mining community, with rough-and-ready entertainments geared to lonely single men.

ABOVE LEFT Whitehorse entertained Governor General Earl Grey, welcoming the visiting dignitary on the docks near the railway depot, August 10, 1909.

ABOVE RIGHT This optimistic advertisement appeared in the *Whitehorse Tribune*, November 10, 1900.

PLANNING THE COMPANY TOWN

The owners of the White Pass and Yukon Railway had set up a variety of linked corporate enterprises to handle their many interests. Eventually, these came under the umbrella of a group known as the White Pass & Yukon Route. Three separate companies were registered by the group within the two countries and three different jurisdictions traversed by the railway: Alaska, B.C. and the Yukon Territory. From the outset, the syndicate of investors was looking well beyond simply operating a railway. In a letter to Prime Minister Wilfrid Laurier dated March 20, 1897, one of the railway's advisors had written: "We ask no

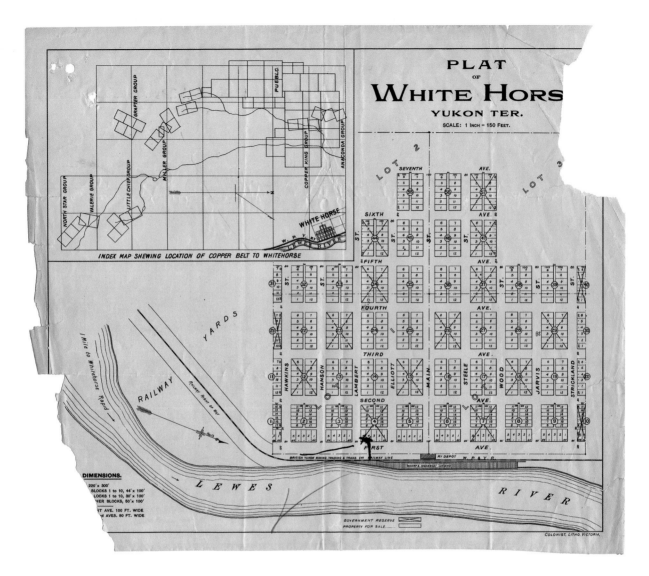

PLAT
OF
WHITE HORS
YUKON TER.
SCALE: 1 INCH = 150 FEET.

INDEX MAP SHEWING LOCATION OF COPPER BELT TO WHITEHORSE

DIMENSIONS.

Plan of Whitehorse, ca. 1900. The inset shows the many claims that had been staked in the copper belt west of town.

money from the government, simply a guarantee of 3% on $1,250,000 for which we will build the line, place ten steel steamboats and 50 barges on the Yukon, and open 9,000 miles of river tributaries and 192,000 square miles rich in gold."

The officials aspired to create a transportation monopoly that would control all freight moving into the territory, as well as the resources being shipped outside. Initially, the railway syndicate had requested a charter from the Canadian government that would have given it wide-ranging rights, including administrative powers over much of the territory. This aroused immense opposition, however, particularly the prospect of stifling other private enterprises. After several revisions, the Canadian Parliament passed the Act to incorporate the British Yukon Mining, Trading and Transportation Company on June 29, 1897. An important clause set limits on the time allocated to complete railway construction, as well as giving the company the right to build wharves and docking facilities.[2]

Once the initial survey was complete and part of the property was further divided into lots and blocks, the railway set up the British Yukon Land Company to handle property transactions, including the sale of lots in the new community of Whitehorse. As required by federal law, 30 per cent of the town lots were set aside for government use. Some were used for federal offices and services, such as the telegraph office, the post office and the Mounted Police compound; the remainder were sold.

The lands granted or sold to White Pass, apart from the townsite, included 97.12 acres to the south, for railway yards, and eighteen 40-acre tracts that occupied virtually all of the flat along the river valley, along with the right-of-way running three miles along the Yukon River waterfront. This meant that anyone camping or living on the lands adjoining the townsite were now considered squatters on White Pass property.[3]

The railway planners wanted to ensure that the transfer point between rail and river was central to the town, so a site was selected for the railway depot building, warehouses and docks at the foot of Main Street. Unfortunately, railway operations outdistanced construction. The *White Horse Tribune* gave a colourful account of the situation:

This shot of the riverfront in the summer of 1900 shows exteriors of the *Bennett News* building, the Hotel Grand, the White Horse Hotel, the Arctic Restaurant, and the railway depot under construction. Note the piles of lumber to the left of the depot.

Early in June rails were laid into White Horse and then came the rush of freight. The scores of workmen who were hustling up the wharves and warehouses on the water front toiled night and day to keep ahead supplying space for the consignments which were arriving and had all they could do to hold their own. Hundreds and hundreds of tons of goods were being piled up daily until the White Horse water front began to assume the proportions of a distribution point for the whole northern territory... a serious blockade seemed inevitable. But it has been relieved and the hairs on the head of General Manager Elliot which many times during the struggle threatened to turn grey are still flourishing in their natural colour, and some people are wondering how he did it.[4]

By midsummer, the waterfront was lined with hastily erected docks and a long, canvas-covered warehouse. In August, White Pass officials appeared, at least publicly, to have the situation under control. Railway spokesman Erasmus Cornelius Hawkins told a *Klondike Nugget* reporter that the company had completed "the best possible facilities for handling perishables at Whitehorse." He went on to describe the company's facilities:

> A wharf, the best on the river 800 feet long, has been built, and on it a warehouse 40×600 feet which will accommodate about 3000 tons of freight. Three tracks are laid on the wharf and cars coming in loaded are run right down to the steamer's side, and the freight transferred direct from car to steamer, which arrangement possesses great advantages over the old way.[5]

For over 50 years, this site—where rail met water—would be the focus of Whitehorse. Economically it was also a key point for the territory. The *Tribune* would prove prescient when it described the site as "the distribution point for the whole northern territory."

THE RIVER DIVISION

Early rail operations, particularly the handling of freight, came with unique challenges. In his memoir, the first president of the White Pass and Yukon Railway, Samuel H. Graves, described the situation when goods and passengers were offloaded at Whitehorse.

The *Victorian* was one of the vessels purchased by the BYN from the Canadian Development Company.

At White Horse we turned them over to an irresponsible mob of river steamers that competed for the business in much the same fashion as cab-drivers outside an ill-managed railway station. Innocent passengers were fought over, through shipments of goods were split up, Customs papers lost, goods stolen on the boats, and in short perfect anarchy prevailed. Many of the boat owners were not responsible financially, so that the passengers with through tickets and the goods owners with through bills of lading naturally preferred to make their claims against us, leaving us in turn to recover from the delinquent boat owner—if we could.[6]

In his memoirs, Graves suggested that White Pass was forced to set up its own River Division because of the chaotic practices of other shipping companies. More likely, this was part of the company's overall strategy. As a single carrier handling both rail and river transport, the company would have a virtual monopoly on upper river traffic. The British Yukon Navigation Company (BYN) was created over the winter of 1900–01. The new company set up a shipyard downstream from its docks and warehouses. Scores of shipwrights began building three sternwheelers: the *Dawson*, the *Selkirk* and the *White Horse*. The machinery and fittings from three former CPR boats were hauled in over the railway while shipwrights fabricated the hulls and superstructures in Whitehorse.

In May 1901, shortly before launching its new ships, White Pass announced the buyout of the vessels and facilities of its major competitor, the Canadian Development Company (CDC). By then the gold rush had abated, the population was dropping, and many smaller shipping companies had shut down. The White

Pass & Yukon Route was now a major player in the territory's economy, with its revenues linked to the prosperity of the Yukon. Conversely, the company was able to affect the profits of local businesses through layoffs and high rates for passengers and freight.[7]

The BYN moved to consolidate too. Within two years, the company owned all but three boats on the upper river between Whitehorse and Dawson. The BYN had greater ambitions, however. In 1913, the company built two new steamers— the *Alaska* and the *Yukon*—designed for lower river traffic, the communities below Dawson and into Alaska. In 1914, after a fierce tariff war, BYN prevailed and bought out its main shipping rival, the Northern Commercial Company.

THE OVERLAND TRAIL

Part of the reason that White Pass had bought out the CDC was to take over the profitable contract for summer mail delivery by sternwheeler. With this came the responsibility to deliver the winter mail from Whitehorse to Dawson and points between. For two years, the CDC had moved mail and light freight in winter using dogsleds and, later, horses to relay between roadhouses along the way. In the summer of 1902, White Pass contracted with the territorial government to build a winter road. This 330-mile route, built at a cost of $129,000, was completed by late fall. The first stage of the Royal Mail Service left for Dawson on November 2. From then on, winter sleighs and stages departed for the Yukon's capital three times a week bearing mail sacks and passengers, a trip that could take from three to ten days, with five days as the average. This service ensured that Whitehorse continued to be a distribution centre year round.

"H" DIVISION HEADQUARTERS

By the end of the gold rush, the North-West Mounted Police had organized the Yukon Territory into two administrative areas. "B" Division, headquartered in Dawson City, was responsible for the territory north of Five Finger Rapids. Most of the division's strength and efforts went into policing Dawson City and the goldfields. To the south, "H" Division was headquartered at Tagish and was responsible for policing an area that stretched from the mountain passes downriver to Five Finger Rapids, west to the Kluane area and even into parts of northern B.C.

MURDER MOST BIZARRE

Convicted murderer Remolo Cesari at Whitehorse in 1915.

IN 1914, the Royal Northwest Mounted Police[8] investigated one case with many bizarre elements: the murder of Dominic Melis, an Italian immigrant. A body, trussed up with branches, was discovered floating near the downtown docks on June 11. The main suspect was Melis's former partner, Remolo Cesari. The two had been arguing bitterly over the rights to an invention they were working on, nothing less than a perpetual motion machine. Cesari had moved on to Dawson not long after Melis disappeared sometime in February.

Doctors estimated that the body had been floating for no more than four to six weeks—an obstacle to investigators, considering the main suspect had been out of town for much longer. But diligent investigation by Sergeant McLauchlan uncovered bloodstained clothing belonging to Cesari, additional blood at the partners' residence, the probable murder weapon and a convincing theory for the state of the body. McLauchlan had located a place along the riverbank, near the rapids, where the stumps matched the sticks tied around the body. According to several witnesses, there had been caverns within the shore ice that year, cold enough to preserve the body until it floated away during spring breakup. Cesari was sentenced to death by hanging but evaded this fate when he was shot to death during an escape attempt from the Whitehorse jail.

Once the railroad was complete, most incoming traffic bypassed the headwater lake system and the police post at Tagish. After only two years of operation, it became apparent that the new town at the railway terminus was a much better location for "H" Division headquarters than the large post on the Tagish River. After some months of discussing the best location, it was decided that the new police headquarters would occupy a large block right in town, on the southwest corner of Main Street and Fourth Avenue.[9]

In an effort to recycle materials, the Mounties dismantled many of the buildings at Tagish, assembled the logs into large rafts and then floated them downriver. At Canyon City, the rafts had to be taken apart and made into smaller rafts to navigate the canyon. Even so, three rafts shattered in the turbulent waters of the canyon and rapids. Most of the building logs floated past White-horse, bounty for those living farther downriver. Finally, the Mounties appealed to the staff of the Department of Public Works (DPW). Using lumber from local mills, the Mounties and DPW employees managed to put up eight buildings by November 1900.

In 1901, "H" Division was made up of 103 members serving at eighteen detachments in the southern Yukon. In Whitehorse, four members were based at the Town Station on Front Street, while Superintendent Philip C.H. Primrose commanded 43 police at division headquarters.

TOP LEFT NWMP tents at Whitehorse, October 1900.

TOP RIGHT Mounties hauling a two-storey building into the Whitehorse compound using a windlass, 1902.

BOTTOM NWMP compound looking northeast from the escarpment. Barracks buildings, residences and other structures were set around a central parade square.

Six teams of horses strain to haul an immense boiler with an estimated weight of 19,900 pounds (9,027 kg) to the Pueblo Mine.

Although the Mounties appear to have put a lot of their efforts into building and heating their large compound, they did patrol the town and outlying areas. Typical cases appearing before magistrate's court included drunkenness, assault, robbery and illegal gambling. In 1901, there were eight cases of men tried for "Supplying liquor to Indians"—fewer than the ten convictions for "Profanation of Sabbath." The occasional murder was easily solved, usually a crime of passion or a partnership gone awry. But all too often the police were called upon to investigate tragic deaths in the workplace due to drowning, freezing, falling, being hit by rock or asphyxiated by gas.

Whitehorse continued to be the headquarters for "H" Division until 1910. At that time, in response to federal budget cuts and a diminishing population, the territory's police forces were drastically reduced, with only 50 Mounties remaining in the entire Yukon Territory. Whitehorse was merged into "B" Division and became a sub-district with just two one-man detachments, Whitehorse Town Station and Carcross. The remainder of the huge sub-district was patrolled by only fifteen RNWMP members.[10]

THE WHITEHORSE COPPER BELT

As early as 1897, prospectors had spotted copper ore just west of Whitehorse, but they were more interested in the Klondike goldfields and so continued north.

PIONEER
COPPER MINERS

Early mining at the Copper King with a windlass and headframe in the foreground.

JACK MCINTYRE from San Bernardino, California, not only filed the discovery claim on the Whitehorse Copper Belt but also helped launch one of its most successful mines, the Copper King. In 1900, McIntyre and his partner, Kentucky native William P. Grainger, sent nine tons of ore to a smelter in Everett, Washington. The ore yielded 46.4 per cent copper, and the future seemed most promising.

Both men came to untimely ends, however. In November 1902, Jack McIntyre and a companion broke through lake ice while delivering mail to Atlin by dog team, and McIntyre's body was not found until the following spring. After a five-year struggle to keep the mine going with a series of loans and mortgages, Grainger was finally on the verge of prospering. Copper prices were high, and outside financiers were prepared to buy or invest in local mines. While preparing the mine, however, Grainger and an employee were overcome by carbon monoxide and died in the shaft. The *Weekly Star* remembered Grainger as "a typical Kentuckian, intensely impetuous but generous to extravagance in his willingness to aid and assist others."

Jack McIntyre gave his name to two prominent Whitehorse features: McIntyre Creek and Mount McIntyre. Grainger's name, in a slightly misspelled form, survives in connection with Mount Granger and the Granger subdivision west of downtown Whitehorse.[11]

Early miners shattered the ore bodies with dynamite and pick hammers then sorted through the rock for copper-rich ore.

The newcomers weren't the only ones with gold fever; there were also reports of aboriginal people bringing ore samples to Canyon City in 1898. They may have thought they had found gold, but to more experienced prospectors the glittering rocks were evidence of copper ore. On July 6, 1898, Jack McIntyre staked the first claim, the Copper King. Over the following weeks and months, several other important discovery claims were staked: the Ora, the Little Chief, the Big Chief and the Anaconda. In 1899, several more significant claims were staked: Last Chance (later renamed the Best Chance), Rabbit's Foot, Arctic Chief, War Eagle, Grafter and Valerie. Even Chief Jim Boss got involved; he worked with prospector H.E. Porter to locate the Pueblo property, eventually the largest mine to be worked on the Copper Belt in this early period.

By 1902, nearly 400 claims had been staked in what became known as the Whitehorse Copper Belt, a broad band of copper deposits approximately 30 kilometres (19 miles) long, running along the western slopes of the Yukon River valley. The Copper King, Anaconda and Pueblo were under development, with two roads under construction to the new claims. Equally important in attracting investors was the presence of a nearby railway to ship in mining equipment and then help deliver ore to outside smelters.[12]

To say the copper claims generated great excitement is an understatement. The headlines were delirious. According to the *Dawson Daily News*, "White Horse Copper—A Railroad Terminal... A Population of Nearly Ten Thousand Expected There Next Summer as the Result of the Rich Copper Ledges

Uncovered in that District." The *Daily Klondike Nugget* predicted that smelters would be built. Newspaper articles enthused that the "fabulous developments" would bring "immense capital and the employment of thousands of men," predicting that the Pueblo Mine would be "one of the greatest mines in the world."

These wild predictions amounted to little. Development and production costs were high, and it was difficult to attract capital since the extent and the quality of the ore bodies were largely unknown. Moreover, the mine owners bewailed the high cost of transport. In 1902, the Grafter Mine earned $29 per ton for a shipment of ten tons of ore. Expenses, however, amounted to $30, with the following cost breakdown: sacking, $7; hauling, $7; freight charges, $10; and treatment, $6. Responding to numerous complaints, the railway lowered its rates slightly, but they were still high. The mine owners continually had to weigh the current price of the metal on world markets against the many expenses of ore extraction.

During a boom period in 1907, the White Pass and Yukon Railway began building a spur from Macrae (now "McCrae") to the principal mines. Work stopped for sixteen months when copper prices dropped and mining declined, but in 1910, the twelve-mile line was completed to the Pueblo Mine.

The Pueblo shipped the most ore, but it too shut down in October 1910, and then reopened under new ownership in 1912. It would close briefly in 1914, at the onset of World War I, but then, along with the other mines, go into high production to meet wartime copper demands.

The boom times in the Copper Belt enriched Whitehorse. More workers moved in to work the mines. Local merchants profited from supplying the mines, and there were spinoff benefits to workers such as the woodcutters, the operators of the horse-drawn wagons and sleighs that connected the mine to the town, and the government workers who built and maintained the roads. A reduction or stoppage of mining activity, however, usually meant less business and a drop in the town's population.[13]

TRADITIONAL WAYS UNDER SIEGE

Faced with this new economy and culture, not to mention the occupation of many of their traditional lands, the aboriginal people of the Whitehorse area were forced to adapt to the changes. Despite all the hoopla over the new mines, the fur trade continued to be important, and now people could trade their furs

Southern Tutchone men with pack dogs at Silver City on Kluane Lake, n.d.

at Whitehorse establishments such as Taylor & Drury. Most families continued to spend the majority of their time on the land, coming to town to trade their furs for food staples such as tea, flour, sugar, salt and dried vegetables, as well as whatever they needed to earn their living: sewing supplies, clothing, traps, snares, shells and rifles. Other stores relying on aboriginal trade included the Arctic Trading Company, operated by Captain Paddy Martin; John Sewell's general store; and William Puckett's hardware store.

The Whitehorse butcher shop, P. Burns & Company, sold beef from cattle that had been shipped north on the hoof to be slaughtered at the stockyard at the north end of the waterfront. It also offered wild meat, fish and waterfowl purchased from local hunters.

Many aboriginal men began working seasonally as longshoremen and deckhands on the riverboats, and on section crews for the railway. For example, Billy Lebarge was employed by the railway, while Ned Boss, George Dawson and Frank Slim worked on the steamboats. Entire families moved to the wood camps to fall, buck and stack cordwood. These enterprises were essential to supply the insatiable appetite for fuel: for the riverboats, for the mining industry and for wood stoves in homes and businesses. The hide and fur clothing crafted by women—ideal for the bitter winters—was always in demand.

Handwritten note on photo: Natives Skinning Moose White Horse Y.T.

Skinning a moose on the banks of the Yukon River at Whitehorse, 1909. Note the old telegraph office across the river.

When aboriginal people came to town, they camped on the riverfront above and below the settlement, or across the river near the present hospital site. In addition to the Southern Tutchone–speaking people based in the Lake Laberge and Marsh Lake areas, people from farther afield travelled great distances to town to trade. These trips were also occasions to meet, feast and celebrate. Both the police and the *Whitehorse Star* wrote about an especially noteworthy gathering that took place in 1905, when Chief Jim Boss and the Atlin Chief led their people in several days of festivities at their camp across the river. The two groups then moved farther downriver to meet representatives from Little Salmon, Dalton House and Tagish for a potlatch.[14]

People also came to town when they were sick or in need. During a smallpox epidemic in 1901, patients were kept in quarantine in the former telegraph office across the river. For several years afterwards, this building served as a hospital for victims of infectious diseases, many of whom were aboriginal people, and the log building became known as the "Pest House." As the main representatives of the Canadian government, the North-West Mounted Police found themselves in charge of Indian welfare and dispensed blankets and food to those in need.

During hard economic times in the Yukon, aboriginal people suffered the most. When jobs were scarce, they were the first to be laid off and the last to be hired. Inspector J.A. Macdonald wrote about a particularly harsh period in his 1911 annual report. The Pueblo Mine had shut down. The White Pass & Yukon Route had laid off 20 per cent of the railway crew and half the River Division staff. He went on to state:

> The Indians were in poorer circumstances, probably, this year than they ever have been since the advent of the white men, in any numbers, in the country. The fur catch in the southern Yukon last year was very small [and] together with their inability to obtain the employment they got in other years rendered their lot a hard one. Until the salmon run commenced this summer we had to issue more or less relief each week. We had to look after completely, a number of cases requiring medical treatment until they were in a fit condition to hunt and fish.[15]

As noted earlier, Chief Jim Boss—a man of foresight—opened negotiations with the Canadian government in 1902 to protect his people's traditional lands. Through a local lawyer, he later wrote another letter on behalf of all the territory's aboriginal people, showing how their populations had been greatly reduced since the coming of the white man.

In his letter to the Superintendent General of Indian Affairs, Jim Boss identified the people of the region and estimated population figures for the following communities (present-day locations in brackets are from Cruikshank, 1991):

Lake Marsh (Marsh Lake, M'Clintock River)	15
Tagish (Tagish)	30
Hoochi (Hutshi)	200
Kluchoo (Kloo Lake)	25
Iseag (Aishihik)	250
Klukshoo (Klukshu)	80
Gaysutchoo (Big Salmon/Gyò Cho Chú)	50
Tatsuchu (Carmacks?)	15
Kloosulchuk (Minto)	55
Haseena (Ross River)	90
TOTAL	810

Jim Boss noted that in previous years these groups had numbered in the thousands before the arrival of newcomers who encroached on hunting and fishing grounds and carried deadly diseases for which local people lacked resistance.

Communities close to the Yukon River had lower numbers than more distant communities such as Aishihik and Hutshi.[16]

Some reserve land at Lake Laberge was set aside, albeit much less than the amount requested. There were many examples from this time of aboriginal and white people living and working together harmoniously. But in Whitehorse, for the most part, the two cultures lived very different lives that rarely intersected.

MORE RUSHES, FEWER RICHES

The miners and entrepreneurs who travelled north during the Klondike gold rush were always on the alert for the next rich strike. Early in the century, two major discoveries triggered staking rushes of hundreds of prospectors, the opening up of new country, predictions of great developments and, within a few years, near-abandonment of the affected areas. In each case, Whitehorse played a key role as a supply centre and jumping-off point.

In 1903, gold was found on Ruby Creek, near Kluane Lake. The discoverers were none other than Skookum Jim and Dawson Charlie, the Tagish men who had located the first major gold finds in what became the Klondike goldfields. A few months later, 43 ounces of gold were mined from nearby Bullion Creek. This triggered the Kluane gold rush, and by March 1904, over 2,000 claims had been staked in the area. The territorial government built a road from Whitehorse to the shores of Kluane Lake at the new settlement of Silver City, following the route of a traditional aboriginal trail. Whitehorse merchants were kept busy provisioning the miners. By 1905, however, only a few hundred men were left in the area, and ten years later, Silver City was almost abandoned.[17]

Whitehorse residents were also alert to mining activity to the southeast, particularly near the new mining town of Conrad. This tent town was located about 100 kilometres (60 miles) southeast of Whitehorse on Windy Arm, part of the Yukon River's headwater lake system. Since 1899, a number of significant silver and gold deposits had been staked on nearby Montana Mountain. The flamboyant American entrepreneur Colonel John Howard Conrad began to consolidate and develop a number of these claims in 1904. Over the next two years, he raised an enormous amount of capital to construct buildings, tramways, a concentrating mill, telephone lines, docking facilities and roads to serve the mine. There was so much activity that a new Conrad mining district had to be established in 1906, with a mining recorder's office at Conrad City.

Captain Martin's store at Conrad ca. 1906. Captain Martin is standing at right.

Whitehorse merchant Patrick Martin joined the rush in February 1906, setting up a temporary store on the waterfront and even staking out a townsite. A new branch of the Arctic Trading Company took its place alongside hotels, barrooms, a combined tent church/reading room, new wharves, a warehouse and at least three other stores. That year marked the peak of activity in the town's short history.[18] There were difficulties among the owners in Conrad's consortium as early as 1907. By 1909, Martin's store, described as a "well-built substantial building" was one of only two structures that still occupied the townsite, the other being a hotel. Not long after, Martin gave up the store "owing to the dullness of trade."[19] Despite expending vast sums on infrastructure, the investors in the Montana mines saw few returns. By 1912, Colonel Conrad was broke, and his operations had shut down. The town of Conrad had long since been abandoned, and Patrick Martin had moved back to Whitehorse.[20]

In 1909–10, a rush to the Wheaton valley area southeast of Whitehorse had a similar outcome: extravagant predictions and a short-lived operation. Livingstone Creek, a tributary of the Big Salmon River, was first staked in 1898 by George Black, a lawyer from New Brunswick who later became Commissioner of the Yukon and then the territory's Member of Parliament. Black's placer mining enterprise did not prosper, and the next excitement from the area came in 1901, when the Larose brothers filed discovery claims on a creek that was reported as a major new gold strike. Over the next decade, the mining camp boomed and the merchants and tradesmen of Whitehorse were alert to this potential new bonanza. Community leaders lobbied hard for the construction of a road to the new camp, eventually resulting in construction of a winter road via Lake Laberge. The gold output fluctuated, and eventually the diggings at Livingstone subsided to a small operation that saw more activity when gold prices were high.[21]

THE BOARD OF TRADE

Since Whitehorse remained unincorporated, the town was unable to raise funds through local taxation for public works such as road building and maintenance, or firefighting equipment. Instead, townsfolk relied on the Yukon Council to disperse funds for basic municipal services. Local civic leaders recognized the need for a strong voice to lobby on behalf of the town. The Whitehorse Board of Trade, formed in the summer of 1900, took on the combined role of chamber of commerce—promoting the local economy and seeking to create a favourable climate for business—and a city council, representing the townspeople in advocating for necessary services. The two roles were evident in a detailed petition that the Board of Trade sent to Yukon Commissioner William Ogilvie in September 1900.

The petitioners pointed out that it was difficult to collect on debts with the nearest court in Dawson and no local magistrate or justice of the peace. Petitioners requested both a magistrate able to rule on debts of up to $1,000 and a deputy judge able to handle criminal cases. They identified the need for a hospital and a school, given that at least 50 children lived with their families in Whitehorse, and perhaps just as many had been sent to schools outside—as far away as France, in the case of the Jacquot family. The petitioners also requested a variety of municipal amenities, including a sidewalk on Front Street, funds for a fire hall and equipment, a park or playing field near the newly built North Star Athletic Association, and a new road to the copper mines west of town.

Dawson was the centre of power for the territory, but for many decisions government officials had to consult employees of the Department of the Interior in Ottawa, a process that often took months, even for small decisions such as increasing the salary of the post office cleaner. It was a continuing source of frustration for Whitehorse residents to have critical decisions about their community made by distant powers with no personal knowledge or appreciation of local conditions. In 1903, the electoral district of Whitehorse was created, giving the southern Yukon representation on Territorial Council.[22]

REPRESENTATIVE GOVERNMENT FOR THE YUKON

Eligible Yukon citizens—white British male subjects—were able to vote for a Member of Parliament after 1902, as well as for some Councillors. After 1909, the Council of ten was wholly elected. The Territorial Council remained separate from the Executive, and it had only limited powers to pass the budget and legislation forwarded to it by the Commissioner. Whitehorse, with its small population of just a few hundred people, elected two representatives to the Council. Although Council elections were not run overtly on partisan lines, everyone's political persuasions were known, since federal elections were hotly contested on party tickets. Whitehorse residents elected Liberals Willard Phelps and Robert Lowe to the Council in the early years, and then switched loyalties to elect some Conservative Councillors after 1912, when prominent Conservative George Black was appointed Commissioner of the Yukon by the new federal Conservative government.[23]

THE *WHITEHORSE STAR*

The town's first settlers had barely pitched their tents when the first newspapers were established to report on their progress. Issue number one of the *White Horse Tribune* hit the streets on July 21, 1900. Its front page headline, "A Rapid Growth," set the tone for this short-lived publication. Nearly half the paper's front page featured advertisements for the hotels, stables, ships, lumber companies and cafés setting up shop in the fledgling town. After less than a year, the *Tribune* went out of business, giving way to an energetic competitor.

Like many newcomers, the founder of the *Whitehorse Star* had come north with the gold rush and then stayed on, attracted by new prospects. Percy Scharschmidt was a medical doctor turned miner. On his first trip north in 1897, he was a special correspondent for the Victoria *Colonist*, sending dispatches from Skagway, Dyea and, a year later, Dawson City. Together with L. Dumar, Scharschmidt set up a printer in a tent in Bennett City and published the first issue of the *Bennett Sun* on May 24, 1899.

Scharschmidt planned to publish a second paper from Bennett, the *Northern Star*, for residents of the new town at the railway terminus. But once the railway was completed, this way station to the Klondike had no purpose, and Bennett soon became a ghost town. Scharschmidt moved his printing plant and tent to Whitehorse, and on July 18, 1900, he launched the first issue of the *Whitehorse Star*. The tent eventually became part of a small frame building on Main Street.

Scharschmidt moved on to become superintendent of the White Pass River Division, selling out the paper to his manager, Albert Miller Rousseau, and printer, Angus Bernard McEacheran. The *Star* was run by a succession of editors, including E.J. "Stroller" White, the Klondike newsman who edited papers in Skagway, Dawson and—from 1904 to 1916—Whitehorse. Over the years, the *Star* came out weekly, semi-weekly or daily. In the early 1920s, it shut down for some months. Nonetheless, it continued to bring out the news during difficult economic times and went on to become the Yukon's longest continuously operating newspaper, providing an invaluable historical record.[24]

EARLY SPORTS AND RECREATION

Sports and recreation have always been cornerstones of community-building. They enable new arrivals to fit in, and they represent the shared values of unity, respect, friendship, equal opportunity, the pursuit of excellence and honest effort.

At the beginning of the twentieth century, however, many sports had no real home. A ten-round boxing match between Dawson City's Curley Carr and Mike Donovan of Boston, Massachusetts, was held in Whitehorse's Jackson McDonnell Hall in April 1901. (Carr won the decision.) Handball and basketball were played on the dance floor in the Arctic Brotherhood (AB) Hall, located at the intersection of Front Street and Hanson. Ping-Pong tournaments at the AB Hall featured live musical interludes between matches.

The first curling match took place in a White Pass & Yukon Route warehouse in 1906. Ice hockey thrived when and where it could. After freeze-up, players used a pond at the north end of town. Later in the winter, they played either on man-made rinks at the NWMP barracks or beside the Yukon River, just south of the train depot. The first championship hardware for hockey was put up by W.P. Renwick, manager of the White Horse Hotel. There were two trophies: a silver-plated urn for competition among teams from Whitehorse, Dawson, Bennett, Atlin and Skagway, and a set of seven gold-lined, silver-plated drinking cups for a series of games between Whitehorse businessmen and saloon-keepers. The saloon-keepers won the series.

Hockey players were not overly affected by falling snow. When it got too thick, they stopped the game, shovelled the snow over the boards, and resumed play. Small change-shacks were heated with little pot-bellied wood stoves. Fans warmed up by the stove while the players were out on the ice. Otherwise, bundled up in fur coats, they stamped their feet to keep them from freezing and drank coffee spiked with overproof rum.

Competitive walking was also a popular winter activity. In 1903, during a relaxed "looping the loop," contestants walked a designated route through downtown, starting and finishing at the Bank of Commerce. Individual times were recorded and judges patrolled the course to ensure there was no cheating. E.A. Dixon completed the circuit in 41 minutes and 45 seconds. His time included a five-second penalty imposed after he slipped and took several false steps to recover his balance.

Most sport matches were invitational, such as the challenge issued to the women of the White Horse Basket Ball Club in March 1902 by a men's team. The women accepted but cautioned they weren't going to be pushovers. Their letter warned that "surgeons and stretchers will be in attendance and a special supply of arnica [a medical ointment used for sport injuries] will arrive on Tuesday's train." While the women had an organized team, the men didn't, so they had to find a coach and quickly learn how to play the game. No records remain of the outcome or whether medical assistance was needed.

Running was probably the first semi-professional sporting activity held in Whitehorse. In races run in December 1907 and February 1908, three men

Outdoor hockey rink in the North-West Mounted Police compound.

competed for a purse of $50 (the equivalent of three months' income) at each event. The "sprint" was five kilometres (three miles) in length, starting at the post office and then going to the British Yukon Navigation barn and back three times. The three competitors were Kenney Hicks, a professional road racer; Patsy Forest, "the most renowned musher that ever burned a northern trail," according to the *Whitehorse Star*; and "Whitehorse Johnny." Operators of the Copper King Mine complained that the latter contestant had trained on their road so often that the snow had melted, making it difficult to run their ore sleds out to the railhead.

The town's only sports organization was the North Star Athletic Association (NSAA), which began life in 1900 as the North Star Athletic Club. Early on, its members identified the need for a centralized recreation complex. A ball held at the AB Hall in the winter of 1901 became infamous because the thermometer showed the indoor temperature to be minus-30 degrees. The only way to stay warm was to keep dancing.

Plans for a new recreation building, designed by Norman Macaulay, were unfurled at the NSAA meeting on June 16, 1903. Total construction costs were estimated at $3,000. The site for the new facility was an empty block of land on the north side of Main Street, between Third and Fourth Avenues. Capital for the new entity was raised through the sale of 1,000 shares at $10 each. Willard Phelps and Robert Lowe drafted an incorporation ordinance, with Lowe sponsoring its passage through the Yukon Territorial Council in July of that year. The NSAA moved into its new facility—which included a gymnasium, a reading room and two meeting/viewing/dining rooms—in the fall of 1904. The following year, the NSAA added dressing rooms and outdoor tennis courts that became skating and hockey rinks in winter. Adjacent buildings went up to house bowling lanes and a covered curling rink.

Introduced in 1906, indoor baseball also became wildly popular. The league's inaugural season featured a schedule for four teams: "townies," sponsored by the British Yukon Navigation Company; two police teams; and a civil service team. With teams playing regularly before rabid fans, rivalries quickly emerged. Over the years, the sports and the team names often changed, but the "townies"-versus-everyone-else mentality persisted.

The new facility also played a key cultural role in the community. At one end of the gymnasium, a stage hosted productions by local drama clubs and visiting performers. Many Whitehorse children watched their first moving pictures in the NSAA Hall. A projection room was installed upstairs, and audiences sat on wooden benches. A long silent film was a true test of an individual's tolerance. People played cards on the main floor, with alcohol served in a nearby games room. Family dances and formal balls had Whitehorse residents whirling around the gymnasium. A decade after opening its doors, the NSAA Hall was the heart of Whitehorse's social, performing arts and sporting life.

TOWN SERVICES

While the merchants, mining promoters and other major figures of early Whitehorse were boosting the town as a modern community worthy of investment, its basic services could only be described as primitive. Water was either bucketed from the river or delivered by one of the town's draying firms, run by the Ryder and the Cyr families. Indoor plumbing was a rarity, and even the most elaborate homes had small outhouses in the back yard. The only electricity was generated by a wood-fired boiler housed in a small log building on the waterfront. Poles and lines conducted the power to a handful of downtown structures that enjoyed electric lighting for a few hours a day. A telephone exchange, started early in the century, was soon taken over by Yukon Electrical Company but this service was likely limited to a few major businesses and prominent homes.

Garbage disposal was informal. In 1912, the *Whitehorse Star* decried the practice of dumping waste in the woods on the outskirts of town, particularly in the trees bordering the lots northwest of the Roman Catholic church. The paper chastised Whitehorse residents for creating "such a collection of garbage as was

The Telegraph Office at left next to the NWMP town depot, 1903.

never before seen on the edge of a civilized community and tin cans are the most savoury and cleanly articles in the vast aggregation of trash and offal." Instead, the *Star* encouraged people to use the "garbage wharf" to dump their refuse in the Yukon River or on the river ice. In spring, the garbage would float downriver to become someone else's problem. The wharf was likely located near the end of Strickland Street, at the edge of downtown. Eventually the town dump was moved to the riverbank between the stockyards and Kishwoot Island. According to various accounts, however, people continued dumping garbage and discarded machinery at various locations on the fringes of the community.[25]

COMMUNICATIONS

Until 1899, communications between Dawson City and the outside world had taken weeks, if not months. This was a particularly difficult situation for government officials, who often had to improvise a response to local problems long before they received an official directive from Ottawa. In summer, mail was carried by boat. Winter mail was hauled by dogsled, most notably by the North-West Mounted Police in 1898–99. Travelling in the most gruelling of conditions, members of the force logged 103,017 kilometres (64,012 miles) bearing over six and a half tons of mail.

In late 1898, the federal government announced plans to build an all-Canadian telegraph line. Early the following year, Superintendent of Public Works J.B. Charleson travelled north with a crew to tackle the first phase of this work. The plan was to link up with the telegraph line installed along the railway to Skagway, then run the line from the community of Bennett along the headwater lakes and Yukon River valley down to Dawson. Along the way, the crew would set up "loops" to the Tagish Police Post, Canyon City and White Horse Landing, where they planned to build a 40-square-foot log telegraph office. Despite many challenges along the way, including the tragic loss of four crew members who

ABOVE LEFT The fire hall soon after completion in 1901.
ABOVE RIGHT A group of men posing outside Eddie Marcotte's barber shop.

drowned in Five Finger Rapids, Charleson and his crew managed to run 1,000 kilometres (600 miles) of line to Dawson by September 28, 1899. The work was completed in only five months, ahead of schedule and under budget. Dawson and the many small settlements along the way were now linked with the outside world by the line to Skagway and from there to Vancouver via the coastal steamers. Two years later, the sections through B.C. were finished all the way to Ashcroft, completing the all-Canadian route.

A telegraph office was erected in Whitehorse at the corner of Steele and Front Streets. Yukoners could now send messages at a cost of $3.75 for the first ten words and twenty cents for each additional word. Newspapers could run national and international stories that were no longer months out of date.[26]

FIRE PROTECTION

Fire is a very real danger in small communities made up of wooden dwellings that are heated by wood and have no running water. Most winters, the local newspapers reported on at least a few homes that had been destroyed by chimney fires that got out of control. The Board of Trade's lobbying for a fire hall and firefighting equipment paid off in July 1901, when NWMP Superintendent Z.T. Wood, Public Works Superintendent J.-C. Taché and Board of Trade member Robert Lowe selected a site for the new fire hall just south of the railway station. The railway's general manager, E.C. Hawkins, gave the property to the town; he also offered to transport the firefighting equipment free of charge by rail and to donate the services of railway workers to raise the hall. Taché volunteered to

After the fire, people searching among the ruins for anything salvageable. This scene is looking from Second Avenue towards the intersection of Front and Main Streets. The gap between the warehouses was formerly occupied by the railway depot.

prepare plans for the engine shed and to estimate the costs. The police delegated prisoners to clear the site and level the ground. By 1901, a handsome new structure was in place. It housed a large boiler and a second-hand Silsby steam fire engine, together with three hose reels and 600 metres (2,000 feet) of fire hose.

A full-time engineer was hired to maintain the apparatus and keep the pressure up in the boiler. There were equipment problems, however, and by May 1905, the department had dug a well, run a conduit to the river and installed new firefighting equipment. It would all be put to the test very shortly.

FIRE!

Early the morning of May 23, 1905, a fire broke out in Édouard "Eddie" Marcotte's barbershop in the back of the Windsor Hotel. The building was right across the street from the fire hall, and it should have been simple to get the fire under control. Instead, the recently purchased equipment proved to be totally inadequate. Due to insufficient pressure in the steam boiler, the engine could not pump water, and although citizens hastily organized a bucket brigade, the fire raged along Front Street for nearly two blocks. Residents desperately tried to save what they could from the burning buildings, but within two hours, nothing but smoking ruins remained of the railway depot, five hotels, several businesses and a number of poles and lines belonging to the Yukon Electrical Company. The damage was estimated at between $250,000 and $300,000. It was a sign of how much the town had grown that the list of businesses affected occupied several inches of column space in the local newspapers. According to the *Atlin*

Claim, "some of the best stocked stores and finest equipped hotels in the north" had been laid waste.

The people of Whitehorse spent little time lamenting their losses. Within hours, they were combing the smoking ruins to see what could be salvaged. Within a day, most businesses had set up in tents running their operations against a noisy backdrop of hammering and sawing as their new quarters rose out of the ashes. By the spring of 1906, the street had been completely rebuilt, and a handsome new railway depot anchored the foot of Main Street.

Local lawyer Willard L. Phelps and White Pass engineer Hector Sproat had been commissioned to investigate the fire and recommend improvements to the firefighting service. Change came quickly. Within a month, the Yukon Electrical Company had made an agreement with the Yukon Commissioner to install a new fire apparatus and maintain the power plant. The light plant would be moved to a new addition south of the fire hall. Most importantly, the electrical company took on the responsibility of maintaining enough steam pressure that the fire pumps could be operated on five minutes' notice. On August 26, the company's equipment was hauled upriver on flat cars to the new site. When the new plant began operating in early September, the *Star* claimed that the company's machinery was so quiet it could not be heard across the street. Although Whitehorse had no shortage of fires in the years to follow, there was never a repeat of the great conflagration of 1905.[27]

THE CITY'S FOOTPRINT

EARLIEST HOTELS

Two of the earliest notable buildings in Whitehorse were the Hotel Savoy and the Hotel Pioneer, both on Front Street. Some sources claim that the Pioneer was built in the original community of White Horse and moved to the new site across winter ice. Portions of the hotel still stand today in Shipyards Park.

TENT CITY

Many homeowners and entrepreneurs moved quickly from their original tents into frame buildings. Many more people, however, simply built over their tents while continuing to live in them. The first step in making a tent more winter-worthy was to line the walls with newspapers. The frame built over the canvas walls was then covered with whatever materials were available—often the same

ones used in sternwheeler construction. Many a humble tent ended up with fine fir sheathing and was lined with tongue-and-groove cedar panelling.

WHITE PASS AND YUKON RAILWAY DEPOT

The first White Pass Depot was constructed over the summer of 1900. The architect may have been Victor Ignatius Hahn, a railway engineer and chief draftsman who designed many White Pass structures. It was a long, low building with a storey-and-a-half centre block. The high hipped roof boasted three gabled dormer windows along the rear (facing Front Street) and two others on either side of a larger central gable on the track side.

The main floor contained offices, a waiting room, a baggage room, a ticket office and a drug room, where pharmaceuticals were secured. There was also a police office to ensure that outbound passengers were not trying to evade the gold tax. The station agent and his family occupied the second floor.

TOP The Hotel Savoy and the Hotel Pioneer, both on Front Street.

BOTTOM The riverfront side of the White Pass Depot, June 1901.

TOP LEFT The Grand Hotel with the Windsor on the left, anchored the corners of Main and Front Streets from 1901 to 1905.

TOP RIGHT The Post Office, completed in 1901, also housed other federal offices such as Customs, the Department of Public Works and a courtroom.

RIGHT Dog team in front of the Bank of Commerce.

FRONT STREET

By 1901, Front Street was well established as the commercial centre of town. Development extended north from Lambert Street to Wood Street. On the river side, the railway depot was flanked by the new fire hall and giant freight warehouses. Hotels and stores were simple wood-frame buildings, with many owners adding false, or boomtown, fronts to lend an air of substance and elegance. In the case of the two hotels flanking Main Street, the builders went to a little more trouble. The Hotel Grand featured graceful curves, finials and moulding on its facade. The three-storey Windsor sported a bracketed wooden cornice. Both buildings had doors facing the corner of Main and Front, aimed enticingly at the depot and its arriving passengers.

Professional people such as doctors and lawyers had offices in the downtown by 1901. A hardware store, a drug store, a barbershop, restaurants and

even jewellers offered their wares and services. Outfitting services and general merchants had downtown outlets to provide goods to miners, prospectors and citizens alike.

The Post Office, built in 1901, immediately became a landmark with its handsome mansard roofed tower and was the focus of government activity in town. It sat just on the edge of the burn area on Front Street and escaped the 1905 fire unscathed.

The Bank of Commerce extended the downtown business area by setting up at the corner of Main and Second Avenue, its two storeys rising from a sea of low buildings and tents.

DOWNTOWN, POST-1905

Following the great fire of May 23, 1905, the downtown was quickly rebuilt, but its complexion changed slightly. The Windsor was rebuilt as the White Pass Hotel. Across Main Street, the Hotel Grand was replaced by a more modest mercantile establishment owned by Whitney and Pedlar. The White Horse (Vancouver) Hotel was not rebuilt, and part of the lot remained empty for years. The Arctic Restaurant was rebuilt with a fancier, pedimented facade. For the most part, however, the two newly rebuilt blocks of Front Street featured a similar assortment of stores, hotels and small offices.

The White Pass Depot did not survive the fire, though the warehouses were spared. It was the company's busiest time of year, and operations could not be halted. Offices were set up in a tent, and work began on the new depot almost before the ashes had cooled. Perhaps because of the rush to get it operational, the new station lacked the graceful lines of the old building. By July, however, the *Whitehorse Star* was reporting that "the office arrangement of the new building is much better and more commodious than was that of the old. In

ABOVE LEFT Post-1905 White Pass Depot. At right, the steam derrick is hoisting a barge onto a flatcar.

ABOVE RIGHT The town's first hospital, administered by a volunteer board, opened in 1902. It occupied a small single-storey building with a false front on Second Avenue between Main and Elliot Streets. During World War I, it was replaced by this new building on Second Avenue and Hansen Street.

the upstairs are four elegant living rooms, wardrobes, pantry and other conveniences which will be occupied as the home of Agent G.C. Mellott and family. Beneath the building a well has been sunk from which by force pumps, water can be had in all parts of the building. A cellar with concrete floor and wall will contain a furnace by which the entire building will be heated."

WATERFRONT WAREHOUSES

Although the White Pass Depot was an impressive structure in a small town, it was the warehouses, built beginning in 1900, that dominated the waterfront. These two large buildings on the east side of the train tracks were used for the temporary storage of goods being transshipped from the depot. Goods that arrived by rail were moved into the River Warehouse (No. 1) and then onto the sternwheelers at the wharves.

Warehouse No. 2, the upstream building, was known as the Commissary. It contained supplies for the steamboats. The north extension of the Commissary, the "Bennett Shed," held piles of coal for fuelling the steam derrick, among other items. The south end of the building contained White Pass offices and, upstairs, living quarters for unmarried workers.

On the west side of the railway tracks stood Warehouse No. 3, commonly referred to as the "local warehouse" or the "freight shed." It held freight for Whitehorse and other communities reached by road, such as the Kluane area. Goods were loaded onto wagons, and later trucks, for transshipment.

CHRIST CHURCH CATHEDRAL

This simple log building was erected in 1900 by Reverend Richard John Bowen, who had honed his construction skills by building St. James Church at Forty Mile and the first Anglican church in Dawson City. After some months of sleeping in the new church, he built a two-storey rectory next door. Isaac

Stringer was the priest here from 1903 until he was named Bishop of Yukon in 1905. For a short time, poet Robert Service served as the vestry secretary.

SACRED HEART CATHEDRAL

The first Catholics of Whitehorse worshipped in a wall tent while building a more permanent structure. Two Oblate missionaries, Father Camille Lefebvre and Brother Augustin Dumas, travelled from Dawson City to Whitehorse in June 1900 to supervise the building of Sacred Heart Cathedral. Plans were prepared by two government engineers in the congregation, J.-C. Taché and Paul-Émile

Mercier. Materials were shipped north from Vancouver. The new church opened in the fall of 1901.

By 1917, the town's population had declined and, with it, the number of Roman Catholics. For many years there was no full-time priest, and the Roman Catholics of Whitehorse had to settle for occasional visits from the priest in Skagway.[28]

Whitehorse French Canadians were more isolated than their counterparts in Dawson City in these years, with but a few speakers available to share their language and culture. The priests at Sacred Heart Cathedral would continue to be key contacts for many decades as francophone numbers dwindled along with the mainstream population in the territory.

ST. ANDREW'S PRESBYTERIAN CHURCH

From 1900 on, the town's Presbyterians attended services in a frame building at the southeast corner of Main Street and Second Avenue. An important public service offered by the church was its reading room, an alternative refuge for those not interested in spending their leisure time in bars. Up until 1915, six different ministers served the congregation. The last, Reverend C.K. Nicoll, enlisted as a chaplain with the Canadian Forces during World War I, leaving the church without a leader. Most local Presbyterians became members of the United Church of Canada after the merger of four Protestant denominations in 1925. The building on Main Street was sold in the 1930s and later demolished.[29]

LAMBERT STREET SCHOOL

The first school in Whitehorse opened in February 1901 in the reading room of St. Andrew's Presbyterian Church. Reverend J.J. Wright held class for sixteen children aged five to fourteen. He then formed a school committee that hired the town's first teacher, Patrick Campbell, and made plans to put up a permanent school building. The Lambert Street School, a handsome two-room frame building, opened in November 1902. The building was expanded in 1916 when another room was added for high school students. In June 1918, the first two students were ready to write their junior matriculation exams.[30]

AFTER THE RUSH

By the onset of World War I, the territory's population was greatly reduced. The 1911 census figures noted only 8,500 inhabitants for the entire Yukon, as compared to 27,200 ten years earlier. While specific figures for the population of Whitehorse are not available, it is likely the community consisted of only a few hundred people, with population increases in summer, when the sternwheeler crews came to town, or during periods when the mines were active.

Within days of the arrival of the railway, residents were describing their town as the "natural distributing point for the Yukon Territory." Despite its ambitions to become another great mining centre, distribution was to be the town's destiny over the next several decades, and the transportation network of the White Pass & Yukon Route was critical in fulfilling this role.

The Yukon's first peoples continued to follow a path that now included the new trading centre and job opportunities while retaining their connection to the land. The stores of Whitehorse attracted trappers from all over the southern Yukon and parts of northern B.C. This meant that the area continued to be a natural spot for gatherings of diverse people from far-flung groups. The increasing number of gravesites on the hill across the river was a reminder of the many who had come to an untimely end, often due to illnesses against which aboriginal people had little or no natural resistance.

Most of the non-native people who remained in the Yukon after the Klondike gold rush were committed to the North and embraced life in a small, close-knit town. Lacking the amenities of a larger centre, these residents showed the self-reliance and initiative necessary to create a vibrant community. Whether it was through sports, theatre, fraternal organizations such as the Arctic Brotherhood and Freemasons, or community service activities such as running the local library or supporting the town hospital, residents did whatever was necessary to entertain themselves during the long winters and improve their town. These characteristics have persisted, and Whitehorse is still known for its high level of volunteerism and dedicated community spirit.

COMMUNITY PORTRAITS

Doctor Paré and NWMP Inspector Fitz Horrigan sitting in the first automobile in Whitehorse.

SURGEON LOUIS ALPHONSE PARÉ 1848–1918

Like Dawson City, Whitehorse was located in a low-lying area with several nearby marshes and rudimentary water and sewage services. NWMP Doctor Louis Alphonse Paré played an important role in early Whitehorse, not only in looking after the health of the force but also in treating aboriginal people and promoting public health. Paré was born in Lachine, Quebec, and joined the NWMP in 1887. In November 1898, he was notified that he was urgently needed at Tagish Post, where several members were afflicted with typhoid fever. When "H" Division moved to Whitehorse, so did Paré. He remained there until his retirement in 1911.

One of Paré's continuing concerns was to improve the diet of the force with more fresh produce and fresh meat, and to ensure the food was well cooked. In an early report, he observed that "navvies on the railroad" ate better than the police, with their reliance on "evaporated potatoes," bacon and tinned meat. He also expressed concern that most of the town's water came from the river, as opposed to nearby streams. As well as treating the Mounties, he looked after other government employees, civilians and aboriginal people. Many times he expressed concern for the health and sanitation of indigent aboriginal people. "I feel that the immediate necessity of making a systematic and proper provision for the Indians cannot be too strongly urged upon the Government," Paré wrote in 1902. "But it will be evident to you that shelter for the sick, and medicine to cure them, will not feed the hungry and needy, nor will it put blankets upon them to protect them from the cold." Likely the reports of Paré and other concerned individuals helped lead to the appointment of a Yukon Indian Agent in 1914.[31]

TAYLOR & DRURY

The partnership of Isaac Taylor and William Drury began during the Klondike gold rush, when the two men began buying the outfits of discouraged stampeders. After a time in Atlin, the two moved on to Bennett, where Drury, a former shoemaker, made sails for the vessels of northbound gold-seekers. The pair boarded the first train to Whitehorse in July 1900, and then set up a tent store on the corner of Front Street and Lambert. Within a few years, they had set up trading posts all around the territory. They supplied their posts with a succession of small steamboats: the *Thistle*, the *Kluane* and finally the *Yukon Rose*. These vessels travelled up the Yukon's side streams to places like Teslin, Ross River and Pelly Banks. In 1912, T&D partnered with its main competitor, Whitney and Ped-

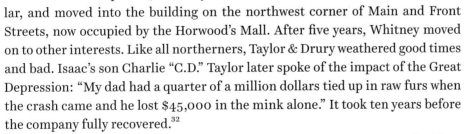

lar, and moved into the building on the northwest corner of Main and Front Streets, now occupied by the Horwood's Mall. After five years, Whitney moved on to other interests. Like all northerners, Taylor & Drury weathered good times and bad. Isaac's son Charlie "C.D." Taylor later spoke of the impact of the Great Depression: "My dad had a quarter of a million dollars tied up in raw furs when the crash came and he lost $45,000 in the mink alone." It took ten years before the company fully recovered.[32]

By 1969, T&D had taken over the Northern Commercial Company building next door to their Main and Front Street location to occupy the entire length of the block. The original partners had become even closer when Isaac Taylor married Bill Drury's sister Sarah. At least two more generations would be involved in family businesses, including a General Motors dealership. In its peak year, T&D's gross sales were $3-million, and the firm employed 85 people. After 75 years of serving Yukoners, the store closed down in 1974 with the retirement of C.D. Taylor.[33]

TOP Early view of the Taylor & Drury store in Whitehorse.

BOTTOM Raising the *Thistle* near Cluett's wood camp, ca. 1920.

JOSEPH-CHARLES TACHÉ 1850–1939

Joseph-Charles Taché was born in 1850 in Rimouski, Quebec, to an illustrious family. His ancestors included senior civil servants, doctors, politicians, merchants, a journalist and even one of the Fathers of Confederation, Sir Étienne-Paschal Taché. After completing his studies in civil engineering, Taché joined the federal Department of Public Works at age 21. In February 1899, he was dispatched to the Yukon, along with Superintendent J.B. Charleson, to act as chief engineer on the telegraph line between Bennett and Whitehorse, as well as to supervise the construction of roads, bridges and navigation improvements on the Yukon and other rivers. Moving just ahead of the line builders, Taché arranged to build a dam at Nares Lake, raising the water level by closing off a slough between Bennett and Nares Lakes. His crews also blasted out rocks in the Six Mile River connecting Tagish and Marsh Lakes. Taché tackled many other river hazards over the next year. These included blasting rock to widen the rocky eastern channel of Five Finger Rapids and building a dam at the entrance to Lake Laberge in an effort to keep the river from silting in. He oversaw various new roads and trails, including two trails between the Whitehorse Copper District and the railway, and a fifteen-mile road from Dawson to Gold Run. He also supported the petition from the Whitehorse Board of Trade to construct a new 49-mile road between Whitehorse and the mining area of Livingstone Creek.

J.-C. Taché on the dock at Skagway, March 1899.

After a trip to Ottawa, Taché returned to the Yukon in July 1900 with his family: his wife, Leda Drapeau, and their two daughters, Marie-Louise and Yvonne. They travelled by steamship to Skagway, then over the newly completed railway. Marie-Louise Taché married one of Taché's employees, Paul-Émile Mercier, son of Quebec Premier Honoré Mercier, on June 28, 1901, in the large canvas tent that served as the temporary Roman Catholic church. According to Marie-Louise's diary, this was the first marriage "entre Blancs" in Whitehorse, a major social occasion.

Although Taché and his family left the Yukon in November 1901, he left his mark on the territory and the early townscape. He designed and helped build the town's fire hall; the first telegraph office, which stood across the river on the original townsite; and the second telegraph office, which is still standing in its original location and is now part of the MacBride Museum complex. With his fellow engineer and son-in-law, Paul-Émile Mercier, Taché also prepared the plans for the town's first Roman Catholic church, Sacred Heart Cathedral.[34]

KÀDÙKIKH/KITTY SMITH CA. 1890–1989

Kàdùkikh (Kitty Smith) was the daughter of a Crow mother from Marsh Lake and a Dakla'weidi father who had been born on the coast, near the mouth of the Alsek River. Her father was Tàkàtà (his English name was Pardon), and her Tagish mother was Tatl'èrma. During Kitty's early years, the family lived at Shaw'ashe, or Dalton Post. When Kitty's father died, Paddy Duncan married her mother and became her stepfather.

In 1898, Kitty's mother was called home to Marsh Lake when her brother was arrested for murder in the infamous Nantuck brothers case, leaving young Kitty with her stepfather's people. Soon afterwards, Kitty's mother became ill with the flu and died. Kitty remained with her stepfather's people, travelling extensively in the southwest Yukon, even rafting down the Alsek River to Yakutat, Alaska, on an epic journey to visit a medicine man.

Kitty witnessed many extraordinary events in her lifetime. Her family walked over the trails to Whitehorse to see the first White Pass and Yukon Railway train. Although they were three days late and missed its arrival, she remembered all the people marvelling at the size and power of the train:

> Another time we went to see that first train to Whitehorse. Not much white people in those days. When they hear train going to come, gee, everybody wants to see train.... Oh... it's coming now.... Ding, ding, ding, ding.... Some people get off there. One boat made it down to Whitehorse, too! After we saw that train, we walked back to Dalton Post. There's a walking road there, for a stage.[35]

When her first marriage—arranged by her family—ended, Kitty decided to leave Dalton Post and rejoin her mother's people at Marsh Lake. She became an

Susie Fred and Kitty Smith,
ca. late 1970s.

accomplished trapper and was able to support herself and her grandmother quite comfortably, for the times. Kitty's second marriage, to Billy Smith in 1916, was a happy one. They lived at Robinson and Carcross, where Billy worked as a labourer and mined, in addition to the hunting and trapping they did as a family. During the building of the Alaska Highway, Kitty sewed mitts, hats and other items to sell to the soldiers, earning enough to help buy a truck for her family. She also created many small carvings that she sold to visitors, some of which are preserved today at the MacBride Museum. When Billy died in 1968, Kitty continued to live on the land as she had always done: hunting and trapping.

During her two marriages, Kitty had six children. Only two survived to adulthood: her daughter May Hume and her son Johnnie Smith. Both married and provided Kitty with a wealth of grandchildren. She helped raise them and taught them about their cultural heritage. Throughout her life, Kitty was a prolific storyteller. She spent many hours recording her history and telling stories to her family and, particularly in her later life, to students, researchers and the general public at heritage conferences and the Yukon International Storytelling Festival. She published a book of her stories, *Nindal Kwadindur—I'm Going to Tell You a Story*, and contributed to several other publications.

Kàdùkikh lived from the land and represented the strength of knowledge, motherhood and Elder-hood; she was an artist, carver, wife, mother and leader. Her life was an adventure. She epitomized survival and the diligence to carry forward the ways, language and understanding of those who had gone before, for the benefit of those coming after her. By the time she died in June 1989, Kàdùkikh was a legend herself.

KATHERINE RYAN 1869–1932

A formidable woman from Johnville, New Brunswick, Katherine Ryan crossed the continent, travelling to the Yukon in 1898 over the infamous Stikine Trail. By 1900, she had settled in Whitehorse, where she opened a restaurant and

Kate Ryan poses for a formal portrait with her nephews.

invested in local mines. That same year, the White-horse NWMP hired Kate Ryan as their first "woman special." She worked as a prison matron to assist the police with women prisoners. She also took on the job of gold inspector, with the tricky task of search-ing women suspected of smuggling gold out of the territory in order to avoid paying the 2.5 per cent gold export tax. According to one story, Ryan even managed to discover a cache of nuggets enclosed in an elaborate hairdo. NWMP Superintendent Snyder described Ryan as being a "warmhearted, affable and efficient" person who carried out her work with tact and good judgment.

Ryan continued in both jobs until 1919, when she moved to Stewart, B.C. An RCMP honour guard attended her funeral in 1932.[36]

EPHRAIM J. HAMACHER 1857–1935

Whitehorse owes much to a man who moved to town in 1900 and documented the life of the community from then until the mid-1930s. Born in Kitchener, Ontario, Hamacher learned the photographer's trade in Washington State. In 1898, he headed north with Eric Hegg to document the Klondike gold rush. When Hegg went on to Dawson City the following spring, Hamacher stayed on in Bennett City. Before long, he ended up in the new town at the end of the railway line.

Hamacher soon became known as the "White-horse photographer." Nothing escaped his inquisitive eye; his images portray panoramic views of the town from the escarpment and across the river, the stages of building a sternwheeler, railway trains, horse-drawn winter stages en route to Dawson, fascinating street scenes, sporting events and various other incidents around the southern Yukon. In his studio, he shot portraits of

Ephraim J. Hamacher.

Shorty Chambers with a visitor
in front of his original roadhouse
at Champagne.

Whitehorse citizens. In addition to his prints and photographic supplies, Hamacher occasionally sold other items. He loved the outdoors: fishing, hunting and travelling the river in his little boat. He was also a musician and played piccolo in the town band.

Upon his death in 1935, Hamacher was remembered for his many contributions to his adopted town. As his obituary in the *Whitehorse Star* recalled, "A gentleman of the old school, Ephraim Hamacher was noted for his courteousness and affability in all circles and will be missed by the entire community, and by the old-timers of the town, who reverently bow their heads in tribute to [the] passing of a grand old man."[37]

HARRY "SHORTY" CHAMBERS CA. 1857–1929

Harry "Shorty" Chambers hailed from Albany, New York. He travelled north to work as a wrangler for Jack Dalton, the former gunslinger who became famous for running cattle to Dawson City during the Klondike gold rush. Chambers arrived in Whitehorse in 1899 and started the Pioneer Livery Stables, where he freighted goods, bought and sold horses and dogs, and supplied feed, wood and ice. Described by the *Whitehorse Star* in 1901 as "the hustling and irrepressible news agent," he also ran newsstands around town and at the railway depot. That same year, Chambers became the second vice-president of the Whitehorse Board of Trade.

Although Chambers was well known in Whitehorse, his main enterprise became his trading post and freighting business in the village of Champagne, 100 kilometres (60 miles) to the west. This had long been an important trading place for the Southern Tutchone and the Coastal Tlingit. Chambers recognized the commercial opportunity and built a log store there, as well as the first roadhouse. Both these enterprises boomed after the building of the government wagon road to supply the Kluane gold rush in 1904.

In 1912, Chambers married Annie Kershaw, an aboriginal woman from Dalton Post. Harry and Annie and their children continued running the freighting business, the stables and the store. When Chambers died in 1929 at the age of 72, the *Whitehorse Star* reported: "His funeral was one of the largest in the history of the town. The businesses were closed during the service." The Chambers family continues to be prominent in the Yukon today.[38]

ROBERT W. SERVICE 1874–1958

People all over the world are familiar with the man who became known as the Bard of the Yukon, and with his epic poems, such as "The Cremation of Sam McGee" and "Spell of the Yukon." Few realize, however, that Service did not reach the Yukon until 1904, well after the gold rush, and that he got his start as a clerk in Whitehorse, at the town's first and only bank, the Bank of Commerce. Service recited popular poems of the day at public events, although he had also been writing his own poetry. It was *Whitehorse Star* editor Stroller White who suggested to Service that he write something about "our own bit of earth.... There's a rich paystreak waiting for someone to work. Why don't you go in and stake it?"

Inspired by stories about the great gold rush told by local prospectors, Service penned "The Shooting of Dan McGrew" in a single night. The poem was a great hit, and many more followed. Service's first book of poems, *Songs of a Sourdough*, was printed in 1907 and went on to become a runaway success. Service finally saw Dawson in 1908, when the bank transferred him. After a year, he left the bank to rent a cabin, where he wrote his first novel.

Service left Dawson and the North for good in 1912. He moved to France, where he married, worked for the American Red Cross during World War I and—after a period in California during World War II—eventually settled in Southern France. He is buried near a family home in Lancieux, Brittany. He is honoured in Whitehorse with a bronze bust sponsored by the Hougen family and a sculpture on Main Street, near the site of the original Bank of Commerce, paying homage to the poet's writing desk.[39]

Robert Service lived in Whitehorse from 1904–08 and in later life in Lancieux, France. Whitehorse became a twin city of Lancieux in 2000 to honour him.

5

THE TRANSITION YEARS

1914–1938

DESPITE LIVING IN a remote northern community, the citizens of Whitehorse were not entirely isolated from the impact of world events. Many young men who worked in the mines and on the boats enlisted to take part in the Great War overseas. Most did not return, either perishing on foreign soil or settling elsewhere after coming back to Canada. The great flu pandemic that swept the world in 1918 also claimed some lives in the Yukon, including a number of Southern Tutchone people at Lake Laberge. That same year, Alaskans and Yukoners mourned the hundreds of northerners who drowned in the wreck of the *Princess Sophia*, a CPR passenger liner that foundered during a bad storm. The Depression of the 1930s brought wage cuts and job losses. All of these factors contributed to a massive drop in the Yukon's population, from 27,000 in 1901 to less than 4,200 twenty years later.

Nonetheless, Whitehorse residents had reasons to be optimistic. The town continued to be the Yukon's distribution centre. The local newspaper focussed on mining activity in the region, headlining every new discovery and promising development—all good news for local merchants, although there were the inevitable downturns due to low mineral prices, high processing costs and mineral strikes that didn't pan out.

Tourism grew after World War I and became an important focus for White Pass summer operations. Increased mining in the Keno and Elsa region ensured that more equipment and supplies were freighted through Whitehorse to Mayo. When aviation came to the Yukon in the early 1920s, the woodlot above the escarpment became first a landing strip and then the town's airport. Air travel opened up the country beyond the river corridors. Mostly, however, the town's

FACING First plane to land in Whitehorse, en route to Nome, Alaska. Mrs. Head holding an infant, Mountie Jack Stewart and another man pose with the pilot, 1920.

economy remained tied to the White Pass & Yukon Route—the transportation company that owned the railway, the sternwheeler fleet and many other associated enterprises. As went the company's fortunes, so went those of the town.

The divide between aboriginal people and non-native town dwellers widened in 1916, when First Nations people were abruptly exiled from their camp on the downtown riverbank to a new area downriver, far from the rest of the community. This forced move underlined their status as second-class citizens and created bitter feelings that would last for generations.

FROM HORSE POWER TO MOTOR POWER

Among the greatest changes during this period were innovations in transportation technology that made the North less isolated. Increasingly, sleds, sleighs and wagons pulled by dogs and horses gave way to cars, trucks and tractors. Small boats no longer relied on the current when travelling downriver, and their pilots were freed from the back-breaking work of paddling and poling their way upstream. Residents were able to purchase outboard motors and gasoline launches from the 1910s on. In 1914, Tagish Jim made the news when he sold his foxes for $1,000 then bought a gasoline launch, or "gas boat." Ten years later, E.J. Hamacher was selling Evinrude outboard motors from his photography studio.[1]

In the early 1920s, horse-drawn winter sleighs gradually gave way to "cat trains," sledges full of freight linked together and pulled by tractors. Tracked vehicles were first used in 1922 by the Treadwell Yukon Company (forerunner to United Keno Hill Mines). Within a few months, a ten-ton Holt tractor hauled 4,500 tons of ore from the company's Keno Hill mines to Mayo Landing, reducing transport costs by up to 75 per cent. These trains were usually self-contained and even featured a heated caboose where crews could sleep and eat along the route. Roadhouses, the traditional purveyors of meals, beds and horses, began to fall into disuse.

Cat trains were first introduced by Greenfield and Pickering in 1924, along a portion of the Overland Trail, between Whitehorse and Yukon Crossing. During the muddy spring and fall, wheeled horse-drawn stages were replaced by trucks, while in winter, the horse-drawn sleighs were supplanted by caterpillar tractors. In 1921, the White Pass & Yukon Route had given up the winter mail contract and ended its operations on the Overland Trail. The company had taken on winter mail delivery in order to obtain the profitable summer mail contract for its

HAMACHER Photo

JOE JOE ROAD HOUSE
MENDENHALL CROSSING.

ABOVE Procession of automobiles on old Hepburn tramline along Miles Canyon, ca. late 1910s.

RIGHT Chevrolets for sale on Front Street in front of the Taylor & Drury Store, ca. late 1920s.

sternwheelers. When the company's last rival on the upper river went out of business in 1918, there was no longer any need to compete for the winter postal contract. A few different private contractors took on this service over the next decade, including T.C. Richards and W.L. Phelps who operated Klondike Airways in the late 1920s.[2]

The greatest change of all was the onset of air travel. By the late 1920s, observers of the local scene were not only listening for train and boat whistles but tilting an ear to the skies for the sounds of incoming aircraft. A rudimentary landing field was roughed out on the escarpment above town, and by the late 1930s aircraft were landing on the ice or water of the Yukon River in front of town. Occasional flights gave way to regular air mail service in the late 1930s.

THE WHITEHORSE AIRPORT

In the spring of 1920, U.S. Army General William "Billy" Mitchell ordered preparations be made to fly four Air Service de Havilland DH-4 biplanes on a 9,000-mile trip from New York City to Nome, Alaska, and back to New York. Such a trail-blazing flight, much of it through remote areas that had never seen an airplane, presented enormous challenges: the placement of aviation fuel along the way, crew accommodation and, most importantly, places to land at each planned fuel stop.

An advance party consisting of Captain H.T. Douglas of the U.S. Army and Captain J.-A. LeRoyer of the Canadian Air Board was sent to Whitehorse, which had been identified as one of the essential fuel stops. Fortuitously, the plateau above the clay cliffs to the west of town had been partially cleared by local entrepreneur Antoine Cyr, who supplied most of the town with firewood. Cyr had also managed to gouge a road into the clay bank of Puckett's Gulch in order to haul the loads down from his woodlot. In a letter dated June 17, 1920, the U.S. War Department confirmed a verbal contract with Robert Lowe to prepare and mark a 500-by-125-yard landing field for the sum of $1,500.[3]

On August 16, 1920, three of the four army biplanes appeared on the south horizon and zoomed low over Whitehorse, much to the delight of excited residents. The fourth aircraft arrived early the next morning, after a delayed departure from Wrangell.

For the most part, Tony Cyr's modified woodlot worked just fine for the historic arrival and departure of the four surplus World War I bombers. Upon

landing on the primitive airfield, however, one of the heavy biplanes tore open a tire. The damage was hastily "bush repaired" down at the shipyards by wrapping the wheel with many turns of rope, then lacing the torn tire over it. On August 17, the eight airmen continued north, arriving at Dawson in the midst of Discovery Day celebrations.

Over the next seven years, a few intrepid American flyers made landings at the Whitehorse airfield during historic flights to and from Alaska, but it was not until 1927 that the field saw use by Canadian registered aircraft. A Yukon entrepreneur by the name of Clyde Wann gathered enough investors to form Yukon Airways and Exploration Company, the first attempt at offering a commercial air service in the Yukon. Their aircraft was a sleek silver Ryan monoplane christened the *Queen of the Yukon* and flown by A.D. "Andy" Cruickshank.

The following year, Treadwell Yukon bought a Fairchild aircraft for their company use. Klondike Airways, a cat train service operated by T.C. Richards and W.L. Phelps, bought a small de Havilland Moth aircraft, which they turned over to Treadwell Yukon to operate. All three of these Yukon-owned aircraft were frequent users of the Whitehorse airfield in the late 1920s.

In 1935, the British Yukon Navigation Company (BYN) commenced a commercial air service based in Whitehorse, using the river during the summer, when their aircraft was on floats, and the airfield (and the frozen river) during the winter, when the machine was on skis. That same year, Pacific Alaska Airways, based in Fairbanks, inaugurated a thrice-weekly scheduled air service connecting Whitehorse to Fairbanks and Juneau. The company leased land and

purchased Treadwell Yukon's maintenance building on the east side of the field. Pacific Alaska would be absorbed by Pan American Airways in 1941, and Alaska-Yukon air service would continue through a succession of companies, including Wien Alaska, Trans North and Air North.

By 1936, BYN had decided that both flying seasons would best be carried out from the airfield. That summer, the company built the first hangar to appear on the airfield, a T-shaped structure large enough to accommodate their Ford Tri-motor or their single-engine Fairchild 82.

WIRELESS TELEGRAPHY

Up until the early 1920s, the sole communication link between the North and the outside world was the Dominion Telegraph line. Messages were transmitted via a single-line steel wire on poles that traversed thousands of miles of rugged wilderness terrain from Dawson City through Whitehorse and northern B.C. to points south. In small cabins at twenty-mile intervals along the line, lone operators relayed messages in Morse code. Their most important duty was patrolling and maintaining the line, constantly under threat from both the elements and wildlife.

In 1923, the federal government contracted the Royal Canadian Corps of Signals to set up wireless stations at Mayo Landing and Dawson City. Messages from Mayo were relayed south via the Yukon Telegraph line. Over the next few years, a relay station set up at Fort Simpson, Northwest Territories, was linked to a terminal and transfer station at Edmonton, thereby connecting these northern communities to CN and CP telegraph lines across the country.

It was over a decade, however, before wireless telegraphy reached Whitehorse, a development triggered by the intervention of an American airline. In 1935, Pacific Alaska Airways (PAA) began air service between Juneau and Fairbanks and arranged to break up the 700-mile flight with a fuel stop in Whitehorse. Alaska representatives asked the Canadian government to supply Royal Canadian Corps of Signals personnel to operate the communication equipment

ABOVE LEFT August 17, 1920: First take-off from the primitive White-horse airfield, as one of the four U.S. Army De Havillands departs for Dawson City on its 9,000-mile flight from New York to Nome and back to New York. Note the faint outline of Golden Horn Mountain in the distance.

ABOVE RIGHT The inauguration of scheduled international air service to the Whitehorse airfield, April 1935. Local residents, young and old, admire the sleek Pacific Alaska Airways Lockheed 10A Electra, which has just arrived from Fairbanks en route to Juneau.

installed by the airline. On February 25, the station went on air in the PAA hangar. Two years later, Signals staff received their own equipment and moved into an unused police building downtown, from which they communicated with Dawson and Mayo as well as running the PAA station. In 1941, all airport control duties were taken over by the Canadian Department of Transport, but Whitehorse was home to a downtown telegraph office until the 1970s.

THE CREATION OF LOT 226

In 1914, the Canadian government appointed the Yukon's first Indian Agent, Anglican priest John Thomas Hawksley. Reverend Hawksley had extensive northern experience as a pioneer missionary, having served in the Northwest Territories and northern Yukon for nearly 25 years. Most of his experience was with Gwich'in- and Hän-speaking people, and apparently he was fluent in the Gwich'in language. He had little personal experience of First Nations issues in southern Yukon, yet soon after his appointment, Hawksley was called upon to intercede in a sensitive matter at Whitehorse.

Since the founding of the town, First Nations people had set up their tents and various other simple shelters at various locations on the outskirts, as well as on the east riverbank, across from downtown. In the fall of 1912, some families moved to the west bank of the river, just south of downtown near the rail yards. Within weeks, the *Whitehorse Star* published an inflammatory editorial, the beginning of a campaign to move the settlement far from the downtown

ABOVE LEFT From 1911, many aboriginal children from the Whitehorse area attended this Anglican-run residential school in Carcross.

ABOVE RIGHT This detail from a 1913 riverfront photo shows the tents of the aboriginal community above town.

LEFT First Synod of Diocese of Yukon at Whitehorse, Sept. 1907. Rev. John Hawksley is in the front row, third from left.

area. The writer, editor E.J. White, described the locale as a "flat, pestilential and mosquito-breeding swamp," raised alarms about the camp's location just above the town's water intake, and predicted the camp would soon "be reeking in disease-breeding filth and pollution of all kinds." White went on to describe the First Nations people as trespassers on White Pass land, and he called on the railway authorities and the police to "oust" them "without delay." [4]

The paper's position appeared to mirror the attitudes of many influential people in town. A year later, John Hawksley met with White Pass officials V.I. Hahn and William Gordon and RNWMP Inspector Bell to select a new site for the aboriginal settlement, about three kilometres (two miles) north of town. No aboriginal people were consulted; the only communication was an eviction notice issued to each family. Stories tell of families being loaded with their belongings onto White Pass barges to move them to the new location. Adding insult to injury, White Pass officials discovered that the new site was within one of the great blocks of land purchased by the company. Yet again, aboriginal people were evicted and moved still farther downriver.

In June 1916, Crown Land Agent R.G. Miller submitted an application to designate this area into a reserve, making it clear that the land "had little prospective value for any other purpose." When the reserve request was formalized some years later, Lot 226, or Whitehorse Indian Reserve No. 8, occupied 282.3 acres on a flood plain. Many First Nations people did stay there when travelling to town, and for a few weeks in 1916, the inhabitants were quarantined during a town-wide measles epidemic. Other people found more convenient places to camp and eventually spread out around the outskirts of town.[5]

FUR FARMING

> The live fox industry has created a great deal of interest among the Indians, as well as among the white trappers. Prices have ranged from $40 to $50 for an ordinary cross fox, up to $1,600 for a young black fox, which was the amount one of the Indian boys received.
> —*Northern Lights*, September 1913

The 1910s saw the arrival of a new industry in Canada and the Yukon: the ranching of fur-bearing animals, particularly foxes. The combination of high prices for pelts and breeding stock, plus a plentiful supply of inexpensive food that could be hunted or fished from the territory's lakes and rivers, made the venture an attractive proposition for many local business people.

Foxes native to the Yukon were heavily furred and somewhat larger than animals found elsewhere in the country. Especially prized were the silver and cross foxes found in remarkably high numbers in the Yukon River basin. One breeding pair of silver black foxes was worth as much as $10,000.[6] Would-be fur farmers acquired property, built pens and got started with animals that were either live-trapped in the wild or purchased from other operations. The animals were then bred and sold for their fur or sold as breeding stock.

There were many success stories of First Nations people obtaining high prices for fox pelts and even more for the foxes they live-trapped. In 1913, two men from the Pelly River area arrived in Whitehorse by steamboat with sixteen

Display of fox furs.

foxes, eight pelts and eight live animals. Anticipating the large amount of money they would receive, they had booked passage on the steamer *White Horse*, something few locals could normally afford. The late Angela Sidney recalled a time when her family stayed on the Whitehorse riverfront in 1914. During a trip downriver, her father and three companions live-trapped a black fox and her pups. With part of his share of the sale price, her father bought Angela a new sewing machine and a gun for her brother Johnny Johns.

Over the next two decades, many Whitehorse residents tried out this new enterprise. Among them were local businessmen such as Édouard "Eddie" Marcotte, Captain Paddy Martin, J.P. Whitney and J.R. Alguire. In the fall of 1925, Charlie Baxter bought ten pairs of foxes and ranch equipment from Sam Chambers in Carcross, with plans to set up the pens at his ranch north of town. Most of the fur farms were located near the Yukon River, including operations on the east bank across from Whitehorse. Other ranches were located north of downtown, and George Wilson had an operation upriver, near the present site of McCrae. Bert Cluett had a fox ranch at his wood camp by Croucher Creek. Chief Jim Boss set up a fur farm at Lake Laberge, and for some years there was a fur farm at Fish Lake. As well as foxes, some ranchers raised mink, or even a combination of the two. Frederick and Frances Langholtz had a mink ranch across the river, as did woodcutter Ole Wickstrom. Jim Geary ran a fox and mink ranch north of town. Henry "Shorty" Roil, who lived in the area that is now Rotary Peace Park, had a mink ranch southeast of town, across the river.[7]

According to Laurent Cyr, these operations changed hands several times over the years, so it is not always clear if early accounts are referring to separate operations or to different owners of the same farm. As in any speculative business,

Feeding time at a Whitehorse area fox farm in 1937.

the fox farmers prospered or failed depending on the ever-changing fur market. The market did eventually plummet, and by the late 1920s or early 1930s, most of the ranches had closed.

SPORTS AND RECREATION

Whitehorse was somewhat sheltered from the Depression of the 1930s, but by the same token it did not derive a great deal of benefit from the boom of the 1920s. The North Star Athletic Association building remained the focal point of community activities, but with the town's population dwindling, it became financially difficult to maintain the facility.

Parts of the building were turned into storage areas. Other rooms fell into disrepair. The NSAA still hosted dances, and men went on playing cards and drinking in the games room. There were banquets and movie nights, and students walked to the NSAA once a week for gym classes. For the most part, however, the lights were left off.

There is little evidence of much sports activity during the years between the World Wars. Once immensely popular, indoor baseball disappeared completely. A short-lived sport-governing body, the Whitehorse Athletic Club, was formed in the late 1930s, with representatives from basketball, badminton, baseball, tennis and hockey. By the end of the 1930s, the local hockey league was down to two teams, White Pass and the Town.

Skiers monitored the *Whitehorse Star* for regular updates as to where and when they might be able to safely venture onto the river ice. When the ice was solid enough to cross, they skied or walked across the river and up an old wood road to a fork at the top of the first hill. From there, one could turn north to the Ski Bowl, the preferred destination for experienced Whitehorse skiers; or south to the Pot Hole, favoured by kids. The Ski Bowl was simply a cluster of steep, open areas where people could ski without fear of colliding with trees. The skiers didn't carve their way down the slopes; the hills weren't high enough for that. They simply pointed their skis and went hell-bent for leather in a straight line.

TOP LEFT Curling in the NSAA hall.

TOP RIGHT Playing hockey on an outdoor ice rink in Whitehorse, ca. late 1930s. Two of the men are Don Murray and "Burpee" Anderson.

BOTTOM The Ski Bowl, ca. 1940s.

EARLY TOURISM

The magnificent scenery, the big game, the fox farming industry will be attractively featured with a view of bringing to the Yukon tourists, sportsmen, settlers and investors, rendering a service to them, to the loyal and liberal supporters of the paper and to the territory we aim to serve.
—Editorial, the *Weekly Star*, April 4, 1924

Although construction of the White Pass and Yukon Railway was inspired by the gold rush, railway owners were quick to realize the potential for tourism. As early as 1900, the company published a booklet entitled *Scenic Railway of the World,* with numerous photographs and fulsome prose extolling the beautiful scenery, the challenges overcome by the railway builders, and the pleasures of the sternwheeler trip to Dawson City, during which passengers enjoyed every comfort.[8] Most of the White Pass literature stressed the role of Whitehorse as an efficient transfer centre, although there was some mention of its gold-rush past, with a focus on the hazards of Miles Canyon and Whitehorse Rapids.

Over the next three decades, the White Pass & Yukon Route invested heavily in the tourism market, advertising rail and river trips and building or renovating vessels geared for the tourist trade, notably the *Whitehorse*, the *Casca* and the *Tutshi,* out of Carcross. These efforts gradually paid off, and in 1928, over 6,000 passengers travelled to Dawson by sternwheeler. Nearly 7,400 people stopped at the Carcross railway station to take a side trip to Atlin via the headwater lakes.[9]

By 1924, Whitehorse residents were considering what they could offer visitors during the intervals between the arrival of the trains and the departure of the boats. They were strongly encouraged in this by the new editor of the *Whitehorse Star*, J.D. Skinner. Backed by local merchants, the *Star* continued to report on comings and goings, social events and mining operations within the southern Yukon. It also followed the town's annual cycle, from the arrival of boat crews to the eventual freeze-up and close of navigation. Most critically, the newspaper continued to be the town's greatest booster, extolling its scenery, mineral wealth and new opportunities through fur farming and tourism. It exhorted local citizens to maintain a clean and wholesome town and to make every business "a model for service and value." There was even some mention of winter tourism. Editorials encouraged regular community clean-ups, especially in spring, and efforts were made to deal with the "mosquito nuisance." At the

KODAK PICNIC IN MILES CANYON

time, the accepted method for controlling mosquitoes was to cut back brushy areas, and then pour used motor oil over nearby ponds and standing water.

There is no record of the effect of these efforts on local commerce. White Pass records do show that tourism reached a peak in 1927, and then—with the onset of the Great Depression—steadily declined into the mid-1930s, with only 1,229 passengers travelling the riverboats to Dawson City in 1935.

SETBACKS AND DISASTERS

The war years and the post-war period were difficult times for Whitehorse and the Yukon. Costs kept rising for everything from groceries to replacement parts for mining equipment, while wages remained low.

The Yukon's population kept falling too. By 1921, it had reached a low of just over 4,000, only 25 per cent of the 1901 figure. Of these, approximately 2,500 were aboriginal. The largest drop occurred between 1901 and 1911, when large Klondike mining concessions were granted to a few large companies, and independent miners moved on. The federal government felt it could no longer justify the high costs of supporting Yukoners and their infrastructure. The government

Wreck of the sternwheeler *Dawson* at Rink Rapids, 1926.

workforce, everyone from Mounties to administration officials, was cut radically in 1919, and the territorial budget was reduced to 36 per cent of the 1914 amount. The post of Commissioner was one of many positions cut, with the Chief Executive Officer duties added to those of the Gold Commissioner. That position was abolished in 1932, when the administration was further downsized, and the Comptroller was designated the senior official, with another revision in name to "Controller" in 1936.[10]

The Yukon had contributed significant manpower and financial support to the war effort, and so, not surprisingly, Yukoners felt betrayed by their country. According to a letter addressed to Prime Minister Robert Borden by the Yukon Development League, "Yukon gave more men and money per capita to the Dominion for war purposes than any other section of Canada without receiving a cent of war business... and why the government should now try to put Yukon almost entirely off the map of Canada, the loyal and patriotic subjects here cannot understand."[11]

The Whitehorse copper-mining industry did well during the war years, with the worldwide demand for copper leading to higher prices. By the early 1920s, however, copper prices were too low to justify the high costs of exploration, mining and transportation.

This was also a challenging period for the British Yukon Navigation Company. Many of its seasoned old-timers had died or retired, and other workers had left to enlist in the war overseas. The Superintendent's Annual Report of 1910 noted that the company's operating costs were up due to many accidents. The 1916 report lamented the shortage of good firemen and deckhands, with "most of our regulars having enlisted and gone to the Front." Along with hundreds of other northerners, key BYN men died during the sinking of the *Princess Sophia* in 1918. This left many important crew positions in the hands of untried newcomers, which led to several accidents and a number of wrecks, including the wreck of the *Tanana* in the Thirty Mile River in 1915 and the sinking of the steamer *Dawson* in Rink Rapids in 1926. A particularly devastating year was 1936, with the loss of the *Casca* II in the Thirty Mile River and the wreck of the first *Klondike*, which hit a rock a few kilometres below Hootalinqua.

Armistice Day was declared on November 11, 1919, and the long years of the Great War were finally over. The joy and celebrations marking the official end of the war were muted by the losses overseas and, much closer to home, the *Princess Sophia* fatalities only a few weeks earlier.

THE PUEBLO
MINE DISASTER

The three survivors of the Pueblo disaster in front of Whitehorse Hospital on April 1, 1917. In no particular order, they were Harry Graham, Tom Davis and Nick Radovich.

MINING IS a dangerous occupation, and this was particularly so in the Whitehorse Copper Belt during the early years. The many back-breaking tasks involved in early mining included shovelling, breaking up rock with a pick, hand drilling, timbering and sorting rock. Underground work took place in dark, damp and poorly ventilated spaces. The candle and carbide lamps shed little light. The Pueblo was a notoriously "wet" mine, filling with 500 to 600 gallons of water per minute, which required constant pumping. In 1916, the Pueblo reached peak production, sending out ore with a value of $763,586. It had also become a very dangerous place to work. In three separate incidents, three men died after being hit by heavy objects underground.

There was worse to come. During an underground inspection on March 21, 1917, Superinten-dent Berg learned that the support timbers at the 400-foot level were "taking weight." He evacuated workers from the 400-foot level stope, but neither he nor the mine manager considered the situation serious enough to take further precautions. An hour later, rock caved in between the 200- and 400-foot levels, trapping nine miners.

Rescue efforts began immediately. A diamond-drilling crew pushed an 85-foot drift through solid granite in a record time of 72 hours to reach three survivors. Rescue efforts continued until March 29, when the shaft conditions were declared too unsafe to continue. The collapsed mine became the final resting place for the remaining six miners.[12]

THE SINKING OF THE
PRINCESS SOPHIA

Many northerners were seasonal residents, moving south after construction projects and dredges had shut down, navigation season had ended and businesses had slowed down or closed up after the busy summer. Most migrants left just before freeze-up. They would steam up to Whitehorse on one of the last sternwheeler runs, then ride the railway to Skagway and travel south on one of the coastal steamships.

The *Princess Sophia* marooned on Vanderbilt Reef.

The passenger liner ss *Princess Sophia* steamed out of Skagway on the evening of Wednesday, October 23, 1918, fully loaded with 353 passengers and crew. The steel-built *Sophia* was part of the coastal fleet of the Canadian Pacific Railway, one of seven Princesses built for CPR between 1907 and 1914. While steaming down the Lynn Canal, the vessel encountered a blinding snowstorm and heavy winds, then ran aground on Vanderbilt Reef. Several smaller boats hastened to the scene to evacuate passengers and crew, but rough weather made it impossible to transfer people between vessels. After an anxious day and night, followed by another day of gale-force winds, blinding snow and heavy seas, the *Princess Sophia* slid off the reef and sank late in the afternoon of October 25, taking all aboard with her. Only a dog survived.

Northerners were overwhelmed by the tragic news. As many as one in ten Dawson City residents had been lost in the wreck. Alaskan communities were similarly devastated, and the BYN lost nearly 90 crew and dependents.[13]

Among the many expressions of sorrow was this note from BYN Superintendent Bill Gordon:

> We are... mourning the loss of a great many employees who went down with the ill fated *Sophia*; among whom were some of our most capable officers, some being with this company since its inception.... This loss will be keenly felt next spring when we start up once again and miss the many familiar faces that were identified with some of our boats for so many years. It will be impossible to replace some of these men for several years to come, if at all.[14]

THE YUKON COUNCIL, 1919–1939

The other blow to Yukon in 1918–19 was the news that the federal government would amend the Yukon Act to eliminate the representative Yukon Council, reverting to an appointed advisory body. After much protest about the undemocratic nature of such changes, the federal cabinet relented, instead reducing the Council to three members. Whitehorse had one member. Dawson City and the Klondike districts also had one each, and the latter was eventually assigned to the new Mayo District when the silver boom took off there. The two northern mining districts frequently combined to vote funds for their areas, to the annoyance of southern residents. This was a cause of great concern in the mid-1920s, when the Council voted to move the Territorial Assay Office from Whitehorse to Mayo.

THE BRITISH YUKON NAVIGATION COMPANY SHIPYARDS

The railway may have been the reason for the founding of Whitehorse, but it was the shipyards and sternwheelers of the British Yukon Navigation Company that really powered the town. White Pass kept its major railway shops in Skagway, where most rail workers were based, but Whitehorse was essential to maintaining the company's upper river fleet. Along an extensive stretch of downtown waterfront, White Pass had installed all the facilities it needed to build ships, overwinter the sternwheelers and do everything necessary to prepare the boats for the spring launch.

Many early waterfront photos show the imposing presence of the sternwheelers drawn onto the sloping wooden "ways," then blocked up and levelled with "cribbing." Judging from the scale of nearby structures and the small figures moving about beneath, these vessels were the equivalent of the town's skyscrapers, dwarfing the humble dwellings nearby.

Early spring marked the return to Whitehorse of the boat and shipyard crews. In late March, townsfolk gathered at the end of Main Street to greet the daily train and the return of friends back for another season.

For ten-year-old John Scott, the shipyards were a magical place. In a 1992 interview, he shared his boyhood memories of the Whitehorse waterfront in the 1920s. The whole character of the town changed each spring as the waterfront became livelier and noisier. The town's population doubled from approximately 350 to 700 people. The steam whistle at the shipyard power plant once again

ABOVE Four sternwheelers blocked up on ways during the heyday of the Whitehorse shipyards. L-R: the *Columbian*, the *Sybil*, the *Yukoner* and the *Canadian,* ca. 1905.

LEFT Launching the *Dawson*, May 28, 1906.

ABOVE LEFT BYN employees pose in front of the carpentry shop.

ABOVE RIGHT A close-up view of some of the shipyard workshops.

became the town timepiece, with everyone setting their clocks and watches by the morning, noon and closing whistles. The wooden sidewalks drummed under the heavy boots of workers marching to the Whitehorse Inn Cafe at mealtimes.

About 60 people worked in the shipyards in spring to ready the boats for launching. The first arrivals cleared ice and snow from around the ways and off the decks. Next to arrive were the steamboat engineers and firemen, who looked after any necessary repairs and maintenance on the ships' boilers and engines. Then the shipwrights got to work. Hulls were scraped, damaged planks were replaced, and boards were caulked and tarred before repainting. Of particular concern was the "knuckle plank," set at a 45-degree angle between the side and the bottom of the boat. This piece of wood, which took a lot of the strain on the hull, was bolted in place, allowing for easy replacement. After all repairs were complete, the carpenters pumped water into the hulls to test for leaks, then drained it out before launching.

Launching was a big operation, requiring the help of the entire shipyard crew. Boats sat on blocking and had to be lowered onto "butterboards," which were skids set upon the ways. In the days before hydraulic jacks, the workers used screw jacks, "great big things that weighed about 80 pounds."[15] Approximately 20 jacks were set along one side of the boat. A designated worker blew a whistle, and the jacks were turned. After one side had been lowered slightly, the jacks were moved to the other side of the vessel. The skids were well lubricated with tallow and grease, making them a tasty target for ravens and the town dogs. When the boats finally settled onto the butterboards, they slid down the greasy ways to land in the water with a great splash. Long lines steadied the boats until they righted themselves in the water.

By the time the ships were launched, their entire crews were ready to go: captains, pilots, pursers, engineers, firemen, galley crew, stewards and deckhands, all set for a busy season of attending passengers, loading firewood and freight,

fuelling the boilers and ensuring the safe passage of the majestic boats along the ever-shifting main channel of the Yukon River.

In fall, as the weather chilled and ice formed along the shoreline, the ship-yard workers prepared to haul out the sternwheelers and barges for another season. Ships were first steered parallel to the ways. Then a "heaving line" pulled four heavy straps (made up of about four wires each) around each boat. Each strap was fastened to a tow strap, which in turn was fastened to one of four winches on shore. The heavier stern end was pulled in first, and then all four straps were winched in evenly along the length of the boat. In the early days, the boats were hauled in by horse-drawn capstans. These were replaced by steam capstans in 1917. According to BYN Superintendent Bill Gordon, this meant a tremendous saving in time. A crew could now haul out a boat in a mere two hours, a task that had previously taken an entire day.[16]

In 1907, a railway spur was laid through the yard, easing the transport and handling of timber, machinery and coal. At the downstream end of the shipyards was the "boneyard," where derelict vessels were permanently dry-docked. On rainy days, carpenters sat in the hull of the old *Bonanza King*, twisting oakum and gossiping. Various buildings inland from the boats housed the steam plant that powered the yard, a large workshop, a paint shop, the tin shop, a steam chest used to bend planks, and crew bunkhouses. Young John Scott's favourite place was the blacksmith's shop. He watched in fascination as blacksmith Pat Murray and his helper, Joe Bolderson, devised a great variety of intricate metal parts from bar iron and iron plate. Well before modern welding techniques were invented, blacksmiths joined iron parts by heating the metal until it was white-hot and then hammering it together.[17]

Former ship carpenter Walter Jensen described the ways as "big huge things" requiring at least ten men to shift them. Nonetheless, the company regularly repaired, relocated, rebuilt and levelled the awkward structures, sometimes

ABOVE LEFT Building two stern-wheelers, ca. 1913. The hull has been laid for the foreground boat, while the superstructure has been started on the vessel in the background.

ABOVE RIGHT SS *Keno* in 1945.

The second ss *Klondike* in 1946 at the BYN dock in Whitehorse.

moving thousands of cubic yards of dirt and railcars full of rock to grade the area to a uniform slope and reinforce the ways.

Even 70 years later, John Scott recalled the names of other BYN shipyard workers, many of whom returned year after year. Charlie Groundwater was the fireman who handled the boilers at the steam plant. Jack Rose headed the machine shop, Al Stewart was the painter, and Steve Martin was the bull gang boss. The carpenters were Joe Gardiner, Alex MacIntosh, George Corkell, Frank Wilson, Norman Murray and Jim Delgarneau. Cam Smith was a gas engine mechanic and often skipper of the *Loon* or the *Sybilla*, the small gas boats that went out early each spring to mark the channel.[18]

The BYN purchased some ships when it went into business in 1900–01, but one of the company's great strengths was that it built riverboats and barges specifically designed to navigate the Yukon River and its side streams. Lumber, engines, boilers and other machinery were shipped in by rail. Often, machinery was salvaged from disused or wrecked vessels. In 1901, BYN launched the first three vessels built in its shipyards: *White Horse*, *Dawson* and *Selkirk*. In 1910–11, the company decided to rebuild the *Casca*, after determining that the hull of the original vessel was "practically worn out and useless."[19] In 1913, the *Yukon* and the *Alaska* were launched from Whitehorse. These sister ships were destined for the lower river service, a separate entity known as the American Yukon Navigation Company (AYN). The *Alaska* was renamed the *Aksala* when it went back into Canadian service.

Two icons of sternwheeler history were fabricated in the BYN shipyards: the *Keno*, completed in 1922, and the original *Klondike*, built in 1929. When the latter was wrecked in 1936, an identical second *Klondike* was built and went into business the following year. With a draft of only three feet, the *Keno* was designed to haul ore sacks from Mayo to Stewart Island on the Stewart River. In 1937, the *Keno* was lengthened by another ten feet, allowing more freight capacity. In optimum conditions, the sternwheeler could carry 120 tons while pushing a barge loaded with another 225 tons. Design modifications to the *Klondike*, including a specially designed hull and compound condensing engines, meant that the boat could efficiently carry up to 300 tons of ore on the run from Stewart Island to Whitehorse without pushing a barge.[20]

WOOD CAMPS

Until the end of World War II, most Whitehorse homes and businesses were heated with firewood. Wood also powered the hungry boilers of the sternwheeler fleet. Yukon sternwheelers ran on wood, lots of wood, burning an average of a cord an hour going downstream, and one and a half cords going upstream.[21] In 1915, the BYN fleet burned 8,000 cords. During the 1930s, woodcutters were paid $5 per cord, all cut with handsaws. A good woodcutter could cut three cords a day and earn up to $500 for a season's work.

Since a sternwheeler could carry only some of its fuel, it made frequent stops to take on firewood, about ten to twenty cords at a time. Wood camp locations changed as the tree supply was exhausted, but most were situated at intervals of 80 to 160 kilometres (50 to 100 miles). Deckhands moved the wood aboard using handcarts.

Woodcutting was a major Yukon industry and an important source of cash for First Nations families. The Ryder family, who had several wood camps in the Whitehorse valley, relied on First Nations woodcutters, often working with the same families over many years. This was a flexible arrangement, with families taking breaks during the salmon run and hunting season.

MARSH LAKE DAM

THE NAVIGATION season was a brief window during which hard-working boats and crews had to transport thousands of passengers and a year's worth of supplies to communities downriver. Every day of delayed shipping meant a drop in income to the shippers, the merchants and White Pass. With this in mind, the BYN carefully tracked the navigation season, recording break-up and freeze-up dates and water levels from early spring to late fall.

Even after the river opened in front of Whitehorse and at the Thirty Mile River below Lake Laberge, the thick ice of Laberge remained frozen for another two to three weeks. To hasten the season, freight was sledded over the lake ice to smaller sternwheelers that had overwintered at Lower Laberge and Hootalinqua. For a few years, BYN laid a "lampblack trail" of used oil along the lake to rot the ice.

The most effective solution, however, was the construction of the Marsh Lake Dam, completed in 1924. When its gates were opened in early spring, the dam released extra water to float the stern-wheelers over the shallow stretches before and after Laberge. Most importantly, the extra water floated out the lake ice, advancing navigation season by as much as two weeks.[22]

The Department of Public Works replaced the rotting dam in 1952, but by then the sternwheeler era was ending, and the dam was of little use. In 1975, the Northern Canada Power Commission built the current steel structure, which helps control water flow to the hydro dam at Whitehorse Rapids.

Marsh Lake Dam shortly after completion. The *Gleaner* is tied up upstream of the dam.

Croucher Creek was an important wood camp and First Nations base about ten kilometres (six miles) downriver from Whitehorse. Bert Cluett ran the operation in the 1920s. Once the Ryder family took it over, it became known as Six Mile Camp. Elder Louis Smith recalled that this spot was also a base camp for First Nations hunters travelling inland to the mountains.

Loading wood aboard the steamer *Columbian* at Croucher Creek wood camp. Union Sunday School excursion to Lake Laberge, July 17, 1906.

WEATHERING THE CHANGES

The period from the onset of World War I until the eve of the Second World War was a transitional one for Whitehorse. The town's great strength continued to be its function as the territory's distribution centre and home to the BYN shipyards. Travel options improved with the advent of motor vehicles, gas boats, tractors and aircraft, but Whitehorse stayed a quiet, peaceful town that became a busier, more exciting place during navigation season. No one could have foreseen the tremendous upheavals that would come in the early 1940s.

COMMUNITY PORTRAITS

BILLY AND JENNY LEBARGE CA.1880–1939 & 1890–1978

Billy Lebarge came to Whitehorse from Fort Selkirk at the time of the gold rush. His wife, Jenny, was related to Klukwan Coastal Tlingit, Carcross Inland Tlingit and Southern Tutchone people at Lake Laberge. The couple had a cabin and outbuildings west of the tracks at the White Pass and Yukon Railway Yard Limits, at the south end of Whitehorse. Here they raised a large family from the early 1900s to the 1940s. Their daughter, Violet Storer, remembered that her father combined seasonal subsistence activities with occasional wage employment.

Following in the footsteps of their ancestors, the whole family travelled to Fish Lake in winter and spring, often with Jenny's aged mother, who was renowned for her gopher-snaring skills. In late summer, Billy set fish nets below the rapids, catching enough salmon for family use and trade. For part of the year, he worked on the railroad, as did Violet's brother and other family members. Whitehorse Billy and his family lived nearby. Jim Boss and other kin visited during trips to town, contributing to the busy social life at Yard Limits.

Each year, after the Lebarge family had harvested salmon in midsummer, they set off on shakat. *Shakat* is the Southern Tutchone word used to describe the late-summer hunting trips taken by interior Athapaskans. During these extended sojourns, they put up enough food to last them through the winter. The family would travel lightly, taking only a tent fly and bedding. Their food staples were fish and meat harvested along the way, plus a little flour, sugar and tea. The Lebarge family crossed the river by boat, and then followed a trail to the east of Grey Mountain, into the hills. They hunted moose and then dried the meat from four to five animals, storing it in caches along the way. With the help of their dogs, they later packed the meat to the upper reaches of the M'Clintock River and drifted down to Marsh Lake on rafts. Several families arrived at M'Clintock Bay around this time. They all stayed together for a month or more, setting nets for whitefish and trout, drying their catch for winter, and visiting.

As autumn closed in, the men hunted in the surrounding hills for fresh meat. After carefully wrapping the fish in gunny sacks and the moose meat in mosquito netting, the family headed home, rafting down the Yukon to their cabin at Wigan, just above Miles Canyon. From there, they walked the rest of the way to their home at Yard Limits, a distance of about sixteen kilometres (ten miles). In later years, a family member would walk to town to get the Ryders, who would haul everything to town by truck, in exchange for meat and fish. Billy Lebarge was always generous with his moose meat, giving away what the family didn't need.

Violet Storer remembered shakat as a happy time with her family and friends. People celebrated special occasions with feasts, and the usual rules were suspended, so children had more freedom to help with the harvest and to play with other kids they might not see again for another year.[23]

ROBERT LOWE 1868–1929

Many of the entrepreneurs who settled in the brand-new town of Whitehorse were not simply seeking economic opportunities and personal prosperity. They were also community-builders and enthusiastic volunteers, willing to do whatever was needed to create a good home for their families. Robert Lowe was definitely one of this breed. He ran a draying business, using his horses, wagons and sleighs to haul firewood and ice, sell grain and hay, and handle all kinds of deliveries, including supplies to the copper mines. He also had interests in the

FACING TOP Jenny Lebarge and Aline Chrétien at Sourdough Rendezvous, ca. 1969.

FACING BOTTOM Bill Lebarge near Yard Limits, ca. 1920s. Mr. Lebarge used to line his dogs' packs with willow before transporting fish into town for sale or trade.

ABOVE LEFT Stages departing Whitehorse from Lowe's business on Front Street, ca. 1922.

ABOVE RIGHT Robert Lowe campaign poster.

Copper Belt: he owned the Grafter Mine and was part owner of the War Eagle and LeRoi properties.

By 1901, Lowe was president of the Whitehorse Board of Trade. When Whitehorse became a territorial electoral district in 1902, he was elected as its first member by a strong majority. He sat on the Yukon Council from 1902 until 1920 and was elected Speaker in 1909 and again in 1925. Lowe worked hard for his district, gaining appropriations for everything from new roads to the Copper Belt to improvements at the local school and the fire department. His name survives on Lowe Street in downtown Whitehorse and on the Robert Lowe Footbridge, which has spanned Miles Canyon since 1922. [24]

W.L. "DEACON" PHELPS 1867–1951

According to his contemporaries, Deacon Phelps got his nickname because he donated money to build a Methodist church but never actually attended a service. Willard Leroy Phelps was born in Merritton, Ontario, and took his law degree at Osgoode Hall in Toronto. When his short-lived law practice in Toronto failed, he set out for the Klondike to try his luck at gold mining. After an arduous trip to Teslin via the Stikine Trail, and a winter on Quiet Lake, Phelps finally reached Dawson in spring 1899. He worked as a sternwheeler deckhand and ran a hotel in Atlin. When the railway set up the new town, he moved to Whitehorse to establish a law practice. For nearly half a century, he represented key businesses and professional and charitable organizations, as well as a few businesses of his own.

Phelps married Hana Livingstone, a teacher from Ontario, in 1907. They had two children, Dorothy and John. Phelps became manager of the Yukon Electrical Company in 1905 and, within a year, managed to lower power rates from 90 to 50 cents per kilowatt hour. In 1909, he was one of two Whitehorse men to win a seat on the first wholly elected Territorial Council. He chose not to run between 1920 and 1925, but otherwise held his seat until 1943. In the late 1940s, he used his life savings to finance the Fish Lake hydro project developed by his son John and his son-in-law, John Scott, a risky but ultimately successful undertaking.

Willard Leroy "Deacon" Phelps.

Phelps's descendants followed in his famous footsteps. John Phelps won a seat on Territorial Council in 1954. Deacon's grandson, Willard, also became a lawyer. He was elected to the Yukon Legislative Assembly in 1974, serving as Yukon Government Leader in 1985; Leader of the Official Opposition, 1985–91; and Cabinet Minister, 1992–96. The Phelps home on Main Street was later converted and became Murdoch's Gem Shop.[25]

HERBERT WHEELER CA. 1874–1965

For over half a century, the White Pass & Yukon Route dominated the Yukon's transportation history. Much of this was due to visionary, strong-willed leadership by tough-minded individuals such as the legendary one-eyed Herbert Wheeler. Born in England and raised in Ireland, Wheeler moved to B.C. to homestead at age nineteen before ending up in Whitehorse as a clerk with the Canadian Development Company. He supervised the successful inauguration of the White Pass winter mail service in 1902, became the company's general manager in 1915 and then served as its president from 1920 until 1940. In his biography of aviator Grant McConachie, *Bush Pilot with a Briefcase*, Ronald Keith quotes an unidentified minister who spoke of Herbert Wheeler's formidable reputation: "Whitehorse is a company town. Whitepass and Yukon owns it.... They own the railroad to Skagway... they run the riverboats to Dawson, they operate the stage line so they own the town. By 'they,' I mean H. J. Wheeler. He runs Whitepass. He rules Whitehorse. There's the Territorial Council, yes, but Wheeler's king of the Yukon."[26]

Through the transition from horses to steamboats to planes, Wheeler awed his employees, forwarded the company's interests and fended off the competition. After leaving the company in 1940, he helped establish wartime airport facilities. He left Whitehorse at the end of World War II and retired in Victoria, B.C.[27]

Wheeler during the early days on the Overland Trail.

Buzzsaw Jimmy on his home-made sawing machine, ca. early 1940s.

JAMES "BUZZSAW JIMMY" RICHARDS 1876–1967

The town's most unconventional woodcutter was Buzzsaw Jimmy, who first showed up in the records in about 1910. Although he briefly held a sawmill lease on the waterfront, Richards handled most of his business with his homemade buzzsaw-on-wheels, fashioned from an old tractor, a Model T Ford and various other scraps. This machine cut logs in stove lengths at the rate of eight to ten cords an hour.

About 1916, Jimmy accidentally cut off one of his legs, but that didn't slow him down for long. He got fitted for a new wooden leg and went back to work. Some years later, he again fell off his machine, and again his leg slipped under the blade. But this time it was the wooden leg that was cut in half. Jimmy's reaction: "I fooled you that time, you son of a bitch!"

Buzzsaw Jimmy lived a long and colourful, if sometimes dangerous, life, dying in 1967 at the age of 94.[28]

W.D. (BILL) MacBRIDE 1888–1973

William David MacBride was born in 1888 in Butte, Montana. After losing both parents while still an infant, he was raised by his aunt and uncle, Nellie and Frank Miles. MacBride first trained as a teacher, and he taught for two years before taking a business course at Blair College in Spokane, Washington. In 1912, he was hired as a clerk for the Northern Navigation Company, spending two summers in St. Michael, Alaska. When the White Pass & Yukon Route bought out his employer in 1914, MacBride was transferred to Whitehorse. Here he fell in love with Yukon life and, over the years, worked for White Pass as district passenger agent, public relations officer and general historian. In 1919, he married Eva Teskey, a local school teacher, and they had three children: Mary, John and Eva.

MacBride left us a vivid description of early Whitehorse in his memoir, *All My Rivers Flowed West*:

William D. MacBride at the city's first museum in the old telegraph office.

We knew everyone in town and also the names of their dogs. The miners came to town on Saturday nights and made a bit of whoopee but the police had everything under control. Dog teams were a common sight in winter. Indians walked from store to store with skins of beaver, marten, mink, muskrat and lynx, trying to get a higher bid.... In a corner of the old White Pass Hotel was the liquor office of Robert Lowe & Co. In this wholesale office, four 40-gallon barrels of Scotch, rye, rum and sherry lay on their sides with wood spigots and large glasses nearby. This refreshment stand was well patronized by regular customers, but freeloaders were not welcome.[29]

MacBride became an ardent history buff, collecting books, photographs and artifacts relating to Yukon history. In 1991, his good friend, Yukon author, producer and community-builder Roy Minter, shared the following reminiscence about MacBride: "This fun-loving raconteur, who had a passion for writing and preserving northern history, aged but never grew old.... He was known far and wide outside the Yukon, by historians, writers, publishers, and broadcasters, none of whom would think of passing through Whitehorse without contacting Bill MacBride to obtain the latest northern gem for their articles or radio spots."[30]

MacBride was also concerned to see much of the Yukon's history leaving the territory as souvenirs. Together with immigration officer Fred Arnot, Bill

ABOVE LEFT Early photo of the Richards family home, built in 1948.

ABOVE RIGHT Babe Richards at left with her parents, T.C. and Bernadine, in the newly opened Rainbow Room, 1952.

MacBride organized a group of thirteen people to form the Yukon Historical Society in December 1950. Two years later, the society acquired the old telegraph office to house the town's first museum. A much larger purpose-built log museum was put up in 1967 as a Canadian centennial project. The new building was officially opened by Princess Alexandra and named the MacBride Museum in honour of Bill MacBride and his many contributions to Whitehorse and Yukon history.[31]

THOMAS CECIL "T.C." RICHARDS 1889–1961

It is no stretch to say that Thomas Cecil "T.C." Richards was larger than life. Born in Leicester, England, T.C. arrived in Whitehorse in 1915 to manage the P. Burns & Company operation, which included a stockyard and slaughterhouse north of town and a butcher shop on Main Street. In the days before refrigerated shipping, meat arrived on the hoof, and the butcher was expected to ensure it reached its destination as fresh as possible. In 1921, T.C. went so far as to run a cattle drive to Mayo. The cattle were shipped up the Pelly River and herded overland to the mining camps, where they were butchered and preserved in the chilly mining shafts.

In the late 1920s, T.C. teamed up with W.L. Phelps to set up Klondike Airways, a transport company that won the winter mail contract between Whitehorse and Dawson, making deliveries by tractor, cat train and truck. During the soggy period between freeze-up and breakup, they improvised with canoes, small boats and hand sleighs—everything except a plane—to haul mail, meat and freight to Dawson City and other remote communities.

A man who took big chances, T.C. became a hotelier over a poker game in the infamous Snake Room of the Whitehorse Inn, using his winnings to make a $20,000 down payment on the Inn. The business expanded under his management, and it thrived during the war years, when the café was open 24 hours a

Kristina and John Erickson with their daughter Gudrun and family friend, Eric Benson.

day and people slept in the rooms in shifts. T.C. managed the Inn until his death in 1961.

T.C. married Bernadine Piper, originally from Missouri, in 1918. The pair had three children: Cecil, Bobby and Evelyn, or "Babe." When T.C. died, his obituary referred to him as "one of the almost legendary sons of the territory," and his funeral was a major event. In 1998, T.C. Richards was inducted into the Yukon Transportation Hall of Fame.[32]

JOHN OLAF ERICKSON 1878–1974

John Olaf Erickson not only travelled a long way to reach the Klondike but took a very roundabout route. After leaving his home in Sweden in 1898, Erickson worked his way eastward around the globe, rounding Africa's Cape of Good Hope and continuing through Australia. He reached Seattle in 1900 and moved to Dawson City later that year. For the next several years he mined and prospected on Eldorado Creek, and later on Bullion Creek, in the Kluane country. Many stories tell of his exploits at that time, including training horses to walk in deep snow wearing snowshoes.

During a visit to Sweden in 1925, John married Kristina Erickson, a childhood friend. The newlyweds settled in Whitehorse, where they bought and managed the Regina Hotel. For the next several decades, the Ericksons welcomed many guests: sternwheeler captains and officers, Dawson families travelling to and from the coast, and most notably the pilots and American soldiers working on the Alaska Highway. The Regina's lounge, with its piano and pot-bellied stove, was a place to play cards, sing and listen to John Erickson's colourful stories.[33]

The Ericksons' two children—Gudrun "Goody" Sparling and John Erickson—took over management of the hotel in the late 1970s. In 1997, they sold the business. In recognition of his work in the Bullion Creek area, John Erickson was inducted posthumously into the Yukon Prospectors' Hall of Fame in 1988.

P. BURNS & COMPANY

The P. Burns & Company building was the second structure to occupy its Main Street location; the first was destroyed in the 1905 fire. In 1928, Bert Bates built an addition on the west side. Pat Burns began shipping cattle to Dawson City in 1898, driving the animals inland over the Dalton Trail and slaughtering them

The Burns Building on Main Street next to the Whitehorse Inn at left, 1950.

on the Yukon River, just above Fort Selkirk at Slaughterhouse Slough, and then shipping the carcasses to Dawson City by steamboat. Once the railway was completed, Burns set up a stockyard and slaughtering area north of town, and this store on Main Street. Whitehorse legend T.C. Richards managed the business from 1915 until ca. 1960. The building was sold in 1969 and later converted into office and retail space.[34]

A passenger sleigh in front of the Regina Hotel, ca. 1901.

THE REGINA HOTEL

The Regina Hotel began in 1900 as a two-storey log structure that also housed a restaurant and a bakery. In 1901, owners Frank M. Walter and Charles H. Johnson built a frame addition. Two years later, they added a false front that extended across both buildings. The hotel became one of many ventures of Ed Dixon—former Mountie, river pilot and one of the town's pioneer entrepreneurs—when he bought out Walter's share of the business.

After John and Kristina Erickson took over the hotel in 1925, it was run as a family business for more than 70 years. During the 1930s, the Ericksons moved the old RCMP annex to the rear of the building, using the bottom floor as a garage and storage area and the upper floor for staff accommodation. The building was clad in imitation-brick asphalt siding in the 1950s. In 1970, it was demolished to make way for the new Regina Hotel building, which became the current River View Hotel.

Whitehorse Steam Laundry, ca. early 1950s. At this time it was operated by Kai and Inga Gertson.

WHITEHORSE STEAM LAUNDRY

Not long after selling his interest in the Pioneer Hotel, Ed Dixon—together with fellow entrepreneur Cariste Racine—built and ran a small laundry. In 1901, it was replaced with a log building containing a steam laundry plant. With its tall chimney, this structure was a waterfront landmark for over half a century. It handled laundry for the hotels and, in summer, the sternwheelers. For a few years, the town's electrical plant was located in an addition on the north side, but after the downtown fire of 1905, the electrical plant was moved to the fire hall.

Eventually the laundry was replaced by a dry cleaning establishment with small apartments in behind. In its last years, before it burned down in November 1985, the building housed a second-hand shop. Known as the "20-20" after its lot number, the building reputedly contained timbers from its venerable predecessor. Today, the site is home to the wilderness outfitters Kanoe People, one of whose proprietors, Joanne McDougall, is a granddaughter of the renowned riverboat pilot Frank Slim.[35]

RYDER'S FUEL

Some of the town's most essential services were provided by Ryder's Fuel, a longstanding Whitehorse family business. Roland Ryder and his son George delivered wood, water and general freight. George's sons Lloyd, Howard and Gordon also worked in the family fuel delivery business. Over the years, they replaced their horses and wagons with trucks and tractors. The Ryders had a network of up to eight wood camps in the Whitehorse area, providing fuel for local homes and businesses as well as cordwood to power the sternwheeler boilers. Many aboriginal families worked seasonally in the camps, creating longstanding ties. Marny Ryder later wrote about this special relationship: "Just as the different generations of the Ryder family assumed responsibility for the wood camp operation, different generations of the local native people worked as wood-cutters. During the summer months entire families would move out to the wood lots as early as April—green tree cutting had to be completed by September in order for the wood to dry for winter use. During the peak season, 25 to

30 men could be employed at any one camp. This number would vary as the Indian families moved in and out of camp pursuing their own life style."[36]

The Ryder House on the corner of Wood Street and Second Avenue has been continuously occupied by family members since 1921.

WHITEHORSE INN

Built in 1927, the Whitehorse Inn was the largest and most modern hotel of its time, with hot and cold running water in every room. It is indelibly associated with colourful entrepreneur T.C. Richards, who owned and managed the Inn from 1938 on and financed a major addition in 1948. It hosted many gala events, the first years of the Frantic Follies revue, weddings, a bowling alley, a television station and the first Bank of Montreal. Many mourned when the fabled Inn closed its doors and was demolished in late 1970s, to make way for today's CIBC. The distinctive neon sign, first installed in 1955, was salvaged and restored by a dedicated band of volunteers in 2010. Now it shines brightly every evening on the southeast corner of the MacBride Museum of Yukon History.[37]

TOP Lloyd Ryder loading wood on family fuel truck, 1947.

BOTTOM Whitehorse Inn, June 12, 1942. The beer parlour is at right.

The Whitehorse Inn, controlled by Richards, had everything... a restaurant, the Blue Owl café, the Inn ballroom, the Blue Room, Yellow Cabs, the beer parlour, a laundry and of course, the snake pit where legendary characters played poker long into the night. The rooms in the Inn were not much by today's hotel standards, but that didn't bother T.C. He'd laugh when he said it was his job to give tourists hardships—with modern plumbing.
—Les McLaughlin, "T.C. Richards (and the Whitehorse Inn)"[38]

6

WAR TOWN

1939-1945

FACING U.S. Army band plays a concert in front of the White Pass railway depot, 1942.

IT WAS THE spring of 1942, and after a long winter, Whitehorse residents were more than ready for the town to rouse itself to a busier summer pace. A favourite activity was meeting the daily train to check for the arrival of old friends. On April 3, the train-watchers got a great surprise. The locomotives were pulling many more cars than usual, and as hundreds of soldiers disembarked, the streets became "a walking sea of humanity." It was quite an experience for those who had never seen a large crowd of people in their lives.[1] As it turned out, this was the vanguard of the U.S. Army regiments charged with building a highway to Alaska. Within a month, the town's population had swollen to more than 3,000. Men, construction equipment and supplies kept pouring in over the next few months, until the river valley held an estimated 10,000 people. Whitehorse was unprepared and totally overwhelmed.

At the time of this "friendly invasion," Canada had been at war for three years, joining its British allies to fight Hitler's forces in Europe. Many Yukoners enlisted. Their families followed war news via newspaper and radio reports, and community leaders led campaigns to raise funds for war bonds, but the actual fighting seemed very far away. All of this changed after Japanese planes bombed Pearl Harbor on December 7, 1941. The United States was now in the war, and it was anxious to protect the northwest corner of the continent, vulnerable to further Japanese attacks.[2] This led to a barrage of wartime mega-projects: hastily organized, heavily funded, and carried out with what seemed to be an unlimited supply of workers, equipment and resources. Time was of the essence, no expense was spared and northerners were appalled by the ensuing wastefulness.

159

"Tent City," the 18th Engineers Regiment tent camp north of Whitehorse airport, May 6, 1942.

THE MEGA-PROJECTS

The first priority of the U.S. military was to upgrade airports, airstrips and communication stations along what became known as the Northwest Staging Route. This flyway extended from Montana to Fairbanks, enabling American pilots to ferry over 7,000 aircraft to Fairbanks and Nome, all destined for the Russian front. None of this would have been possible without the dedicated support of the radio range operators all along the route, who provided landing, take-off and weather information for the thousands of planes flying through the country in support of the war effort. Every aircraft that flew the route required a flight plan, frequent en route position reports and an arrival message—all accomplished in the absence of landlines or telephones. Every word, every message was handled in Morse code by two radio operators—one sending, one receiving.[3]

Plans were also made to build a highway from Dawson Creek to Fairbanks, linking these airports. The third key element of the scheme was construction of a 960-kilometre (600-mile) pipeline pumping crude oil over the Mackenzie Mountains, from the oil fields at Norman Wells to a new refinery at Whitehorse.

For months before the arrival of the U.S. Army, rumours had circulated that a lot of soldiers were coming to town. The only reference to the planned highway in the local newspaper, however, had been a short paragraph buried on the last page of a February issue of the *Star,* mentioning that the governor of Alaska had urged President Roosevelt to proceed immediately with construction of a B.C.-Alaska Highway.[4] No doubt the newspaper's editor was restricted by wartime censorship regulations on what he could print. Although there had been talk of a highway and discussion of various routes since the late 1920s, nothing had come of it, and White Pass firmly opposed any new transportation corridor that might threaten its monopoly.

TOP Eight members of the 18th Engineers Regimental Post Exchange (PX) posing in front of their tent on May 4, 1942 during a blizzard. L-R standing: Lt. Les Grant, Paul Forestal, "Carolina" Farlow, Sheldon; L-R kneeling: Watson, Nickleson, Evans and Legrand.

BOTTOM Four members of the Headquarters and Service Company—18th Engineers motor pool repairing a jeep along the Alaska Highway northwest of Whitehorse.

The first troops of the invading force were part of the 18th Engineers Regiment (Combat) of the U.S. Army. The seven companies of the regiment arrived in town between April 3 and April 14. During those ten days, nearly 1,500 men disembarked from the train, increasing the local population fivefold. The soldiers had travelled by train from their previous postings in Washington State to either Seattle or Prince Rupert, then by steamship to Skagway. From there, they made the eight-to-ten-hour train trip over the White Pass to Whitehorse. The town made a poor initial impression on them, as the regimental historian Fred Rust later recorded:

162   WHITEHORSE

After 110 miles of narrow gauge uncertainty, we reached Whitehorse and viewed a scattering of shacks and small faded houses dominated by the Government Building and a few cracker-box hotels all served by the oversize red railway station. Near the station on the Lewes, the Yukon River boats were still tied up for the winter. A few whites and Indians went about their business on the plank sidewalks that bordered the half dozen unpaved, unnamed streets and dogs were more numerous than humans and showed the greater interest in our arrival.[5]

The soldiers were much more impressed by the steep climb up the airport road at the end of Main Street to the site of their base camp, a hike that was later described as "the toughest ten minutes of the entire movement."[6]

THE WHITEHORSE AIRPORT

In the summer of 1940, the BYN built its second hangar, a unique structure that became known as the "Steamboat Hangar" due to its flat-roof support cables, which resembled the "hog-chain" braces of the sternwheelers. The company also cut a road into the side of the clay escarpment, commencing at the west end of Main Street. It was a vast improvement over the Puckett's Gulch road. Since it was gouged into the steep side of the unstable clay cliff, it was still disturbingly narrow, and some pilots and passengers were reported to have found it more frightening than their adventures in the air. Traces of the old road can be seen to this day on the escarpment.

On December 9, 1940, the BYN T-hangar burned to the ground, taking with it the company's newest aircraft, the huge Bellanca Aircruiser. In later years, catastrophic fires would cause the demise of three other hangars at the airport.

Before 1940, the runway surface and surrounding field had been mere dirt—chokingly dusty on dry summer days, and a quagmire of mud during fall and spring. In early 1942, the U.S. Army moved in en masse and quickly converted the Whitehorse airfield into a modern airport, with two paved runways, a control tower, instrument approach facilities and, on the west side, three enormous hangars—all in aid of getting aircraft and *matériel* to Alaska.

Amidst this boom, the BYN decided to sell its air division to Grant McConachie's Yukon Southern Air Transport, which had offered a scheduled air service from Whitehorse to Edmonton and Vancouver since the late 1930s. By

FACING TOP Wartime construction continues on the U.S. military (west) side of the Whitehorse airport, October 15, 1943. On the far right A Hangar has been completed, while B and C Hangars are clearly works in progress. A few of the thousands of military aircraft ferried through Whitehorse can be seen on the tarmac. On the far (east) side of the field are the RCAF Administration Building (left), the Steamboat Hangar (behind crane boom), and a small Canadian Pacific Airlines hangar (with doors open). The newly built Alcan Highway runs across the bottom of the photo.

FACING BOTTOM The east side of the Whitehorse airport during the late 1940s and into the early 1950s. Two CPA DC-3s are loading in front of the old air terminal. The CPA hangar, which burned down in 1984, can be seen to the right.

mid-1942, with Yukon Southern Air Transport as the catalyst, Canadian Pacific Railway had collected several other pioneer air services across Canada and formed Canadian Pacific Airlines.

On the east side of the airport, the Royal Canadian Air Force constructed a large hangar and an administration building that became the airport terminal building for Canadian Pacific Airlines and Pan American Airways. The building served as the Whitehorse air passenger terminal well into the 1960s, when that function was relocated to Hangar A, one of the former U.S. Army hangars.

TENT CITY

The first army arrivals, members of "A" Company, spent their first night in town on the floor of the North Star Athletic Association Hall. The following day, they set up their base camp in a snowstorm. The rapidly growing tent camp, situated on the escarpment north of the airport, overlooking town, was soon dubbed "Tent City." For a short period that spring, a camp member credited as "J.F.S." submitted columns to the local paper, recounting amusing incidents of camp life. He shared anecdotes about the regimental band, strategically situated at the opposite end of camp from the medical detachment; confusion over exchange rates between American and Canadian money; the competition for adequate firewood for each tent; and the soldier who ended an argument by stating, "Listen. I've stood at attention longer than you've been in the army!"[7]

The second-growth saplings on the bench were cut down and used for supporting the tents and constructing outdoor mess tables at the end of the "streets" lined with hundreds of green pyramidal tents. The soldiers' chief occupation was collecting firewood for the Sibley stoves. This became known as "gopher wood," "because you would put it in the stove and go for more."[8] The camp made such a demand on local firewood supplies that many residents would be forced to burn green wood the following winter, leading to an especially high number of house fires. A May snowfall and spring thaw soon ensured that the site became a "sea of mud."[9]

The soldiers spent most of this first month waiting to move on. They were issued winter clothing and other gear, including World War I campaign hats that later proved useful when draped with mosquito netting. They drilled, cut and collected wood; spent some time wielding picks and shovels on the roadbed north of town; and marvelled at the arrival of the first caterpillar tractors. They

also fed the roving husky dogs that attached themselves to the camp. The members of the 18th were in town until late May, when they moved northwest to work on the highway in the Kluane area.

A ward in the new U.S. Army hospital, ca. 1940s.

SPRAWL, DISORDER AND MAYHEM

Within months, the departing soldiers were succeeded by thousands of civilian contractors, although the military kept a strong presence in Whitehorse to run the railway and airport, and handle logistics and administration. These contractors were part of the U.S. Public Roads Administration (PRA), charged with following the "pioneer" tote road roughed out by the soldiers. Their job was to straighten, widen and grade the roadbed and to work with engineers—some of them Canadian, such as Jimmy Quong—to build more permanent bridges. Other contractors came to work on the Canol pipeline and the new refinery in Whitehorse. The office staff for these projects included many single women who had travelled north for adventure and a good paycheque. More hastily built barrack buildings were put up on the outskirts of downtown, above the escarpment, and at the large construction camp south of town at McCrae, to accommodate the seemingly endless incoming stream of bodies. With the forces came medical personnel, including several nurses, and in late 1942, the U.S. Army built its own hospital downtown, at Second Avenue and Lambert Street. The following year, the town's hospital at Second Avenue and Hansen Street was enlarged with

Highly motivated soldiers rescuing a truck loaded with beer for the 4th of July celebration, 1942. This truck had slid off the Takhini Crossing ferry.

the first of three additions. The expanded facility now contained 60 beds as well as an operating theatre and case rooms.

Gwen Holmes of Winnipeg flew into Whitehorse in May 1944 to work as a field clerk for the PRA. Her first dwelling was a "shaky plywood prefab" building at McCrae that had two squirrels running in and out of its many holes. At night, drunks pounded on the door trying to find out who the new people were. As Gwen wryly stated when describing the irate wife of a PRA engineer, "Spousal dissatisfaction with roughing it was one of the reasons wives were discouraged from coming onto projects like this."[10]

Holmes recounted stories of disorganization and of people under pressure behaving badly. A lieutenant in charge of food supplies, under the influence of alcohol and love, neglected his job to the point that 300 people—army officers, road workers, married construction workers, PRA staff and miscellaneous personnel—went on strike, refusing to return to work after an especially meagre lunch. This prompted quick action, and that evening they were treated to olives, celery and steak. A train excursion to Carcross for a baseball tournament and dance ended up in total mayhem. The soldiers had smuggled in booze from Skagway, and they began drinking on the trip south. The ball game was cancelled since the teams were too plastered to play. The dance was chaotic, with numerous fights, and the trip home a nightmare, with the soldiers smashing train car windows and tramping through the cars on broken glass. As Holmes recalled, "It was a wild fierce indescribable scene."[11] This experience was a radical contrast to the carefully chaperoned dances at mess halls in the various camps, attended by some of the town's young white women.

By 1941, forty people of Asian descent were living in the Yukon. After the Pearl Harbor attack, the RCMP registered all Japanese nationals in the territory with the Department of National Defence as enemy aliens. Although there were no internment camps in the Yukon, it was a difficult time. Due to American pressure, particularly from employees of Pan American Airways, the Whitehorse Inn laid off its Japanese cooks in December 1941.

ABOVE Christmas dance in
an army mess, ca. 1944.

RIGHT Office workers at
the Northwest Service
Command, ca. 1944.

168   WHITEHORSE

With the arrival of the soldiers, many locals were encountering black people for the first time. Three of the seven regiments building the highway were made up of black troops commanded by white officers. Many of these officers were from the American South, and their racist attitudes came north with them. When the boxer Joe Louis visited Whitehorse in 1945, he stayed at the Regina Hotel. A number of officers and their wives refused to stay there at the same time, an attitude the hotel owners—the Ericksons—considered ridiculous.[12]

THE NORTHWEST SERVICE COMMAND

Due to its strategic location and its access by air, rail and water, Whitehorse became one of the major deployment centres for the construction of the Alaska Highway, along with Dawson Creek, Fort St. John and Fairbanks. On September 4, 1942, Whitehorse was designated the administrative centre of the newly established Northwest Service Command, the coordinating authority for all U.S. Army projects in Alaska, the Yukon Territory, the Northwest Territories, Alberta and B.C.[13]

There was much to oversee. By May 1942, the Public Roads Administration had arrived in Whitehorse to let contracts to civilians for the second phase of highway construction. In June 1942, the ambitious and ultimately disastrous Canol project commenced. By August, thousands of civilian construction workers had joined the army in working on the road. A number of these companies erected large camps in Whitehorse, to the north and south of the downtown core.[14] A party of U.S. Army surveyors had visited the territory during the summer of 1942, looking into the possibility of building a railroad into Alaska.[15] In October of that year, the army leased the railroad from White Pass and put it under the charge of the 770th Railway Operating Battalion, which set up a detachment just upriver from the present site of Rotary Park.[16] In 1943, the Signal Corps of Engineers undertook the construction of a $2-million telephone system to Fairbanks. The new refinery, built and operated by Standard Oil, occupied an immense area north of town that was fenced and guarded, and Whitehorse residents were strictly forbidden access.

Every day, planes arrived in Whitehorse carrying military VIPs and civilian dignitaries. Much of the *matériel* that arrived by rail from Skagway was loaded onto sternwheelers to be shipped to locations such as Dawson City, where it was then transferred to Fairbanks for work on the north end of the road, and to Teslin, via the Yukon and Teslin Rivers and across Teslin Lake, to support construction south of Whitehorse. The army grappled with the logistics of sending mail, supplies and equipment to the military camps, since the camps were always being moved and the tote road varied in its driveability. The building of the Canol pipeline added another challenge, and various small riverboats, including the *Loon* and the *Owl*, were contracted to take supplies—shipped by sternwheelers from Whitehorse to Fort Selkirk—up the Pelly River to Ross River.

By the time the members of the 18th Regiment returned to Whitehorse in late December 1942, the town was transformed. The tent camps had given way to more long-term housing. The administrative staff, who had initially taken over the RCMP compound on Fourth Avenue, had since built their own quarters. Large camps sprawled everywhere, south and north of the downtown area as well as the large compound at McCrae. After spending seven months in tent camps in the bush, the soldiers were mightily impressed:

> Whitehorse had grown. The small section of the original town stood as before, but surrounding it were hundreds of new buildings and warehouses. Both army and civilian quarters and storage yards full of big machines and equipment spread out through the valley until the town itself was lost. The big Army cargo trucks, loaded heavily with all kinds of materiel, rumbled through the streets headed for encampments up and down the road. The railroad, taken over and run by the army, was shuttling loaded cars back and forth. Everywhere there was intense activity. Thousands of men, doing thousands of jobs were all working toward one objective, the completion of the Alaska Highway.... Whitehorse was experiencing another "boom"; the town was once again alive.[17]

SPORTS AND THE MILITARY

When the U.S. Army arrived in Whitehorse in March 1942, they took over the NSAA Hall and immediately got involved in the local sports scene. Part of the building's main floor was converted into a warehouse crammed with canned food. The gymnasium was used for men's and women's basketball and badminton until that fall, when the need for more warehouse space forced the players out. The building's second floor served as a temporary hospital for military personnel.

Softball was popular with the soldiers. Their personnel formed most of the teams in town from 1942 until the end of the 1944 season, since local players were only able to field a single team. Basketball also benefitted. As the *Whitehorse Star* noted in March 1942, "Their place in the teams will boost the standard of basketball in Whitehorse considerably."

Boxing matches were held in temporary outdoor rings between 1942 and 1944. Crowds of up to 5,000, including civilians, construction workers, Canadian army and air force personnel and U.S. troops, gathered to cheer on the combatants.

The Special Services Branch of the U.S. War Department also introduced local organizers to up-to-date sports administration and organization practices. As the military presence diminished in 1944–45, civilians stepped into leadership roles.

The Americans weren't terribly fond of winter sports, although curling and men's hockey saw some participation by U.S. soldiers. Organized women's hockey made a reappearance in 1942.

When a young Norwegian named Arne Anderson arrived in Whitehorse in 1942, he decided that the Ski Bowl needed some additional features. He and John Backe constructed three wooden ski jumps, including a long one from which skiers could literally soar. A ski "chalet," in reality just a warming shack, was also built. Trails were cut for cross-country skiers, and downhill runs were cleared through the brush. A ski club called the Yukon Ski Runners was formed. The Ski Runners hosted several events in the Ski Bowl, including the ski events for the first Whitehorse Winter Carnival in 1945 and races with skiers from Alaska and northern B.C.

Military softball team in Whitehorse, June 1945.

TOP LEFT The ski jump in the Ski Bowl. Arne Anderson, builder of the ski jumps, is apparently one of the jumpers.

TOP RIGHT Crowd at boxing match downtown, ca. 1942.

RIGHT The NSAA burns to the ground, December 16, 1942.

On December 16, 1942, 30 men were in the medical ward on the top floor of the NSAA Hall when a fire started at about 5:20 a.m. All of the men dropped unharmed to the ground from the windows, but the building went up in flames. Only the curling sheet, the baseball field, an outdoor change shack and the ice rink survived the inferno.

Some cases of food and many turkeys were hauled out of the hall during the fire and left in the street. For the next two days, people foraged for their Christmas dinners by returning to the scene after dark, loading boxes and frozen turkeys onto toboggans. Eventually, the U.S. Army posted guards around the area.

Although insurance paid out $4,000 for the loss, it wasn't sufficient to build a new complex. The tennis courts and ice rinks were relocated. The ball park was enlarged and renamed the Sports Field. The curling rink remained in operation in winter and in summer served as the right-field fence for the ballplayers.

Line-up of U.S. soldiers and civilian workers at the government liquor store near the White Pass station, October 19, 1943. Liquor was rationed, with each permit holder being allotted one pint a week. Nondrinkers sold liquor privately for $50 a bottle.

SOLDIERS AND CITIZENS

For amusement, the soldiers were permitted to visit Whitehorse daily without passes. They augmented their diet of canned and powdered camp food with meals at the local cafés. They drank the "heavy Canadian beer" in the beer parlours and bought out the stock of local stores, including items such as old housewares and tools that had languished on the shelves since gold-rush days.[18] The town's first movie house, the W.H. Theatre, built in 1937 by J.R. Alguire on the corner of Main and Second Avenue, was jammed. Within days of the soldiers' arrival, it upped its showings from twice a week to twice a night, excepting Sundays, with new movies three times a week.[19] The post office was overwhelmed by the tons of mail that arrived for the soldiers before the army took over its own mail handling. Laurent Cyr recorded this vivid account of the experience:

> I worked in the post office, a dinky building. Just me and the postmaster, and two weeks after the Americans came he had a stroke, so I ran out on the street and grabbed off two local women and I hired them.... Naturally we had no cancellation machine and from maybe 20 letters a day we were shooting out thousands.... I'd hand stamp for 12 hours a day and one Saturday I stamped for 17 hours. Callouses. Dead arms. If you want to know what hard work is, it's stamping envelopes for 10,000 men, 12 hours a day.[20]

A familiar sight at the time was the oft-photographed endless line-up at the government liquor store. An individual's purchases were limited to one bottle of liquor and twelve bottles of beer a month.[21] What could not be procured legally was available from local bootleggers, who either sold commercial brands at highly inflated prices or brewed their own beverages. Others headed north to the capital city, where there was still a good supply of liquor, then packed it back to Whitehorse. Prices for bootleg liquor ranged from $30 a pint up to $110 for a quart bottle, "and not the best brands either."[22]

After their initial surprise at the overwhelming influx of soldiers, Whitehorse residents were generally friendly and hospitable, often welcoming the newcomers into their homes. The softball club invited the soldiers to form their own teams and compete against the locals. Soldiers took in a basketball game and later

TOP Lillian Harbottle with a group of soldiers in front of the Red Cross canteen (United Service Organization Hall), ca. 1942–45.

BOTTOM Chapel choir, ca. 1944.

arranged to use the NSAA Hall two evenings a week for their own games. Any establishment that owned a piano could be sure of a group clustered around a pianist ("there was always somebody that could play the piano") and enjoying a singsong.[23] A Red Cross canteen was established by the local women. Here the soldiers could buy a cup of coffee, play cards and write letters home.

Once more permanent facilities had replaced the tent camps, the military reciprocated the townsfolk's hospitality. They offered their new friends chewing gum, cigarettes and candy from the Post Exchange, or "PX," and gave Whitehorse residents their first taste of Hershey Bars. There were frequent invitations to dinner at the mess halls, and it was not unusual for a soldier to come visiting

TOP Whitehorse premiere of Irving Berlin's movie *This is the Army*. The 600-seat Quonset hut TITA Theatre was named after the movie's title. Carcross Chief at left.

BOTTOM Another scene from the grand opening of the TITA Theatre at McCrae, 1943.

with a turkey or two. When Gudrun Sparling travelled outside to attend school in Vancouver, she impressed her new schoolmates by regaling them with accounts of the abundance of foodstuffs available in Whitehorse while the rest of the country suffered shortages.[24]

Military bands put on concerts for the townspeople in front of the White Pass train station on Sunday afternoons, and occasionally there were variety shows in the NSAA Hall. The camp recreation halls hosted frequent dances, with music usually supplied by jukeboxes. The few single women in town enjoyed great popularity. When they attended army dances at out-of-town camps, such as McCrae and Teslin, they travelled in groups by bus. There were also visits to army theatre at McCrae, which showed much newer films than the local movie house.

The soldiers also enjoyed the great outdoors. By 1943, army officers were chipping in to rent cabins at Lake Laberge, travelling to their hideaways by motor launch down the Yukon River.[25] In off-hours, army personnel commandeered jeeps for excursions to local beauty spots. For those travelling on foot, Miles Canyon and the Whitehorse Rapids were popular spots for fishing trips and picnics, although one such expedition ended in tragedy. On April 28, 1942, Private George F. Wolters drowned when he tried fishing in Whitehorse Rapids and fell into the cold, swift water.[26]

The churches were a haven for many young men far from home. The Anglican church presented lantern slide lectures on the Yukon twice a week.[27] Lapsed Catholics began attending church services to experience the comfort of familiar rituals. In return, many soldiers spent their free time renovating church buildings. In 1942, soldiers replaced most of the siding and repainted the exterior of Sacred Heart Cathedral.[28] Half the congregation at the Anglican church services was made up of soldiers of all denominations. The pastor at the time, L.G. Chappell, described a funeral for a soldier who had died on the highway: "We had a Jewish service for him in the Anglican church, with a Lutheran chaplain in charge."[29]

CONFLICTED TIMES

Everything was nice, before the highway. When the highway moved in, everybody got sick. Water got sick and everything was polluted .... Our lives started to change.
—Leonard Gordon Sr., 1996

To a certain degree, the effects of the Alaska Highway construction on Yukon aboriginal people mirrored those of the Klondike gold rush. Once again, overwhelming hordes of newcomers moved into traditional aboriginal territories, occupying hunting and trapping grounds and damaging the resources through careless campfires, overhunting, overfishing and driving game away from the highway corridor. In some cases, people were not only displaced from their traditional hunting lands but forbidden access to other areas.

Lucy Wren spoke of an unsettling encounter between her mother and a military guard at Hillcrest:

My mom had a fight with one soldier up the hill. She wanted to go grouse hunting up there where Air Force camp. She said, "That's my hunting ground."

He said, "Out of here!"

She couldn't understand why. She said, "I've lived here many years. You just came here. Go home!".... He pushed her away with the rifle. Them days you can't say anything, you just have to go, get out.[30]

For some, this was also a time of new opportunities. As with other Yukoners, many aboriginal people from outlying communities moved to Whitehorse to take highway-related jobs. Some men worked as guides, leading the surveyors who staked the route for the bulldozers following close behind. Others took jobs on the docks or the steamboats. There was a great need for firewood, and the wood camps were busier than ever. Women took a variety of jobs in laundries, hotels, restaurants and the camps. Many women and their families, including Kitty Smith and Lily Kane, made excellent wages selling moosehide clothing to the soldiers and contractors. Kitty Smith was able to purchase a truck with the proceeds of these sales.

A number of men from the Whitehorse area enlisted, including Elijah Smith. When Annie Ned took part in the local wartime volunteer efforts, she thought of her son, so far away:

When war came, my son was in the army, overseas. I was going with Red Cross, that time. I stayed with it, Red Cross. Sometimes those army socks we fixed. You've got to go and pray for your son. I would go there and work at socks—just white people there. Every time I went to Whitehorse, I would go Red Cross....

I'm going to talk about one time when I went to Whitehorse. That's the time the army comes. My son is out! We got letters all the time; policeman used to bring them to me. That time policeman comes to where we were living.

View of a First Nations wood camp, taken by a U.S. soldier. The furs hanging on the racks are bear hides.

"American soldiers are going to come to Whitehorse. You've got to come." Red Cross lady, Mrs. Taylor, is there. I stood right alongside those white ladies.[31]

Many aboriginal women socialized with soldiers. Although there were some marriages, often these relationships ended in pregnancy and abandonment. Despite some economic benefits, the first peoples were again beset by the ills that had come with the invasion of the territory during the gold rush: alcohol abuse, venereal disease, epidemics and even death.[32]

LIFE UNDER THE MILITARY

The sudden influx of thousands of soldiers inevitably caused strains. The flip side of the increased economic activity and general prosperity for Whitehorse was overcrowding, disease and a certain arrogance that arose from the U.S. Army's status as the majority force making most of the decisions.

The army did buy many of its supplies from local retailers. P. Burns & Company dealt in so much volume that the firm found it expeditious to sell meat to the camps "right off the railway tracks."[33] In running the railway, however, the Americans gave priority to military equipment and supplies, causing shortages for the civilian population.[34] Often the required paperwork complicated matters, so that when supplies finally arrived, there might be three times the quantity ordered.[35]

After the belt-tightening years of the depression, Whitehorse residents were amazed both by the abundance of U.S. Army supplies and by the military's profligate waste. When new consignments of frozen meat arrived, the meat already in camp freezers was hauled to the dump. Other foodstuffs were spoiled by being stored outside over the winter. An exception was that American staple, Coca-Cola: the sugar content was so high that the bottled soft drinks did not freeze.[36]

By July 1942, military passes were required for civilian travel to Alaska. A month later, new restrictions were announced, this time closer to home. The restricted military area included part of the Whitehorse Airport, the Ice Lake Road and the highway south of town.[37] Military checkpoints at McCrae and north of town, near the Fish Lake Road, carefully screened all travellers, including local residents, before letting them continue on their way.

The town's small RCMP force was suddenly confronted with all the problems of a major city: drunkenness, bootlegging, theft, assaults and murders. Since

the small detachment could not deal with the boom in crime, the Mounties were augmented by the U.S. Military Police (MP), who took over to the point of telling a carful of uniformed Mounties that they were speeding and ordering them to report to MP headquarters. While watching the departure of a sternwheeler from the waterfront, Gwen Holmes and two friends were arrested for being in a restricted area. They were let off with a warning, but Holmes had trouble taking the incident seriously: "It struck me as excruciatingly funny that people were being murdered up there and getting off and we three women were arrested for the heinous crime of sightseeing."[38]

The streets became more dangerous, and people began locking their doors. One young woman was assaulted by three soldiers while walking the two blocks home from a friend's house. Employees taking money from their place of business to the bank were now usually escorted by an RCMP officer or an MP.[39] Infractions by local soldiers tended to be handled internally by the army, and often soldiers were transferred before they could answer for their crimes, a process resented by the local population. Life within the civilian camps was even rougher, and there were reports of murders.[40]

Locals were not impressed by the difference in pay scale between American and Canadian workers. Not only was the Canadian dollar worth less than the American dollar, but the pay rates for Canadians were substantially lower. In 1942, a visiting journalist heard the oft-repeated complaint from a man who "was cursing the regulations that made him, as a Canadian, work for a Canadian

The riverfront area where the trains met the steamboats.

MHKCB Company's Time Office No. 1. The Metcalfe Hamilton Kansas City Bridge Company was one of many American construction firms working in Whitehorse during the war.

firm as a shovel operator at $1.25 an hour when he could go to any American camp and get $2."[41] For their part, local employers complained that the Americans and their princely wages were undermining the local economy.

There were some long-term benefits from the American presence. The Americans were appalled by the prospect of their troops contracting dysentery from untreated water. Soldiers were forbidden to drink the water in restaurants, and the army set up chlorination plants. Local residents found the highly chlorinated water undrinkable, however. After prolonged negotiations between the army and the Canadian government, the Americans installed the town's first sewer and water system in part of the downtown core in 1943. After a long period during which it seemed that every street was torn up in summer, the town had the rudiments of a piped sewer and water system, a great step forward from the previous "undeveloped island of cesspits."[42]

The army had set up a local radio station to entertain the forces, and when the Americans moved, they left their equipment behind. Canadian forces and local volunteers continued to operate the station. The Americans also constructed many recreation facilities that were later inherited by residents. One of the most important military legacies was the telephone-telegraph line erected alongside the highway from Edmonton to Fairbanks. The U.S. Signal Corps and private contractors worked together to erect 95,000 poles, string 14,000 miles of wire and build 23 repeater stations. As the world's longest open wire communications line, this was another immense wartime engineering feat. According to the *Star*, the Whitehorse telephone system was now "the most up-to-date in the world."[43]

THE WARTIME BUILT LEGACY

From 1942 on, military and construction-related buildings popped up so fast in Whitehorse it was like mushrooms after the rain. Long, low barracks-style buildings, most of them single-storey wood-frame constructions, cropped up around the edges of town and on the escarpment in compounds of a dozen or more. To the north, Bechtel-Price-Callahan erected a large camp supporting the Canol pipeline project. Farther downriver, Standard Oil occupied an immense area to accommodate all the structures for its refinery.

Hastily built and typically uninsulated, these wartime buildings were never meant for long-term use. They were drafty and cold, and residents frequently complained of malfunctioning heaters and frozen water pipes. Many of the buildings endure to this day, however, demonstrating the northern ethic of recycling and adaptive reuse.

The army left Whitehorse with the rudiments of a sewer and water system, a modern airport with a paved runway, the highway and much-improved roads. More than that, however, military construction had created expectations in Whitehorse. Change had come, and soon the rustic loo out the back door would no longer be the norm.

LOG SKYSCRAPERS

Building the log skyscrapers.

BUILT IN 1947, the two- and three-storey log skyscrapers on Lambert Street, near Third Avenue, continue to number among the town's quirkiest attractions. These rental properties were Martin Berrigan's answer to the post-war housing shortage. The cabins are unique in Canada, and in 1999, they were designated as a Municipal Heritage Site. The buildings continue to fulfil their original function: providing a home to both people and small businesses.

TOO BIG, TOO FAST

As Whitehorse grew and grew, the fortunes of non-highway towns such as Mayo and Dawson City rapidly diminished. Almost immediately after the closing of the Treadwell Mine in 1942, Mayo lost its doctor, its hospital, its bank and its diesel light plant. The Mayo hospital equipment was installed in the new addition to the Whitehorse Hospital. Bechtel-Price-Callahan, the contractors in

charge of the Canol project, took over the Mayo light plant for their maintenance camp in Whitehorse. Even the *Whitehorse Star* benefitted from the town's demise; its editor travelled there to acquire a printing press.[44]

There were plenty of jobs available in Whitehorse during this time, but too few workers. Some people held two or three jobs simultaneously. Babe Richards recalls working all day at the P. Burns & Company meat market, then putting in a five-to-midnight shift on the cash register at the Whitehorse Inn Cafe.[45] Inevitably, many workers and businesses left the smaller communities to take advantage of these opportunities. The range of businesspeople moving to Whitehorse included the Dawson City bootlegger, who transferred his distilling apparatus to Whiskey Flats; the Atlin taxi driver, who shipped her car to Whitehorse by boat; and the owner of the Cascade Laundry of Dawson City, who brought his dry cleaning plant to Whitehorse and opened a laundry on Main Street.[46]

While gainful employment was readily available, housing was another matter. Not only was it rare to find a hotel room with only one bed, but hotel beds were often filled 24 hours a day. After one occupant got up in the morning, another weary person immediately took his place. People slept in hotel lobbies, on the floor of the train station and on any sternwheelers that happened to be docked at the wharves. A group of Atlinites, travelling to Prince Rupert to testify in a murder trial, spent 48 hours wandering the streets of Whitehorse until they

FACING TOP LEFT View of the south end of Whitehorse from the edge of the airport, October 4, 1943.

FACING TOP RIGHT The U.S. Army fire hall.

FACING BOTTOM LEFT Quonset hut next to the log skyscraper.

FACING BOTTOM RIGHT Extension of railway and warehouses in area of today's Qwanlin Mall.

ABOVE Another view of the liquor store line-up. Occasionally people who were closer to the entrance sold their place in line.

could catch their train, since there was no place available for them to sleep.[47] Rents skyrocketed. Many workers ended up building squatter shacks around the outskirts of town or along the riverbank. Hundreds of people occupied these informal communities, which became known as Whiskey Flats, Shipyards, Moccasin Flats and Sleepy Hollow.

Housing wasn't the only hassle. The town's hustling atmosphere was offset by the endless hours travellers spent in line-ups, often waiting days for the permits, authorizations and arrangements that would allow them to move farther up or down the road. It was common to stand in line for two or three hours at the town's one bank. Overwhelmed bank employees were kept working until late at night, trying to complete their paperwork. Journalist Gertrude Baskine, who spent eleven days trying to get out of Whitehorse in 1943, vividly captured the frustration of conducting business in the overextended town:

> The cheapest thing on your hands—time. Because for whatever you wanted to do, you had to spend so much of it, waiting, waiting, waiting; waiting in a queue for a meal, or a stamp, or a letter, or a cheque, or the movies, or this, or that. For every activity, essential or otherwise. And the snaketrail at the liquor store just wound around the corner and up the block and all but bit its own tail coming back.[48]

Local entrepreneurs tried to fill the increased demand for services. Several new restaurants opened, including the Alcan Cafe, the S and A Cafe, the Klondyke Cafe and the White Spot. A new and larger movie theatre, the Capitol, was constructed on the southwest corner of Third and Main. New laundries, taxis and Seely's Pool Room all had lots of customers. In 1947, the local Kiwanis Club published a boosterish tourist guidebook to Whitehorse that described the many commercial establishments downtown. The number and variety of businesses listed had increased by nearly 400 per cent compared to the fifteen enterprises advertising in the 1941 Christmas issue of the *Whitehorse Star*.[49]

VISIONS OF THE FUTURE

Many local residents, having tasted the excitement and prosperity of living in a large community, were concerned that Whitehorse would decline once the U.S. Army pulled out. When the closure of the Canol project was announced, Babe

Richards was discouraged from opening a dress shop in town. People felt that her prospects for success were unpromising once the refinery workers and their families departed. The same gloomy predictions would be made when the Canadian Forces left the territory in the 1960s, but in Richards's words, "Whitehorse always goes ahead."[50] Horace Moore, the editor of the *Whitehorse Star*, was much more optimistic. In the heady atmosphere of the summer of 1943, he saw nothing but progress. "We might grow to be a city of 3,500," he predicted.[51]

One of the more accurate predictions made in the 1940s came from a highway worker burning brush on the right-of-way south of Whitehorse, alongside a rough gravel road: "Boy it's hard to believe but someday they'll be driving down

"Christmas in our shack." A group of civilian workers celebrate the season in their Quonset quarters.

here at 80 miles per hour." His listeners, Bill Drury and George Ryder, had trouble swallowing this statement, but Ryder lived to verify its accuracy. In a 1990 interview, he would exclaim, "And here it is today—superhighway!"[52]

The wartime mega-projects made a great impact on the small settlement by the Yukon River. Whitehorse was now established as a major northern town, the Yukon's largest centre, and it would be only a matter of time before this economic power shift was recognized by the powers in Ottawa. The town had also inherited a legacy of wartime waste and pollution. Some sites, such as the infamous Marwell tar pit in the Industrial Area—left behind when the refinery was dismantled—still haunt today's politicians and planners. Most significantly, over the years to come, Whitehorse would turn its back on the river and look to the new highway and the sprawling subdivisions above the escarpments for its continuing prosperity.

COMMUNITY PORTRAITS

LESLIE "LES" COOK CA. 1908–1942

Hundreds of pilots were employed in the northern mega-projects, flying in perilous conditions over unknown country and jury-rigging repairs when necessary. Among this group of daring flyers, Les Cook stood out.

Leslie Cook was born in Pincher Creek, Alberta. After mustering out of the RCAF, he moved to the Yukon in 1937 to work for Northern Airways in Carcross. By May 1942, he was working as a civilian pilot for the U.S. Army. General William Hoge, who flew several flights with Cook, described him as a "crackerjack pilot" and credited Cook's flying skill and intimate knowledge of the country with assisting the selection of the final highway route. In November 1942, Cook made a night flight in poor weather to deliver medical supplies and two army doctors to a Donjek River camp where a soldier was critically ill with appendicitis. The soldier was saved thanks to Cook's daring flight.

A month later, two engineers who had just completed some repairs on a Norseman asked Les Cook to make a quick test flight. At the last minute, they decided to join him in the plane. The plane was barely airborne when it began acting erratically and then plummeted, crashing into Second Avenue. Cook and his companions, Ken McLean and Don Dickson, lost their lives in the crash and resulting fire. The entire community turned out to a full military funeral. Cook was posthumously awarded the Air Medal of the United States Army, and his name survives in downtown Whitehorse, on Cook Street.[53]

Les Cook.

JAMES YEE CHEW QUONG 1917–2003

Born in Lethbridge, Alberta, James Quong, known as Jimmy, studied engineering at the University of Saskatchewan. In 1942, he joined the U.S. Public Roads Administration to design temporary timber bridges along the Alaska Highway. Quong served in Fort St. John and Dawson Creek before moving to Whitehorse. From there, he went on to help design 134 permanent bridges along the same highway.

Jimmy Quong worked for the Americans until 1946, when control of the highway was handed over to the Northwest Highway Service under the Canadian Army. In 1964, Quong moved to Canada's Department of Public Works when the highway was handed over to civilian control. He continued to work on Alaska Highway bridges, as well as helping to design bridges on the Skagway Road and the Dempster Highway. He remained with the department until his retirement in 1981.

Jimmy Quong married Diamond Chan on February 10, 1944. He promised his new bride that they would be moving north for only six months, but the Quongs lived in Whitehorse for 37 years. Here they made many lifelong friends and raised their family: daughters Meiyan, Meilin and Meijane, and son Kenneth. In addition to being a talented photographer, "the Great Quong," as his co-workers called him, was also an artist, a calligrapher and a musician, passions he passed on to his children. His family donated his immense photograph collection to Yukon Archives, and this amazing body of work was celebrated in 2010 with exhibits in no less than four different venues.[54]

FRANK SLIM 1898–1973

Frank Slim was born in a small village at the north end of Lake Laberge, one of five children. His parents, Slim Jim and Ginnie Jim, were based in the Marsh Lake and M'Clintock River areas, and his great-uncle was Skookum Jim. Frank Slim grew up speaking three languages: Southern Tutchone, Tagish and Tlingit. As a boy, he travelled to Whitehorse by paddling a dugout canoe to Canyon City and then walking the trail into town. About 1917, he married Aggie Broeren, from the Lake Laberge area, and the pair had five children: Sophie, George, Irene, Owen and Virginia.

Frank Slim at the wheel of the MV *Schwatka*, 1962.

At age sixteen, Slim started work on the sternwheelers as a deckhand. He paid a non-native man to teach him to read and write and then practised on the boats using the labels on soup cans and other groceries. His ability to "read the river" led to piloting work on many major rivers of the Yukon, Alaska and northern B.C., chiefly for either the British Yukon Navigation Company or Taylor & Drury. In 1937, Slim travelled to Vancouver, where he passed the exam to qualify as a steamboat captain. Under the laws of the time, he had to surrender his Indian status to do this—a great sacrifice. When the sternwheelers were later beached, Frank trapped and mined as well as freighting supplies on the winter road to outlying communities, first with horses and sleighs, then with motorized cat trains.

During the war years, Slim and his entire family flew to Dease Lake to take a job freighting supplies via the Dease and Liard Rivers in northern B.C. He and his crew used two motor vessels and the small sternwheeler *Drew* to move tractors and graders to Lower Post. Operators used the heavy equipment to carve out a road to Watson Lake, then to construct the airport. Once the sternwheeler era had ended, Slim operated ferries while bridges were being built on the Pelly and Stewart Rivers. In later years, he captained the MV *Schwatka*, a tourist boat that ran between Schwatka Lake and the head of Miles Canyon. He also piloted the *Keno* on its final voyage downriver to Dawson City in 1960.

Frank Slim's life and accomplishments were honoured with the naming of Mount Slim, southeast of Lake Laberge, in 1973. He was recognized as a transportation pioneer by the Yukon Transportation Museum in 1997, and in 2009, a municipal structure in the new Shipyards Park was named the Frank Slim building. [55]

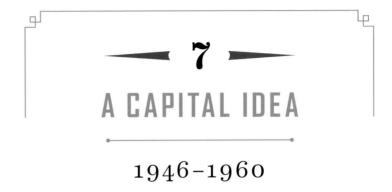

7

A CAPITAL IDEA

1946–1960

THE END OF World War II brought enormous relief and celebration, followed soon after by a sober assessment of post-war realities. Whitehorse residents faced perplexing problems. The town's rudimentary infrastructure was totally inadequate to support the tenfold population increase. The Alaska Highway had opened the southern Yukon to new commercial opportunities, but neither government nor private enterprise was organized to capitalize on that potential. Shortages of housing, services, utilities and money presented huge challenges in the midst of optimism and grand dreams.

The contrast between bright hopes and desperate circumstances was especially stark for aboriginal people. Their economic and social situation was complicated by long-standing government policies that separated families by placing children in church-run residential schools. Attitudes within the non-aboriginal community often kept the mainstream and aboriginal communities apart.

Change was necessary on many fronts. New ideas surfaced in political campaigns, service clubs and the business community. As the country refocussed on civilian goals, the federal government looked north for the first time in decades, recognizing the need for massive investments to support future development.

A NEW MILITARY COMMAND

The first task for Canada was the resumption of responsibility for its northwest region. Since 1942, U.S. Army officers had controlled the Alaska Highway and much else on Canadian territory. The highway was officially handed over to

FACING The Young People's Association leads the parade up Main Street on Sports Day in May 1946.

191

Canadian authorities on April 3, 1946. Whitehorse was designated the new federal operations centre in the Yukon, with the Canadian Army in a commanding role.

On a cool, crisp day filled with brilliant sunshine, visiting luminaries joined thousands of residents and military personnel to witness the historic event, while a regimental band played sentimental favourites. An honour guard of Canadian Army, RCAF, RCMP and American personnel marched to the speakers' platform. L.H. Phinney, Special Commissioner for Defence Projects of Northwest Canada, introduced dignitaries including Canadian General A.G.L. McNaughton and American Major General W.N. (Bill) Hoge.

The U.S. Ambassador to Canada, Ray Atherton, handed over the Canadian highway section and facilities to General McNaughton, who announced that the Canadian government had already repaid the American government $77-million and spent $30-million to improve the rough gravel road for future public travel. Major General Hoge paid tribute "to all those who bore the brunt and the burden ... during the construction period."[1] Later, E.F. Pinchin, president of the Whitehorse Men's Council, which represented the town's business and professional elite, hosted a glittering dinner for 200 guests at the American mess hall. Yukon MP George Black and Controller George Jeckell joined the official Canadian party, but it was a day overseen by outsiders, a harbinger of many new Yukon realities to come. Within days, American troops had packed their bags and left town. The Canadian Army occupied the U.S. wartime barracks and operational facilities to begin maintaining the highway.[2]

When the U.S. Army relinquished control of the Alaska Highway, the telephone system was one of the assets handed over to the Canadian military. Within a year, the federal government contracted the Canadian National Telegraph Company (CNT), later renamed Canadian National Telecomunications, to operate and maintain the system. In 1958, after several years of negotiation, CNT acquired the Whitehorse telephone exchange, part of the Yukon Telephone Company owned by Stan Barker. In 1979, Whitehorse became home to a separate northern-based major telephone subsidiary, with major investments in upgrading and expansion. This new corporation was christened Northwestel, and a decade later was sold to its current owners, BCE Enterprises, the parent company of Bell Canada.[3]

Responsibility for the post-war administration of the northern territories was still situated in the Department of Mines and Resources, which had managed northern affairs since the mid-1930s, when the government reorganized

the old Department of the Interior. Northern agencies would be reconfigured several more times, with successive departmental names reflecting Ottawa's shifting perceptions of the North. The Department of Resources and Development assumed overall responsibility for northern administration from 1950 to 1953, and was renamed as Northern Affairs and National Resources from 1953 to 1966. Health services for aboriginal people transferred to the Department of National Health and Welfare in the late 1940s; many other aboriginal programs moved to the Department of Citizenship and Immigration in the early 1950s. Northern and aboriginal programs were reunited in 1966 under the new Department of Indian Affairs and Northern Development. So many departments had a hand in northern administration that a special Advisory Committee on Northern Development was set up in Ottawa to coordinate federal activities, but the growing plethora of programs and officials created confusion for northern people as they tried to steer their course to the future.[4]

American and Canadian military officials shake hands during ceremonies to mark the handover of the Alaska Highway at Whitehorse on April 3, 1946.

Squatter neighbourhoods were home to many people but the jumble of unorganized shacks, abandoned equipment and other hazards were a concern to health officials and other citizens. Whiskey Flats, ca. 1950s.

SEPARATE REALITIES

While some aboriginal people no doubt watched the ceremonies, they had no official spokesperson or role. The *Star* mentioned nothing of aboriginal participation in wartime projects. People had suffered profound losses, with women and children especially vulnerable in the disjointed society that followed.

The 1941 Census had listed about 3,500 non-aboriginal people clustered at Whitehorse, Dawson and Mayo, with some 1,500 aboriginal people living in small groups around the territory. In 1948, officials counted roughly 6,000 non-aboriginals, including many transient construction workers, and 1,600 aboriginals, with a modest increase in the numbers living in and around Whitehorse.[5] Wartime projects had displaced people from their familiar hunting areas, and more aboriginal families moved to town after the war as labour shortages created work opportunities. A few entrepreneurs hauled wood or guided big-game hunters. Women earned money by sewing garments for local people and visitors, while continuing to care for children and Elders.

People settled with extended family in town or squatted on White Pass and federal lands at Whiskey Flats, Moccasin Flats, the Shipyards and Sleepy Hollow, building small, ramshackle homes from materials scrounged or purchased from meagre incomes. Streets wound around shacks, privies, woodpiles and abandoned vehicles in a haphazard jumble. Frequent fires destroyed homes, killing or injuring people. Some families kept dog teams or pack dogs to trap and hunt in the hills beyond town, balancing the new cash economy with familiar subsistence routines.

Living among their white neighbours, aboriginal people were separated from them by laws and practices that defined their lives from birth to death. Status Indians were wards of the federal government, with no right to vote or to run in territorial or federal elections. They received limited medical care at federal expense in a separate ward at the Whitehorse Hospital. Welcomed by some businesses, aboriginal people were shunned by others. Some men had given up their status to join the armed forces. Confusion over identity, rights and distinctions grew as more aboriginal women married white men, losing their status and the associated minimal benefits for them and their children.

Laws prohibited Status Indians from buying, possessing or consuming alcoholic beverages, with fines or jail time for infractions. Alcohol consumption increased despite the laws and overtook many aboriginal homes, leading to social problems, violence and even deaths. Young aboriginal women had babies who were unacknowledged and abandoned by men who returned to the south, adding to the burdens of struggling families.

As before the war, at age five, Status Indian children were taken to either the Anglican residential school at Carcross or the new Roman Catholic residential school near Lower Post. Their parents were left lonely, confused and heartbroken. The new federal mothers' allowance paid a small amount for each child—provided all school-age children attended school. This brought welcome income but increased pressure on mothers to allow their children to be sent away to school. Mixed race children were ineligible to attend residential schools and yet were sometimes unwelcome at the public schools in Whitehorse, leaving numerous young people roaming the streets.[6]

TOP Some families kept their dog teams in town, finding space near the clay cliffs, recycling barrels and other materials for dog houses. Whitehorse, ca. 1946.

BOTTOM Aboriginal children in downtown Whitehorse, ca. 1946.

Students and staff in front of the Whitehorse Baptist Indian Mission School, ca. 1950.

In 1947, Baptist missionaries Harold and Lydia Lee arrived in Whitehorse to establish a church, but they soon decided instead to start a school for aboriginal children, regardless of status. The Whitehorse Baptist Indian Mission School opened with 40 students in classrooms and residences cobbled together from leftover army barracks and heated with barrel stoves. Some people condemned the new school as a fire trap. Anglican and Catholic officials protested that children were being lured away from their own residential schools. The Baptist school grew nonetheless, being the only option for some kids and for parents who didn't want to send their children away. The Lees received no government funding, but army officials, service clubs and businesses donated cash, food and other assistance. When Reverend Lee was killed in a highway accident in 1952, Mrs. Lee carried on the school with help from Baptist fundraisers outside, and many local supporters.[7]

The federal government had one Indian Agent, who travelled sporadically around the Yukon Territory. By the late 1940s, federal staff in the region also included public health nurses and visiting medical teams looking after health programs for aboriginal people. The spread of tuberculosis was rampant as more aboriginal people moved to town and their children entered schools. A major campaign to eradicate the disease was both welcomed and feared, with free X-ray labs visiting every Yukon community. Hundreds of aboriginal people, including many children, were sent to southern hospitals. Some were gone for years or died alone, far from home. The TB epidemic heightened fears among non-aboriginal neighbours, generating more societal barriers.[8]

The Indian Agent and other federal officials struggled to provide assistance to the aboriginal people flooding into Whitehorse from various communities. For administrative convenience, officials decided in 1956 to amalgamate people

First Nations performers at the winter carnival in 1948. Chief Jim Boss is third from left in his regalia.

from Lake Laberge, Marsh Lake and other areas as the "Whitehorse Indian Band" under an elected Chief and Council, ignoring the traditional groupings and leadership that had existed for generations. Reserve No. 8 had been set aside to provide residential land for aboriginal families north of town. As the former site of the Canol refinery and other industrial facilities, lacking water, sewer and electrical utilities and sitting below the Camp Takhini sewer outfall, the site was an unhealthy environment, and these problems persisted for decades.[9]

Despite all the problems they faced, aboriginal people joined in on special events and community fun. They drew strength from their cultural traditions and family connections to survive in this new urban setting.

POST-WAR DILEMMAS

Non-aboriginal old-timers and newcomers also grappled with rapid change, high costs and shortages. As more attention centred on Whitehorse, other Yukon communities languished in uncertainty. People in Dawson City, Mayo and other isolated settlements, connected to the rest of the territory only through summer river transport or expensive air service, faced difficult choices. Mining and related industries were short of investment capital. Fur prices were down and wood camps less busy, with dwindling sternwheeler traffic. Employment opportunities grew in Whitehorse, but housing was scarce, and living conditions were unpleasant for families used to the quiet peace of smaller communities.

FACING TOP LEFT Whitehorse
Hospital on Second Avenue, 1948.

FACING TOP RIGHT Wooden
sidewalks and unpaved Main
Street in front of Taylor & Drury
Store, ca. 1945.

FACING BOTTOM The fire at the
Corps of Royal Canadian Electrical
and Mechanical Engineers
(RCEME) shop, 1947.

The Yukon itself was stuck with an archaic administrative regime in Dawson City, the capital city, and a jumble of new federal agencies in Whitehorse handling mining, forestry and geological surveys, all reporting to departments in Ottawa. Controller George Jeckell and his small staff managed territorial programs from Dawson City, where three Yukon Council members met for a few days once a year to pass a budget and ordinances.[10]

Whitehorse was by far the Yukon's largest community, but it had just one Territorial Agent to manage liquor sales and permits, plus a road foreman. There was no municipal organization of any kind. The old Lambert Street School was overcrowded with elementary classes, and the makeshift Dowell High School, located in a wartime barracks, housed the senior grades. Both survived on meagre territorial grants. A volunteer board oversaw the hospital, and volunteers from the Imperial Order of the Daughters of the Empire ran the small public library. Private entrepreneurs supplied electrical power and telephones to the few who could afford them. Local businesspeople handled water delivery, sewage disposal and garbage removal by truck. The water and sewer system installed during the war was limited to the downtown core, so most homes had outdoor privies.

The streets of Whitehorse were dusty and rutted, with wooden sidewalks. Territorial work crews performed limited maintenance using antiquated graders or borrowed army equipment. Fire protection was skimpy, with a volunteer town crew operating old pumpers supplemented by the army fire station. The equipment was woefully inadequate to protect the growing population and the many homes heated by wood stoves over long, extremely cold winters.[11]

By contrast, both the Canadian Army and the RCAF built new, fully serviced homes on the bluffs above town. The Camp Takhini army base and the Hillcrest air force community flourished, with civilian officials housed in another federal subdivision called Valleyview by the mid-1950s. Townspeople envied the perks for military and federal officials' families in "Upper Whitehorse": subsidized food from outside suppliers sold in the PX store, low-cost housing, indoor plumbing, modern furnaces, recreational facilities and secure incomes supplemented by northern allowances.

A mostly friendly rivalry developed between the town and the military. Merchants loved the extra business, but some residents believed local prices were high because of government wages. The town's elite prized invitations to the officers' mess. The military contributed much to the community, supplementing

ABOVE LEFT Aerial view of army base housing at Camp Takhini, 1962.

ABOVE RIGHT Newly constructed Air Force houses in Hillcrest, ca. late 1950s.

fire protection, augmenting medical services and supporting town fundraisers. The army supported a local radio station, CFWH, with volunteer military and civilian deejays playing records supplied by local stores, along with pre-recorded American Forces Radio programs flown in from Los Angeles and weather reports from the local Department of Transport. Daily evening news reports and hockey and World Series broadcasts were supplied by Canadian National Telecommunications.[12]

Horace Moore, who had been publisher and editor of the *Whitehorse Star* since 1941, still produced it weekly, carrying news of local affairs and world events. The paper's new banner announced the town's growing significance: "On the Alcan—Voice of the Yukon—On the Trail of '98." Readers followed troubling trends worldwide—fears of Communism, terrifying threats of atomic weapons and the "Cold War"—alongside stories of Canadians grappling with post-war adjustments. The *Star* expanded with the town, carrying colourful written accounts and photographs. There was no shortage of copy as residents rolled up their sleeves and went to work on modernizing their town.[13]

A COMMUNITY OF CLUBS

With no municipal structure in place, volunteer clubs launched a series of campaigns to improve Whitehorse. A Yukon Winter Carnival was organized in 1945 by a short-lived group calling itself the All-Union Committee, with many volunteers, including some involved with the local Canadian Commonwealth Federation party. The event was hugely successful, featuring a dog derby, ski jump competitions, cross-country ski races, a queen contest and nightly dances, generating over $2,000 for the hospital. In subsequent years, more events were added to the extravaganza, renamed the Whitehorse Winter Carnival, with an ice palace, amateur boxing matches, basketball games, figure skating demonstrations, a curling bonspiel and excursion trains from Skagway to expand attendance. In 1949, insurance difficulties forced cancellation of the festivities,

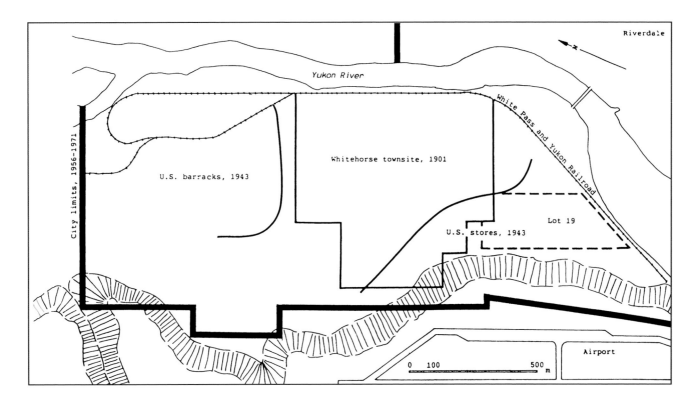

Riverdale

Yukon River

White Pass and Yukon Railroad

City limits, 1956–1971

U.S. barracks, 1943

Whitehorse townsite, 1901

U.S. stores, 1943

Lot 19

Airport

0   100   500
                  m

but residents and businesses rallied to reinstate the carnival the following year, generating $12,000 for local projects.[14] By that time, volunteers were burnt out and the carnival was not held in subsequent years.

The Whitehorse Men's Council was the de facto official town voice, critiquing government proposals and promoting civic projects. Members included business and professional leaders such as Gordon Armstrong, Bill MacBride and Bob Campbell. T.C. Richards hosted their monthly luncheons at his Whitehorse Inn Cafe, and it was at these gatherings that Ottawa officials announced road projects, hydroelectric developments and federal funding to fuel development. In 1947, members dissolved the council to form a new group, the Whitehorse Board of Trade, a precursor to the Whitehorse Chamber of Commerce.

By then, a host of other clubs were sponsoring community projects. A Masonic Lodge, founded in the early years of the town, still met, with newcomers gradually increasing its membership.[15] Many other clubs formed in the late 1940s, initiated by recent arrivals. Elks, Kiwanis, Lions, the Legion, and later the Whitehorse Lodge of the Yukon Order of Pioneeers were established with help from their parent organizations, some including women's auxiliaries. The Yukon Fish and Game Association sponsored derbies, stocked lakes with fish, and imported exotic species like pheasant for hunting. Fundraising for new sports facilities was a key focus of service clubs after the war. Military teams enjoyed modern gyms and arenas in "Upper Whitehorse," but civilians had to organize elaborate campaigns to raise money and volunteer labour for the downtown Civic Centre, opened with much fanfare in February 1953.[16]

City limits, 1956–71.

The Graduate Nurses Club raised funds for hospital equipment and organized social events for nurses. Another women's group started a Supervised Playground and Kindergarten Program. The schools offered no kindergarten at the time, so families welcomed the new project. The Children's Aid Society received modest grants and donations to offer child welfare services in the absence of government programs.

Girl Guides, Brownies, Boy Scouts, Cubs, Canadian Girls in Training and other groups encouraged young people and their mentors to experience outdoor adventure year-round, with camps at Marsh Lake and Scout Lake. Girl Guide and Boy Scout groups organized at the Baptist Indian Mission School brought students together with aboriginal youth at the other residential schools. Sometimes the young people participated in events with their non-aboriginal peers. Piano lessons, bagpipe instruction and numerous other musical and cultural pursuits were available to those with the time and money to participate.[17]

SPORTS AND RECREATION RENAISSANCE

The Young Peoples' Association celebrating Valentine's Day at their clubhouse, 1948.

Without a building, the North Star Athletic Association had virtually ceased to exist by the end of the war. Yet sport in Whitehorse experienced a renaissance. The Young People's Association (YPA) was organized in November 1945 "to provide healthful recreation for the boys and girls of the community and at the same time foster better relations between them." Rolf Hougen was the founding president, working with Bucky Keobke, Betty MacBride, Teresa Porter, Bill Jeffries and Howard Ryder, along with teacher advisors. YPA staged a spectacular May Day celebration in 1946, with a parade, ball games, races and a junior queen contest. They raised money at their Friday night dances to assist the Whitehorse High School Students' Association and other youth groups, purchasing sports, entertainment and recreation equipment. Their clubhouse on the corner of Fourth Avenue and Hanson Street also hosted the Whitehorse Drama Club.

The first YPA sports team was a basketball squad that played two games against a Skagway team during the 1946 Whitehorse Winter Carnival. That summer, the group entered teams in the Whitehorse men's and women's baseball leagues, and in the fall they organized a squad for the town's senior men's hockey league. Starting in 1946, the YPA also organized an annual May 24 Sports Day to showcase "the artistic as well as the athletic talents of the youngsters of the town." Track and field events, mid-distance races, the half-mile, and one- and two-mile runs were all part of the annual celebrations. There was also a soapbox derby in 1949 and 1950.

Intense rivalries developed between sports teams during these years. RCAF and Canadian Army teams were collectively called "Up the Hill." Civilian teams sponsored by downtown businesses were "the Town." Basketball had dwindled during the 1930s to occasional games with Skagway teams. An irregular season was played after the war in RCAF Hangar C, with teams sponsored by the U.S. Army, the Canadian Army, "the Town," the RCAF and the YPA. Later, the games moved to the recreation centre beside the airport. The floor was wildly uneven; a player dribbling the ball could never be sure exactly where it might bounce. On windy days, gaps in the windows could influence which end of the court the teams wanted to defend, depending on the prevailing breeze.

Whitehorse Merchants hockey team relaxing in the change room in Hangar B, ca. 1948.

RCAF Sergeant Andy Gilpin had arrived in Whitehorse in March 1947 to find only one outdoor rink, at the RCAF base, built after the NSAA burned down in 1942. Players also scrimmaged on frozen ponds near the north end of town. Gilpin asked his commanding officer about building a hockey rink inside Hangar B, and his superior approved the request, on the condition that the players build the rink and maintain it, including removing it in spring. Gilpin, Ross King and Len Beech constructed the indoor ice rink late that year. Gilpin and King would become the first Whitehorse-based athletes to compete in the Olympics, playing on Canada's gold-medal hockey team in 1948.

The hockey league had grown to four teams by 1945, sponsored by the RCAF, the Canadian Army, the Legion and "the Town"; the latter team was called the Whitehorse Merchants. Games got rowdy not only on the ice but in the stands as well. Officials suspended a game in January 1953 when the fight on the ice carried over into the penalty box and then into the bleachers, where fans mixed it up. It was two weeks before tempers had cooled enough that league play could resume.

CFWH carried the games live, with RCAF announcer Al Green doing the play-by-play. Bob Erlam later wrote, "We didn't have much back in those days but by God, we had hockey!" In the mid-1950s, when Yellow Cab owner Lloyd Camyre noticed that the army and air force teams were getting the upper hand, he recruited players for the Whitehorse Merchants from the American and Pacific Coast Hockey Leagues, luring them with offers of jobs driving taxis.

It was no different for softball. Bill and Rusty Reid organized a women's league. Terry Delaney set up a men's organization. There weren't a lot of teams, but win-at-any-cost rivalries developed among the "the Town," Porter Creek and "Up the Hill." Men and women alike were offered employment by various businesses, providing they agreed to play for the team their new boss sponsored. The military wasn't above importing outside talent either. Personnel were posted to Whitehorse as much on the strength of their athletic prowess as on their ability to do the assigned job.

A new sport made its appearance at the Yukon Winter Carnival in March 1945. The featured event was a dog derby, with a 64-kilometre (40-mile) dogsled team race on the Yukon River. The next year, the dogsled event was renamed the Whitehorse International Dog Derby. Organizers shortened the race to 16 kilometres (10 miles) in 1947 to make the finish more exciting. Sports dominated the festival in 1948: ski jumping; downhill, slalom and cross-country ski races; and a hockey tournament. Each day started with the dogsled races organized by Alex Van Bibber and Bill Drury.

The absence of the NSAA Hall highlighted the need for a new recreation complex. The White Pass & Yukon Route donated a block of land to the town, located near the Yukon River south of Main Street. It was half swamp and half buckbrush, but that was where town planners decided to group new sports facilities, including a baseball diamond built in 1950. Teams also used the old NSAA ball diamond on Main Street until 1952, when the site was designated for the new federal building.

In 1949, businesspeople and service clubs organized the North Star Civic Centre Club to plan a new downtown ice arena. Designed by John Scott and John Phelps, the Civic Centre was built on the north side of the new ballpark by contractor Bob Campbell using volunteer labour. The new centre, which opened its doors in February 1953, definitely wasn't overbuilt. There was little insulation in the dressing room walls and none at all for the main rink. Terry Delaney broadcast games for CBC Radio wearing earmuffs instead of headphones. Fans bundled in parkas and fur coats, stamping their feet and sipping spiked coffee. The next year, a heated concrete addition accommodated a concession booth and lounge.

Kids at ski lessons on Roundel Ski Hill.

The rink's scoreboard was high on the wall at one end of the ice surface. Whenever a goal was scored, a worker climbed through a small door onto a platform, removed the previous score and replaced it with the new one. Between periods, "rink rats" pushed metal-edged boards around the rink, collecting ice shavings in a heap. Next the "rats" dragged a barrel of hot water with a spigot at the bottom around the rink to flood the ice.

For all its shortcomings, the Civic Centre had a kind of magic as the town's original hockey barn. Legally, about 500 persons could be seated, but it often hosted upwards of 800—with kids hanging from the rafters, and adults standing two and three deep behind the bleachers. It cost 25 cents to go to a game. During playoffs, scalpers would work the lines outside, selling tickets at inflated prices.

The Whitehorse Lions Swimming Pool opened on the south side of the Civic Centre ballpark in August 1958—for eleven days. It was fortunate the weather was warm, because the water in the open-air pool was unheated. The next year a bathhouse was built, with a water filter and heating system, change rooms, and offices.

Skiing continued to be popular. RCAF servicemen in Hillcrest formed the Roundel Ski Club, developing their own facility with a short rope-tow on Roundel Hill. The rope-tow was irresistible for downtown skiers. The Ski Bowl was gradually abandoned, and its ski jumps were torn down in the 1950s.

Golf was a new addition to the scene. U.S. Army personnel had hit golf balls around a field on the Annie Lake Road in the 1940s, but owner Steve Veerman never stopped using the site as a cow pasture. Cattle were deemed hazards;

hitting an animal gave a golfer a free drop, especially if the ball ended up in an unplayable patty. Veerman relinquished rights to the land when a group of Whitehorse residents incorporated as the Whitehorse Golf and Country Club in June 1955. Shares were priced at $200 for males, $50 for females and $10 for juniors, but the cost could be reduced by the "rendering of service, labour and skill at the Society's premises or course" at the rate of $1.50 an hour. The work consisted of clearing fairways, digging out and building sand greens, constructing tee boxes and filling up gopher holes. Over time, members developed eighteen holes on the course, which purists described as "4,000 yards of rough with eighteen sand traps." The first tournament was held in 1955.

The Whitehorse Curling Club formed in 1953, with Bert Boyd elected as the inaugural president, but they had no ice downtown on which to play. The only curling rinks at the time were an outdoor sheet on Ice Lake, maintained by the RCAF, and the rink at the Garrison Curling Club at Camp Takhini. Extra sheets were available at temporary rinks in Hangar B in 1949 and Hangar C in 1952. Curlers identified a narrow piece of land beside the new Civic Centre as the perfect size for a new four-sheet curling rink. Their club sold shares, raised funds and solicited donations. Volunteers completed the rink in 1954, and the club hosted its first bonspiel in February 1955. The biggest problem for curlers was hockey fans, who flocked in from the rink next door for post-game celebrations in the club lounge, which served alcohol. Things got so bad that in December 1958 City Council banned hockey fans from the curling club.[18]

TAXATION AND INCORPORATION

Neither volunteer efforts nor business contributions were sufficient to tackle the many critical issues facing Whitehorse and the rest of the territory. Federal officials knew as well as old-timers did that cutbacks during the Depression, followed by wartime sacrifices, had left the territory with worn-out equipment, tired civil servants and less industrial activity to support services, employment and taxation. The Alaska Highway beckoned to prospectors, entrepreneurs and potential investors, but new developments and the growing population could not thrive without improved infrastructure on a massive scale. Capital for such projects simply did not exist in the Yukon.

Change was imperative. In return for huge infusions of cash for roads, hydro dams and schools, however, Ottawa was insisting on higher local taxation and

CFWH on air with volunteer announcer, ca. 1950.

new municipal organization in the largest communities. Residents and local politicians resisted, on the grounds that Yukon costs were higher, conditions were more difficult and the federal government accrued all mineral royalties. Controller Jeckell introduced an ordinance to incorporate the City of Whitehorse at the 1946 Yukon Council session.

Initially, the *Star* supported incorporation so that Whitehorse could fulfil "its destiny." Straw polls in coffee shops soundly rejected the idea. Whitehorse existed on $13,000 annually in taxes, and territorial grants of $30,000 for schools and roads. Meanwhile, liquor revenues for 1944 topped $250,000. Pundits suggested that this money belonged to the town, and that the income from liquor sales would override any need for incorporation or increased taxes. The incorporation ordinance stipulated that only property owners could vote, since they would bear any increased taxation after incorporation, meaning that 250 owners out of 3,000 residents were eligible to cast ballots. Of those, 160 people actually voted in the plebiscite, with most soundly rejecting incorporation and just 24 voters in favour of the idea.[19]

Controller Jeckell retired later that year with the taxation dilemma unresolved. Mines and Resources Deputy Minister Hugh Keenleyside persuaded Yukon Magistrate John Gibben to accept the job, reinstating the title of Yukon Commissioner for the Chief Executive Officer in 1948, in recognition of the territory's growing stature. Gibben's legal training was critical in negotiating new financial agreements with federal officials and then persuading the Yukon Council to accept more local taxation in return for infrastructure funding in the three main settlements. The Commissioner's job was fraught with tensions, however, and five different appointees from Ottawa would cycle through the office over the next few years.[20]

It certainly helped that business was booming in Whitehorse, with military housing under construction, expansions downtown, mineral and oil exploration, and a growing population. Civilian travel restrictions on the Alaska Highway ended in 1947, bringing increased tourism. Airline service improved. The federal government announced plans for an all-season road to Mayo and a new school at Whitehorse. The pipeline from Skagway reopened to convey petroleum products inland. The Governor General visited Whitehorse in 1947 and again in

1949, as did Northern Affairs Minister Jean Lesage. Thomas Bain moved from Vancouver as the new owner of the *Whitehorse Star* in 1950, expressing his confidence in the town. An energetic entrepreneur who had edited the *Cambie News* for over a decade and had also been active in the Vancouver Chamber of Commerce, he soon plunged into Whitehorse civic activities.[21]

The Yukon Council passed a new municipal ordinance in 1949, establishing municipalities and a new taxation structure in Dawson, Mayo and Whitehorse. A property evaluator from outside the Yukon was hired by the territorial government to prepare assessments for revised taxes throughout the territory. Residents of the three communities voted in plebiscites to decide whether to incorporate under an elected mayor and council, or not to incorporate but still to elect a mayor and council. This time, any resident of Whitehorse could vote who was over the age of 21 and owned property (or whose spouse did) or paid annual rent of at least $200. Despite numerous explanations offered in the *Star*, people still found the issues confusing, and once again, and even with increased voter eligibility and turnout, incorporation was defeated. On June 1, 1950, the city officially became a municipality without incorporation. The next step was to elect a Mayor and four Aldermen.

Growing tourism traffic on the Alaska Highway led to the growth of many new businesses including Yukon Tire Shop on Front Street run by Ernest and Doris Lortie, ca. 1948.

Over the summer, a public meeting nominated a non-partisan slate of candidates billed as "men who have backbone to express their beliefs... who will not waste time... [with] arguments on details of minor importance." Gordon Armstrong, the manager of the Burns meat market, was elected the first Mayor, along with Aldermen James Norrington of Pan American Airways, Sam McClimon (owner of the movie theatre), George Ryder (owner of Ryder's Fuel) and Bill Hamilton (manager of White Pass.) They were sworn in to office in September 1950. There was no shortage of issues: Whitehorse still had limited water and sewer service, no fire alarms, old firefighting equipment and a huge number of squatters living in unhealthy conditions.[22]

MOVING THE CAPITAL

In October 1950, rumours surfaced that Ottawa had decided to move the Yukon's capital to Whitehorse. The *Star* sympathized briefly with outraged Dawson residents but asserted: "The Territory cannot be run economically on tradition or tourist attractions. Taxes are the largest contributor to the treasury and Whitehorse surely surpasses Dawson with her contributions."[23] Dawson had just 800 residents, while Whitehorse had over 4,000 citizens plus hundreds of transient military personnel.

In March of the following year, the federal government confirmed the move. Yukon MP Aubrey Simmons wired the news to the *Star*, which immediately printed a special edition of 200 copies, all sold within hours. Dawson residents protested vehemently, making snide remarks about Whitehorse being a disorganized dustbowl that lacked the requisite housing for officials and the space for

New federal building under
construction, early 1950s.

government offices. Those factors did delay the move for two years, but they did not change any minds in Ottawa. The one crumb thrown to Dawson was a promise to extend the Mayo Road to the Klondike in coming years.[24]

Money poured into Whitehorse to construct a federal office building at the old sports fields on Main and Fourth. The project exacerbated frustrations over residential utilities; the *Star* said the federal government should fund sewer and water services for the whole downtown while extending lines to the new building. Instead, Robert Winters, the Minister of Resources and Development, announced more federal housing construction in "Upper Whitehorse," citing substandard town services. The paper's editor blew his stack: "We don't like it!... While the lavish spending of money goes on the people of Lower Slobovia will continue to pay their taxes in order that Mr. Winters may build his new homes in dusty heights."[25] After months of tough negotiation with the new city government, federal officials allocated $1-million to a cost-sharing agreement for modern services in downtown Whitehorse.

The *Star* welcomed Yukon Commissioner Wilfred Brown and the employees of the territorial government and their families when they moved from Dawson in March 1953. The new Whitehorse Elementary and High School had opened the previous fall, so the old Lambert Street School served as headquarters until the federal building was completed. Conditions were impossibly cramped for the eight officials and their files. The Yukon Council met in the dusty and airless courtroom at the old post office on Front Street, the focus of considerable grumbling by Councillors used to the stately chambers in the old Territorial Administration Building at Dawson City. As a capital city, Whitehorse had little to recommend it, and more hard times lay ahead.[26]

Indian Affairs provided small homes at Whitehorse Indian Village, with families of five or more people crowded into one or two rooms. Whitehorse, ca. 1950s.

TENSIONS AND TEARS

Tensions mounted through the mid-1950s as numerous fires swept through poorly constructed homes. Among the injured and dead were young children. Insurance premiums for business owners and residents were high, owing to the unsafe conditions. Sanitation Inspector G.I. Cameron, along with local doctors and nurses, deplored the state of sanitation, with pit privies, garbage and industrial waste polluting the town and the river. Jim Smith, who served as Alderman from 1956 to 1958, would later characterize Whitehorse as "a prosperous mess" in those days.[27]

Each spring, municipal officials and the *Star* urged people to "paint up, clean up Whitehorse," but the combination of poverty, transient tenants and uncertain land titles owing to haphazard surveys left many areas in poor condition. The Board of Trade began to promote the idea of cleaning up Whiskey Flats and other squatter areas. White Pass owned the land on Seventh and Eighth Avenues, and rumours circulated that the company planned to evict squatters and sell the lots to people wanting to build homes.

The *Star* suggested that evictions were not the answer, proposing that loans be offered to squatters to build low-cost residences. A letter in the paper urged squatters to protest and to form a council of "white, breed and Indian," asking: "Where can you go if you are evicted?"[28]

In May 1953, a serious outbreak of polio brought an end to the discussions. Schools closed early for the summer, and public meetings and social events were cancelled in the wake of dozens of polio cases and several deaths.[29] In June, the city declared Moccasin Flats and other squatter areas unsanitary and ordered a clean-up. It was a horrendous time both for residents and for Sanitation Inspector G.I. Cameron, who had to enforce the health regulations. The *Star* headline read, "Tears Shed as Bulldozer Pushes Condemned Shacks into Slough." A reporter chronicled the unfolding misery:

> Many a tear fell Monday and Tuesday as citizens, Indian and white watched their rickety homes being crushed under the might of a bulldozer.... The scene resembled an evacuation, wheel barrows and wagons were piled high with dishes, bedding and clothing. Those... [with] cars and trucks were busy loading, most with a glum resentful frown on their faces and above the roar of the menacing bulldozer sounded the ripping of boards as possessions were pulled from the walls.[30]

Sturdier homes were towed to the north end of town to the swampy parcel of land set aside for First Nations people in 1916. First surveyed as Lot 226, this parcel was now called Whitehorse Indian Reserve No. 8. Others were left at the edge of White Pass property for owners to claim if and when they located a site somewhere else. In coming years, there would be more evictions—almost always accompanied by regret and controversy—to "clean up" the city, clearing the former squatter areas for parks and civic projects.

GROWING TOGETHER

The clearing of squatter neighbourhoods underscored the deep fractures in the community arising from distinctions between people of different origins, social status and income. Finding ways to bridge those gaps proved difficult and sometimes contentious, but ultimately new attitudes and opportunities paved the way for more integration.

People from the aboriginal community garnered admiration and even adulation as heroic figures. Big-game guides Johnny Johns, Buck Dickson, Alex Van Bibber, Bobby Auston and others donated wild meat to Fish and Game Association dinners, attracted wealthy hunters to the territory and entertained

The new Whitehorse General Hospital located across the river near Riverdale was huge compared to the old hospital.

at public events. Sisters Sue Chambers, Belle Desrosiers and Babe Southwick were legendary women with many outdoor skills. With more intermarriage came blended families, shared experiences and cross-cultural connections.

As the new Civic Centre neared completion in 1950, the *Star* reported that some organizers wanted to exclude aboriginal people. Citing examples of the Gestapo murdering Jews and the beating of black people in the U.S., the newspaper's editor condemned the idea:

The habit of shunning one's neighbour... because he is of a different colour or nationality leads to a narrow minded individual.... Man was born equal, regardless of colour; if they live in the same country they should have equal rights.... What has the Indian done that he should be punished by being barred from the Civic Centre?[31]

Additional inducements to integration came from Ottawa. The clearing of squatters had produced a few building lots, but nowhere near what was required by the booming town. People speculated about how and where expansion could occur, given the confines of the river, the bluffs and poor road access between downtown and the Alaska Highway. A partial answer came in 1954 with the breathtaking announcement of federal funding for a new subdivision on the east side of the river, including a bridge, a hospital and a school.

Gordon Robertson, Deputy Minister of Indian and Northern Affairs, who served simultaneously as the appointed Commissioner of the Northwest Territories, firmly insisted that the new facilities be available equally to all citizens. He met resistance initially from some local politicians, but many citizens supported the worldwide movement to end race-based segregation. The Yukon Council passed an Ordinance to Fund Schools in Whitehorse in 1955, formally ending the discrimination against aboriginal students that had existed since the gold rush.

The inclusion of aboriginal children in publicly funded schools did not end the separation of children from their families, however. Smaller communities had no schools, and families living on the land had to send their kids to school or risk legal prosecution. Robertson was determined to end church control over aboriginal education in both northern territories, insisting the future depended on equal opportunities and a modern education for all northerners. But church officials exerted pressure on Ottawa, resulting in the construction of two government-funded residences in Riverdale, the new Whitehorse subdivision, to provide accommodation for aboriginal students from all over the Yukon. Coudert Hall (for Roman Catholics) and Yukon Hall (at first Anglican, then designated as non-denominational) housed hundreds of children for decades to come, with staff and students facing the challenges of life in an institution far from home and family.[32]

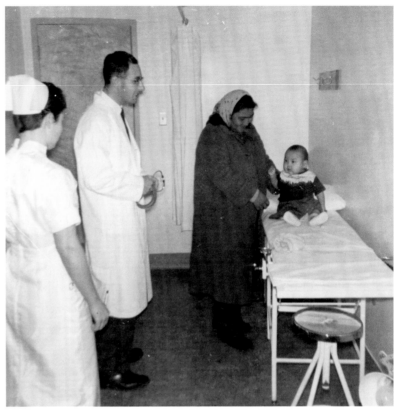

Dr. Boon greets an aboriginal woman and her baby at the new Whitehorse General Hospital, ca. 1958.

The Roman Catholic community in Whitehorse also pursued their right to separate, religious-based schools. Catholic families throughout the territory could send their children to Dawson, where St. Mary's School operated until the mid-1950s. The Sisters of Providence began offering day classes and boarding for students in Whitehorse in 1948. As the town's population grew, so did the number of Roman Catholic families and the demands for a separate school.[33]

Bishop Coudert was a forceful presence in the community, along with parishioners Jim Hanna and others who pressed the territorial and federal governments to fund Catholic schools. The Yukon Council balked at duplicate facilities, but persistence and political savvy prevailed. Built with church funds, the first Christ the King School opened in the early 1950s, next to the Catholic cathedral. When more space was needed, the territorial government agreed to purchase all Roman Catholic schools from the diocese and build new ones. Separate schools received support from the Territory for operations and maintenance, while staffing and curriculum remained the purview of the church.[34]

Most francophones were Roman Catholic, and the cathedral and parish hall hosted most of their cultural gatherings. Joyful weddings and sombre funerals for prominent pioneers drew people together. Daily masses and special services were most often conducted in English, as the majority of parishioners were anglophone, but many priests and most bishops were from Quebec or France, so the church facilitated some linguistic connections among French-speakers. For many long-time residents, like the Cyrs, the Jacquots, Émile Forrest and others, these occasional conversations kept the memory of their French origins alive as they mixed with the mainstream community. However, newcomers were often puzzled to meet residents of French-Canadian descent who spoke little or no French. The priests who provided spiritual leadership and the sisters who taught young students continued to be important anchors for the small number of French-speaking people in the town and in the territory over the next two decades.[35]

IN THE LIMELIGHT

Whitehorse citizens were buoyed by all the new money coming from federal programs, mineral exploration, tourism and business expansions. They celebrated their good fortune year-round with festivities, fundraising and volunteer efforts to attract visitors and improve life in the city.

Several local young people attended the coronation of Queen Elizabeth in 1952, courtesy of local benefactors. Whitehorse high school students flew to London as part of the Canadian youth contingent. Girl Guide Lena Tizya, sponsored by Anglican friends and merchants, also went to the big event. Patsy Henderson received a Coronation Medal honouring his part in the Klondike gold rush and his popular dance-and-drumming performances for visitors.

It was a heady time of success and progress. Local artist Lilias Farley received a commission to create original artwork for the new federal building. Alex Van Bibber, Johnny Johns and their clients received acclaim in the southern media for world-record game trophies. Whitehorse went wild with excitement in 1955, when Winter Carnival Queen Dalyce Smith won the Queen of the Western Rockies title at Banff, and then the Miss Canada Pageant in London, Ontario. Individuals and families, though, still often struggled to make ends meet.

Various dignitaries visited the new capital city, including Governor General Vincent Massey, members of the Vancouver Board of Trade and officials from Imperial Oil and other big companies. There were so many government announcements, openings, celebrity visits and advertisements for cars, appliances and holiday travel that the *Whitehorse Star* constantly expanded in

size. Harry Boyle took over as owner and publisher in 1955, installing modern presses to keep up with the demand.

Politicians and business owners agitated for the paving of the Alaska Highway and other road improvements. The opening of roads to Mayo and Dawson eliminated the need for the old river byways. Some nostalgic longing for the past surfaced with the last sailing of the ss *Klondike* in 1955, the end of the steamboat era. Most people were keen to experience the personal freedom promised by the booming automobile industry. Bill MacBride and others established the Yukon Historical Society and a museum, adding visitor attractions and preserving local history and its rapidly disappearing artifacts.[36]

The decade closed on a high note in 1959, with the visit of Queen Elizabeth and the Duke of Edinburgh. The royal couple enjoyed a tour of the museum; a ride on the White Pass train to McCrae, past the storied Whitehorse Rapids and

In 1955, the whole town celebrated the homecoming of Dalyce Smith, winner of the Miss Canada pageant. Seen here in front of the airport terminal, she was welcomed by the Commissioner, the Mayor, the Board of Trade and townsfolk. That fall, she rode in the Grey Cup parade, bringing more attention to the city.

TOP Using recycled Quonset huts and barracks, Tourist Services developed the early equivalent of a motor hotel along with a supermarket. It was indicative of the changing times that these accommodations were not located on the waterfront or Main Street but were on the main route into town on Fourth Avenue near the base of Two Mile Hill.

CENTRE LEFT Along with the construction of impressive public works, this was also a time when hospitality and entertainment facilities expanded. Interior of Yukon Theatre on Wood Street, 1954.

CENTRE RIGHT Murdoch's Gem Shop as it appeared in 1962 on Main Street. Founded in Dawson City by George Murdoch in the 1940s and moved to Whitehorse in the '50s, it was then bought in the '60s and operated by Mike Scott and Bill Weigand for several decades, and in recent years by Chris Sorg.

BOTTOM The Yukon Travel Agency and a Mercedes Benz dealership were established on Main Street west of Fourth by Eric Wienecke, who emigrated to the Yukon after WWII. The family-owned travel agency is still in business today, in a larger building at Main and Third.

the new hydro dam; First Nations cultural presentations; and meetings with pioneer residents. Mayor Gordon Cameron captured international media attention by charming a warm laugh from Her Majesty as they strolled along Main Street. People speculated for years about just what he had said to her.[37]

A MODERN TOWN

The look and feel of Whitehorse changed dramatically during this period. During Alaska Highway construction, cheap, temporary shelters and housing had been thrown up all over the city and along the highway. In the post-war period, the federal government built for the long term. With the handover of highway administration to the Canadian Army and then, in 1964, to civilian control, there came a commensurate need for infrastructure. More permanent maintenance facilities were required and, in turn, the service industries to support them. An industrial zone began to take shape in the former refinery area. With better roads that actually went somewhere, more service stations and car dealerships appeared. The service and hospitality industry expanded to meet the demands of an increasing number of visitors and tourists.

The single greatest factor contributing to the town's growth and change was the transfer of the Yukon's capital to Whitehorse. The town's most imposing buildings—the railway station, the post office and the Whitehorse Inn—were immediately overshadowed by the new federal building, completed in 1953. The construction of Whitehorse Elementary and High School created another imposing mass in the north end of town. Following quickly on the heels of the secular school, Christ the King School was built on Wood Street, eclipsing the rebuilt Sacred Heart Cathedral by its sheer size.

After the city was named the capital, Bishop Tom Greenwood moved his headquarters to Whitehorse. The Old Log Church became the diocesan cathedral for seven years until it was replaced by a larger structure just up the block and the old church became a museum of church history. Apart from the telegraph office, the Old Log Church Museum is the oldest structure in Whitehorse still in its original location. The modern lines and design of the new churches symbolized the move from pioneer town to modern city.

With a booming town came an increased thirst for electric power. The Whitehorse Dam increased electrical capacity and forever changed the river and surrounding landscape. The Whitehorse Rapids were calmed, and an

instant lake covered a former berry-picking meadow, named Schwatka Lake
after the early U.S. Army explorer. Soon after, the Robert Campbell Bridge was
constructed, giving access to the east side of the river, the new community of
Riverdale and a brand-new hospital.

As the town's dependence on roads grew, the focus on the riverfront diminished. The shipyards and their attendant buildings were now anachronisms,
and dismantling of the waterfront infrastructure began. The town spread south

and west, squeezing up against the clay cliffs until it could go no farther. Once the bridge was built, expansion to the east was a natural next step, and the level land on that side of the river soon filled with houses—the new Riverdale subdivision. Takhini, Hillcrest and Valleyview subdivisions anchored settlement above the river flats on the bluffs overlooking the town.

THE WHITE PASS AND YUKON RAILWAY DEPOT

In the late 1930s, White Pass decided to increase its office space on the second floor. At some point between 1935 and 1938, the company made two extensions to the upper floor on the north and south sides, adding about 2.9 metres (9.5 feet) at either end, squaring off the hipped ends in the process and leaving a plain gable roof.

In 1943, the depot was expanded to accommodate military operations. A new addition to the north end of the building added 4 metres (14 feet) to the main floor and 8 metres (27 feet) on the second floor.

An extension was made to the south end of the depot in 1953. This is when it received its split-log siding and various other improvements to make it more appealing to the tourist trade. In trying to explain the concept to the company's general manager, the Superintendent of the Rail Division wrote: "On exterior of building, we are working at a log cabin style, or what you might call a hunting lodge effect, maybe Swiss Chalet, damned if I know."[38]

In 1991, the Yukon government bought a substantial portion of White Pass property along the riverfront, including the depot and some associated buildings. After interior renovation, the train station was occupied by the offices of various non-profit organizations. Great care was taken, however, to retain the distinctive exterior of this Main Street landmark.

FACING TOP LEFT Whitehorse Elementary and High School, 1955.

FACING TOP RIGHT The Northwest Highway System was set up to oversee the continued development and maintenance of the Alaska Highway. With headquarters in Takhini, this building became the centre of a nearly self-sufficient enclave that included federal government offices, a steam plant, recreation centre, store, school and housing for families and single men.

FACING BOTTOM LEFT Newly completed Federal Building on Main Street, ca. 1956.

FACING BOTTOM RIGHT The new Sacred Heart Cathedral, 1962.

ABOVE NCPC hydroelectric dam shortly after construction, 1959. At left is the 366 metre-long fish ladder built to assist salmon upriver to their spawning grounds, believed to be the longest wooden fish ladder in the world.

THE WHITEHORSE AIRPORT

TOP LEFT The depot in 1943.

TOP RIGHT BYN bus and car parked in front of the depot, 1949. According to Laurent Cyr, Don MacPhail was the driver unloading parcels from the back of the bus with Dick Carswell stepping out of the door.

BOTTOM LEFT The depot, ca. mid-1960s. White Pass created a bus division after the Alaska Highway was built. For a time, the depot served as the town's bus and train station as well as the office for Canadian Pacific Airways.

From after the war until the mid-1960s, small air charter companies, including the Yukon's first flight training school, were based on the east side of the airport. Two locally owned air services, Yukon Airways and Whitehorse Flying Service, opened for business in 1947, fighting over the meagre charter market until 1949, when they amalgamated under the name Whitehorse Flying Service, which was bought by Pacific Western Airlines in 1955.

During the 1950s, the federal Department of Transport (DOT) established its Whitehorse facilities, including aviation weather services and housing for its personnel, on the east side of the field, near the escarpment. On the south end of this development stood the Yukon's VIP House, a large home used to accommodate visiting dignitaries, with a view south to the hydro dam and Schwatka Lake. It was in this lofty abode, during the royal visit of 1959, that Queen Elizabeth and Prince Philip learned that they were expecting another child, the future Prince Andrew.

The Steamboat Hangar was destroyed in a windstorm in the late 1950s, and what remained of the structure was torn down. The DOT complex was dismantled, with some of the buildings relocated to a new subdivision north of town, known as Porter Creek. By the mid-1960s, all aviation activity had been relocated to the west side of the airport. The small round-roofed hangar at the southeast end of the field (constructed by Canadian Pacific Airlines in the

ABOVE Whitehorse Airport in the 1950s; military operations on the west side (foreground), and civilian operations on the far (town) side.

LEFT In 1947 on the east side of the airport George Milne started the first flight training school in the Yukon, with his brand-new Canadian-built Fleet Canuck CF-DPM. Among his first students were Moe Grant, Bud Harbottle and Gordon Cameron. He was soon joined by Cameron and Harbottle as partners in Whitehorse Flying Service.

FACING Erik Nielsen greets John
Diefenbaker at the Whitehorse
Airport, 1961. Diefenbaker was
the first Canadian Prime Minister
to visit the Yukon.

1940s) was dismantled in 1965 and re-erected on the Atlin airfield, where it
stands today. For a time, the large CPA hangar served as a warehouse for steel
construction material. The VIP House, purchased by private interests, was
moved downtown to 611 Alexander Street.

VOTING FOR CHANGE

In 1958, Progressive Conservative leader John Diefenbaker won a majority government with a promise to pursue Canada's northern destiny. He promoted
more "roads to resources," including an ambitious plan for a highway to the Arctic Ocean that would link the Klondike Highway with the new town of Inuvik
in the Northwest Territories. Erik Nielsen was elected as the new Progressive
Conservative MP for the Yukon. As the former legal counsel for the City of
Whitehorse, Nielsen was well versed in the ongoing challenges of the capital city.

Yukon aboriginal people were ready for change as well, anxious to fulfil their
destiny as equal citizens in their homeland after decades of displacement. Communication with aboriginal politicians from outside also sparked interest in
social reform. Frank Asu, B.C. president of the North American Indian Brotherhood of Canada, ran ads in the *Star* promoting the aboriginal right to vote.
In 1949, Nisga'a activist Frank Calder was elected as MLA for the B.C. riding of
Atlin, becoming the first First Nation member of a Canadian legislature. The
Yukon Indian Advancement Association formed in the late 1950s in Whitehorse
to organize cultural events and help struggling families.

Many people were alarmed by changes to territorial game laws and other
measures that affected their lives on the land. The Yukon government insti-
tuted controversial regulations requiring trapline registration under individual
ownership, disrupting the traditional sharing of resources according to clan
and extended-family practices.[39] Territorial welfare authorities seized aboriginal children under various child protection measures, in some cases placing
them for adoption with white families outside the Yukon. Ongoing destruction
of squatters' homes contributed to growing distrust and the need for political
influence.

Yukon aboriginal people were still barred from voting or running for office.
Once again, Deputy Minister Gordon Robertson urged reform; he called upon
the Yukon Council to extend the territorial franchise to all residents, regardless
of race or status. It took several years of discussion in Council, but finally the

Elections Ordinance was revised in 1960, granting aboriginal people the most basic of democratic rights.[40]

As the 1960s dawned, Whitehorse was at the forefront of change. With a booming economy, positive social reforms, local political zest and growing national recognition, the capital city's citizens looked forward to organizing a bright future together.

COMMUNITY PORTRAITS

Émile Forrest was a longshore-man and pilot who died preparing the ss *Keno* for its final trip to Dawson, 1960. Forrest is likely the man working in foreground of the image.

ÉMILE FORREST
CA. 1889–1960

Émile Forrest was born in Quebec and moved to the Yukon with his parents and two brothers in 1901, when he was twelve years old. He attended St. Mary's School in Dawson for several years. He and his brothers were all avid sportsmen, playing hockey, baseball and basketball.

In 1910, at age 21, Forrest went to work as an assistant pilot on a motor launch, freighting cargo on the Yukon River between Circle and Fort Yukon, Alaska; he worked on the river for most of the next decade. When silver mining boomed in the Stewart valley after World War I, Forrest staked claims in the region and later prospected in the Carmacks area as well. He lived in Mayo throughout the 1920s, working as a mechanic for White Pass and for the Treadwell Yukon Company. In 1923, he drove the first caterpillar tractor over winter trails from Whitehorse to Mayo, ushering in a new era of mechanized transport in the Yukon. He was always popular, contributing to sports and entertainment wherever he lived—for many years he built a rink on the river at Mayo, enjoyed by the community's youth, and he organized a women's baseball team there in 1939. He played percussion in a small orchestra at Wernecke Camp and owned one of the first movie cameras in the Yukon, showing his films to delighted audiences.

During World War II, Forrest moved to Whitehorse to work as a mechanic. With all the action related to Alaska Highway construction and other projects, he was soon working on the river again, first as the engineer on the *Neecheah*, and then as the captain of the *Loon*, employed by the BYN to chart safe passage for the big steamboats. After the war, river transport gave way to the new road network; the *Loon* was dry-docked in 1947, and Forrest went to work as a night watchman for White Pass. Like so many others, he was sorry to see the last of the big boats pulled out of the water in 1955. One more trip on the river beckoned in 1960, when he was hired as the pilot for the last voyage of the ss *Keno*, destined to become a heritage attraction in Dawson City. Forrest spent his final

day supervising preparations for the launch of the boat. All the exertion proved fatal to the 71-year-old river man; he suffered a massive heart attack and died on the day the *Keno* slid into the water for the last time.[41]

GEORGE AND RACHEL DAWSON
1902–1989 & 1902–1976

Having first met as children at Fort Selkirk, and later reacquainted when he was working on the steamboats, George and Rachel Dawson were married on July 28, 1923. They lived at Fort Selkirk until Rachel's mother died in 1927, when they moved to Whitehorse.

George and Rachel Dawson depart for a holiday in Seattle after winning a Tourist Services contest in 1962.

George Dawson was born at Long Lake to Tusáxal (Jenny Boss) and Dawson Jim of Lake Laberge. George's uncle was Chief Jim Boss and his grandparents were Mundessa and Łande. During the building of the Alaska Highway in 1942, George Dawson took an active role in guiding the American engineers through traditional routes that would later become part of the highway. He also worked on the docks at Whitehorse, supervising an aboriginal crew of stevedores. After the war he continued to combine trapping and hunting with wage employment in Whitehorse, working for the federal government for many years as the care-taker at the post office building. He gave up his Status Indian designation to acquire that job, and so that his children could attend the public school in the late 1940s.

George served as the Hereditary Chief of the Ta'an Kwäch'än (Lake Laberge) people later in his life. Dawson was also an active member of the Chief Mundessa Club during the 1970s, responsible for erecting the grave fences at the gravesite on the east side of the Yukon River at Whitehorse.

Rachel Dawson was born in Dawson City in 1902 and settled with her parents at Fort Selkirk during her childhood. Rachel is remembered as an accomplished storyteller and historian. Along with Angela Sidney and Kitty Smith, she recorded her Northern Tutchone stories, published in the 1977 book *My Stories Are My Wealth*.

Rachel and George Dawson were pillars of the Yukon community during their lives, and raised a large family, many of whom live in Whitehorse today.[42]

LILIAS FARLEY 1907–1989

Artist Lilias Farley was born in Ottawa and moved to Vancouver with her family in 1924, where she studied art at the Vancouver Art School and the B.C. College of Art. She was friends with renowned Group of Seven artists Frederick Varley and J.E.H. MacDonald. During the 1930s, she taught art at the B.C. College of Art and also worked in theatrical design. In January 1948, she visited her brother Arthur, who was working in Whitehorse. Captivated by the vibrancy of the place, she accepted a position as art teacher in the old Dowell High School, where she was prized as a skilled and caring art instructor. When Yukon Commissioner Fred Fraser dismissed Farley in 1952 as a cost-saving measure, the whole town rallied to have her reinstated. She continued to inspire art students until her retirement from F.H. Collins Secondary School in 1972.

Farley was an accomplished artist, working in several genres, including sculpting and painting; her work was exhibited in Vancouver galleries. In 1950, she received a prestigious commission to create a large mural for the courtroom in the federal building under construction at Whitehorse. The mural depicts the history of the Yukon; it was preserved when the building was torn down, and it hangs today in the Elijah Smith Building foyer. Farley received the Centennial

Medal in 1967 for her service to the arts. She continued to support the development of art and artists all her life, welcoming each new development in the Yukon cultural field with enthusiasm. She died in Whitehorse in 1989.[43]

The Santa Train sponsored by Hougen's was an annual highlight for Whitehorse children.

GEORGIANNA LOW 1950–

Georgianna Low's childhood days in downtown Whitehorse were full of adventure and fun. Her father, Doug Low Sr., moved from Telegraph Creek with his own father just after World War II, and they worked as wood contractors, hauling fuel to city homes. Doug worked for Ed Jacobs and Canadian National Telecommunications before establishing a successful outfitting business. Low's mother was Ida Sidney, daughter of George Sidney and Angela Johns from Carcross and Tagish. Ida worked at the Whitehorse Hospital. Born in 1950, Georgianna Low was the oldest of five children.

The Lows lived west of Second Avenue, on Jarvis and later Alexander Street. They had many neighbourhood friends. Downtown kids spent most of their time outside year-round. The clay cliffs and the rest of downtown were playgrounds for hiking, biking, tag, hide and seek, pick-up ball games and road hockey. The kids rode their bikes to Riverdale and then along the old tramway trails, crossing the narrow bridge on top of the dam as the water thundered beneath, and heading back home past the rapids. Sometimes they biked to Ear Lake for picnics. Outdoor sports events were part of the town's May Day celebrations, and on Canada Day there were three-legged races and games at the ball fields. Low belonged to the Anglican church choir, Girl Guides and Pathfinders, and she enjoyed camps at Chadburn and Marsh Lakes.

In winter, the whole gang skated outdoors at Christ the King School. Some of the boys played hockey in one corner, while other kids played tag and crack the whip or tobogganed on the clay cliffs. The Santa Train, offering free candy, was an annual holiday hit.

At the Lows' home, evenings were spent doing puzzles and playing board games. There was no TV, just radio with its few children's programs. Grandpa George was a big hockey fan, so the family listened to Saturday night hockey broadcasts and often went to the Civic Arena to watch games. Low remembers that the corner store at Fifth and Strickland sold jawbreakers, bubble gum, Tootsie Rolls and snacks for a nickel or a dime apiece. Teens went to Kenny's Drive-In for burgers, fries and soft drinks. On weekends, movie matinees cost ten cents.

Georgianna Low's childhood was special in many ways, with weekends spent at her father's Tagish ranch, riding in the hills with her cousins the Bakers, the Sidneys, the Wedges and the Austons. Her grandmother Angela, Grandpa George, Uncle Johnny Johns and Auntie Dora Wedge taught Low and her siblings and cousins the history, stories and legends of their ancestors. For the most part, Low felt acceptance in her hometown, with friends from all backgrounds. Downtown kids were safe: people knew everyone else in the neighbourhood.[44]

T.A. FIRTH & SON LTD.

Thomas Andrew Firth stampeded to the Yukon with thousands of others in 1898, looking for gold, but he soon found that "his pen was mightier than his pick." Born in Owen Sound, Ontario, in 1867, the son of a Baptist minister, he

was only thirteen when he left home. Little is known of his travels prior to hiking the Chilkoot Trail, but he was a literate man, unlike many of the miners in the goldfields. He started to earn a living by helping people complete the government forms for staking and maintaining their claims. In 1906, he founded a business as a broker and financial agent in Dawson City, laying the foundation for the insurance firm that is now the oldest family-owned business operating in the Yukon.

The company, like its three generations of owners, has weathered the many boom-and-bust cycles since the gold rush. Thomas Firth made enough money to travel back to Ontario in 1909 to marry his childhood sweetheart, Delia, after a courtship by correspondence lasting sixteen years. The couple returned to Dawson City, where their son, Howard, was born the following year. Howard grew up in the Klondike capital, graduating from high school at age sixteen and

Businessman Howard Firth moved the T.A. Firth Insurance Company from Dawson City to the new capital in 1954, seen here in its first location on Main Street.

immediately going to work in the local Canadian Bank of Commerce. From there he transferred outside to work in various B.C. branches, meeting his wife, Nancy Hughes, in Fernie. They were married in 1937 and moved to Dawson City, where Howard joined his father's firm, taking over when the elder Firth died in 1941.

Howard and Nancy Firth were active participants in community life while also raising their six children. Howard conducted the Victory Loan drive during the war, was a member of the B.C. and Yukon Chamber of Mines and the Dawson Curling Club, and ran for election and won as the youngest Mayor ever elected in Dawson City. The whole family loved their Klondike home, and they were sorry to leave in 1954, but the move of the capital to Whitehorse had forced the issue. Howard later mused that "we would have been pretty hungry... if we had stayed in Dawson."[45]

Howard Firth opened his Whitehorse office in a small building on Main Street, and the family made their home in the back of the building for the first few years. When the Riverdale subdivision opened up, the family moved to a new, larger home. Though they missed Dawson City, both Howard and Nancy Firth quickly joined in the activities of the bustling new capital. Howard contributed to many sports and other community organizations, as well as serving on City Council for five years. Nancy Firth was active especially in the Catholic Women's League, doing volunteer work for the parish and for Mary House (a charitable organization that ran a thrift shop and offered shelter to those in need), and working to establish a YWCA in Whitehorse.

T.A. Firth & Son Ltd. moved again, first to an office on the other side of Main Street, then to a new building at Steele and Fourth Avenue in the 1970s. Howard and Nancy Firth's sons, Tom and Howard Jr., joined the firm in 1965. The third generation of Firths continue to operate the company more than a century after their grandfather first saw opportunity in the land of gold.[46]

WHITEHORSE MAYORS

1950–1959

When the first Whitehorse City Council was elected in 1950, the *Whitehorse Star* editor saluted the five men who courageously took up the task of creating a municipality from scratch:

> The tremendous task of setting up an efficient method of dealing with the urgent needs of the community, and then carrying them through to completion falls on the shoulders of our new civic government. They will be taking office without a proper place to meet, without funds whatsoever and without any organizational setup behind them. In fact, they will be bucking a brick wall to start.[47]

Commissioner Andrew Gibson and his assistant, Vic Wylie, flew from Dawson to attend their first meeting and offer cogent advice, though not much financial support. Within a few months, the Council had hired Percy Hewitt as the first City Clerk and adopted a miniscule budget for the Council ($1,540), City Clerk ($8,585), legal department ($560), public works ($12,436) and fire department ($13,225)—the grand total was $36,346. The Mayor received $500 per year and each Alderman $200. With such meagre resources, the councils of the 1950s had to volunteer enormous amounts of time, with the Mayors in particular taking on huge responsibilities. The men who took up the challenge were legendary for their positive spirit and civic pride. By the end of the first decade, the municipality had a new sewer and water system, a new subdivision and an expanding tax base to support more improvements to city services.

GORDON ARMSTRONG 1950–1958

Gordon Armstrong was the community's unanimous choice as the first Mayor of Whitehorse. He was swept into office by acclamation and went on to serve four terms. Armstrong had all the right stuff for the onerous duties thrust upon him—business acumen, having worked since his arrival in 1929 as a butcher and then manager at the Burns meat market; experience with the heady boom days of World War II; and most importantly, a great sense of humour. These plus perseverance and a zest for work were essential qualities for tackling the countless issues facing the community.

Born in 1905 at Whitehead, just before Saskatchewan became a province, Armstrong was familiar with frontier life, including the volunteerism that

Judge Gibben swearing in first Whitehorse City Council. L-R: Bill Hamilton; George Ryder; Mayor Gordon Armstrong; Judge Gibben; Sam McClimon; and RCMP officer, Hank Neufeld, 1950. Missing was James Norrington. George Ryder died a short time later and Ernest Lortie was elected in a by-election.

kept small towns ticking. He and his wife, Peggy, and daughter, Pat, were avid participants in community clubs and events, revelling in a whirlwind social life from their small log home on Wood Street. As the economy took off in the 1950s, Armstrong left Burns to start Yukon Sales, delivering goods to communities along the new highways. Armstrong and his fellow Councillors, as the city's pioneer politicians, accomplished huge gains for citizens in less than a decade through hard work and determination, always promoting a bright future for Whitehorse. Gordon and Peggy Armstrong retired to Vancouver in 1962, returning often to visit. He died in Vancouver in 1993.[48]

GORDON ROBERTSON CAMERON 1958–1959

When the affable Gordon Cameron was acclaimed the city's second Mayor in 1958, he was well aware of the heavy workload facing him, having already served as Alderman for two terms. An aircraft mechanic by trade and a businessman by instinct, Cameron used charm and persuasion to accomplish seemingly impossible goals.

Born in Nova Scotia in 1921 and raised in Vancouver, Cameron came north in 1941, seeking adventure in the budding air transport industry. He and his wife,

HRH Queen Elizabeth leaving the MacBride Museum with Mayor Gordon Cameron, 1959. Patsy Henderson and his wife Edith are to the left in the crowd.

Bonnie Hunter, started their family life in Whitehorse in small shacks, as did so many others. With four boisterous boys born within a few years, the Camerons eventually acquired more substantial housing. Cameron worked for several air services over the years, as well as starting his own small businesses, including a marine supply store and a Volkswagen dealership. Bonnie Cameron joined numerous clubs and was especially devoted to acting in Whitehorse Drama Club productions.

The most difficult issue Cameron faced as Mayor was the ongoing squatters' dilemma. He dreaded the demolition of condemned buildings and worked hard to develop new housing options. After he had served one term in office, business and family required all his time, and he did not stand for re-election. In 1962, opportunity came knocking. Prime Minister John Diefenbaker appointed Cameron as Yukon Commissioner. For four years he had the ear of senior Ottawa officials, promoting infrastructure development and governance reform. Cameron resigned as Commissioner in 1966, accepting a position with Canadian Utilities in Edmonton and moving there with his family. He returned often to Whitehorse as a director on various corporate boards and to visit family and friends. He died in 2010 in Edmonton.[49]

8

BOOM TOWN

1961–1980

WHITEHORSE TOOK OFF in the 1960s, with thriving businesses, booming construction and a rapidly multiplying population, yet uncertainty gripped many citizens. Trucks and planes replaced the steamboats, creating new jobs for some and eliminating the livelihood of others. The military housing in Upper Whitehorse and the new Riverdale subdivision accommodated people with the means to pay. Yet a third of all residents still lived as squatters, facing eviction from shacks erected along the river and fringes of downtown. As the Cold War heated up, new technologies refocussed military strategies. The Alaska Highway was no longer a primary defence corridor, and rumours of the military's departure created ongoing jitters in the business community.

The city's efforts to build an identity as a capital were circumscribed by a meagre tax base with no major industries and too few homeowners. Raucous debates raged in political circles over autonomy, home rule and local control of Yukon's destiny. With the issues of equal opportunity, identity and self-government at the top of their agenda, aboriginal citizens began organizing new groups to represent their needs and demands.

Education had become essential for people of all ages and backgrounds. As the new decade dawned with the economy firing on all cylinders, Yukon was awash in projects and headed for the delirious pipeline dreams that would characterize the 1970s.

FACING Bulldozers hauling the sternwheeler SS *Klondike* from the shipyards through the streets of Whitehorse in June 1966. The boat was relocated in a new park on waterfront land donated by WP&YR, formerly occupied by Whiskey Flats residents.

237

Whitehorse was at the hub of the massive change affecting every region of the Yukon in the early 1960s. The city's old economy—based on rail-to-river connections serving mines at Dawson and Mayo—had realigned with the shift to road and air transport. A new highway network joined over twenty small communities, supporting mineral exploration and small enterprises. The exception was the community of Old Crow, which was still served by river barge as well as planes.

Ottawa agreed in 1961 to expand the Yukon Council to seven members. (The numbers would be increased in 1974 to twelve, and again to sixteen in 1978.) Whitehorse held the most seats on the Council, in keeping with its population. Politics fuelled spicy debate in cafés, bars and living rooms, and the hotly contested campaigns in municipal, territorial and federal elections provided plentiful grist for local media.

Yukon MP Erik Nielsen was challenged unsuccessfully by several Liberals, a Social Credit candidate and a few NDP hopefuls, but he would hold on to his seat for an unbroken stretch of 30 years. Nielsen frequently addressed Whitehorse City Council, announcing new funding when his party was in power and exhorting Councillors to demand more federal money while the Progressive Conservatives were in opposition.

Territorial candidates ran individually on non-partisan platforms, as did municipal politicians, both groups hedging their bets to ensure support from all parties in Ottawa.[1]

From the outset, mayors were sometimes acclaimed in Whitehorse, the prevailing view being that the remuneration was too little for the time and headaches involved. Lawyer Vic Wylie succeeded Gordon Cameron as Mayor in 1960 but did not run again, saying "there was a lack of oneness" in the community.[2] Businessmen Ed Jacobs and Howard Firth each served terms in the 1960s, followed by Bert Wybrew, who held the post from 1969 until 1974, when Paul Lucier was elected. Ione Christensen was the first woman to be elected Mayor, in 1975, and she won again in 1977.[3]

Few candidates ran for Alderman during the 1960s, so some Councillors also won by acclamation. In 1962, Jan Montgomery became the first woman on Council, serving seven years altogether. City Council was also a training ground for advancement to senior government. Gordon Cameron, Ione Christensen and

former Aldermen Jim Smith and Doug Bell were all later appointed as Yukon Commissioners. Paul Lucier became Yukon's first Senator in 1975, with Ione Christensen succeeding him in 1999. Tony Penikett served on City Council in 1978, and then was elected to the Legislative Assembly that same year; he was Premier of Yukon from 1985 to 1992.[4]

Whitehorse still lacked basic organization and infrastructure in the early 1960s. House numbers were added in 1964 to assist firefighters responding to emergencies. Whitehorse had its own police force by then, consisting of one officer, Constable Jack Macdonald. Among the most dangerous situations facing citizens were mudslides on the clay cliffs, where children played and squatters' homes crowded close together at the bottom. Flooding occurred almost every spring, damaging streets and causing headaches for city officials with limited budgets for repairs. Stormy debates often erupted in Council over street paving, sidewalk construction and parking meters, as officials and residents debated the merits versus the costs of such projects.

Mudslides at the clay cliffs were an ongoing threat to children, who played there, and squatters, who lived below the cliffs.

When Ottawa officials decided in the late 1950s to amalgamate people from Marsh Lake, Lake Laberge and Whitehorse into the Whitehorse Indian Band, Billy Smith was elected the first Chief. After several years without elections, band member Scurvey Shorty was chosen as Chief in 1962. Elijah Smith, Andrew McLeod, Johnnie Smith and Roy Sam held the position in subsequent years. The elected Band Council repeatedly voiced concerns about the appalling conditions on the reserve at the north end of town. Several hundred people were crowded into shacks, with water delivery by truck and no sewer system. The former refinery area was scarred by poor roads, industrial pollution and sewage draining down from the Takhini subdivision. All levels of government made a major effort to relocate people during the 1970s, but the process stalled repeatedly over disagreements about funding and sites.[5]

In Upper Whitehorse, military commanders still managed sewers, water, road maintenance, fire protection and other services. Air force families in Hillcrest elected their own Mayor and Councillors to organize sports and social events. Camp Takhini's elected association organized a library, rink and many

community activities. As more lots opened up in Porter Creek, a community association formed there too, led by renowned motel and bar owner Stan McGowan.

Whitehorse was truly a government town, with a significant proportion of money flowing from federal civil and military programs, as well as through the territorial, municipal and aboriginal governments. City Council hired a Manager in 1963, recognizing the need for more effective planning and policy direction. Centennial year funding was funnelled into the construction of the town's first city hall, consolidating city government in a permanent home.[6]

THE SQUATTERS OF WHITEHORSE

Topping the list of headaches for Whitehorse officials were the squatters still living on Crown land along the waterfront and the adjacent White Pass lots. Ongoing campaigns to "clean up" these areas resulted in a few unoccupied buildings being removed each year, but hundreds of substandard shacks remained. Plans for a public park on the waterfront provided a rationale for clearing squatters from Whiskey Flats, with White Pass donating the land to the City in 1962.

A federal report established the hard facts of the squatter dilemma: ten main sites housed about 30 percent of the total downtown population, with 20 per cent of homes having three or more children. The rest were occupied by single male workers or pensioners. Most household heads worked in seasonal, low-paid and unskilled jobs. A significant proportion of squatters were aboriginal or new Canadians who had difficulty finding work. With inadequate water, sewer and fire protection services, most squatters existed in dangerous, unhealthy conditions, with no ready solutions on the horizon.[7]

Federal, territorial and municipal officials struggled with various proposals to resolve the situation, but the lack of building lots and the meagre incomes of squatters presented big challenges. Faced with mounting pressure to deal with unsafe conditions on their lands, White Pass officials offered to sell Lot 19 to the city for building lots. When two plebiscites failed to win the required two-thirds majority approval from ratepayers to borrow the money from the federal government, the *Star* deplored taxpayers' antipathy towards the squatters, urging a more humane response to neighbours caught in a terrible dilemma.[8]

A group of more prosperous squatters to the west of Eighth Avenue formed an association led by entrepreneur Eric Wienecke and chiropractor Kay

People driving over the new Robert Campbell Bridge passed by the jumbled collection of shacks at Whiskey Flats. In the 1960s, concerns about public health issues and the unsightly appearance of this neighbourhood led to plans for clearing the area and development of a park.

MacDonald. The group asked that city boundaries be extended since residents there had the means to purchase the land on which their homes stood and to pay for water and sewer services, but a plebiscite on that proposal was also defeated.[9]

While debates raged, more homes and lives were lost to fires. A case of typhus and other outbreaks of disease fanned community fears. Some Whiskey Flats residents, led by Jim Fordyce and Gertie Tom, presented a proposal to raise the money themselves to buy Lot 19, with the City holding their funds in escrow and subdividing the land into lots priced between $300 and $500 dollars. White Pass and city officials reached agreement with the group in 1963, but some people in Whiskey Flats were unable to raise enough money, so that plan failed as well.[10]

The stalemate was finally broken as more land and housing became available in the late 1960s and the 1970s. Using federal grants, the territorial government built some low-cost family units in the areas west of Sixth Avenue. Some squatters bought lots downtown, moving their homes there or getting Central Mortgage and Housing Corporation loans to rebuild. Others relocated along the Alaska Highway and in new subdivisions at Porter Creek and Crestview. People

with Indian status were eligible to move into federal housing at Whitehorse Indian Village. Some squatters continued to occupy Crown waterfront reserves north of downtown for another 40 years, however, until the last homes were finally cleared to develop Shipyards Park.[11]

TRAINING FOR SUCCESS

Providing improved educational opportunities for all ages was a major concern for leaders focussed on building a stable, prosperous city. The Yukon government added kindergarten to the school curriculum in the 1970s, ending the fee-based services. F.H. Collins Secondary School opened in Whitehorse in 1961, offering enhanced academic and technical programs. Federal funding supported language training and evening adult literacy programs to strengthen basic skills, allowing people to obtain work as new mines and services developed.[12]

Post-secondary training was a major gap. Few families could afford to send their kids outside to university or trade colleges; that had left a growing number of youth, especially aboriginals, without the required skills to gain employment. Many adults needed to enhance their skills to gain better-paid jobs. In 1963, with federal support, the territorial government established the Whitehorse Vocational Training School (WVTS) in Riverdale. It was an immediate success, offering programs geared to the Yukon economy: carpentry, electrical, heavy-duty equipment operation, mechanics, surveying, hairdressing, nursing assistant, food services, secretarial and accounting training. Renowned artist Ted Harrison, hired as an instructor, introduced an arts program that

ABOVE LEFT The Whitehorse Vocational Training School (WVTS) opened in 1963 to provide the first post-secondary education in the Yukon.

ABOVE RIGHT Food Services student Frances Auston (later Woolsey) receives prize for top marks from Tourist Services Manager Jim Smith. Frances obtained employment at Yukon Hall with her training, a major boost to her income as a single parent with several children.

encouraged many aboriginal youth to develop their talents. A student residence provided accommodation so that youth from communities outside Whitehorse could attend the facility. The school was renamed the Yukon Vocational and Technical Training Centre in 1965.[13]

Business leaders and politicians welcomed the first WVTS graduates as a new wave of homegrown skilled workers with the desire and fortitude to stay in the Yukon. Many students were aboriginal, determined to join the economic boom unfolding all around them. Graduates found jobs in the hospital, at Yukon Hall and Coudert Hall, in restaurants, mines and on construction sites. Some aboriginal graduates had gained skills vital to leading their communities in the emerging land claims movement.[14]

FUN AND FROLICS

Buoyed by success and prosperity, Whitehorse was by now hosting frolics year-round to retain residents and attract visitors. The non-stop entertainment smorgasbord included summer street dances, classical concerts, visiting country music stars, drama festivals, agricultural fairs, hockey and baseball tournaments, curling bonspiels, judo competitions and much more. Events billed as "international" included Alaskan participants. Having fun together smoothed the riffles of disparity among Whitehorse residents. Kids and adults of different backgrounds played on sports teams and celebrated seasonal events together, creating healthy bonds.

The jewel in the crown was the annual Yukon Sourdough Rendezvous, a revival of the winter carnival organized by business leaders and service clubs in 1962. For three days in February, and in later years for a full week, Rendez-vous was a smash hit. Revellers converged on the downtown by the thousands for flour-packing, snowshoe and tea-boiling races, the Rendezvous Queen contest, an aboriginal craft fair, old-time fiddle dances, a Native Folklore Show, vaude-ville entertainers and bands at dozens of bars. People dressed up in various Klondike styles, men grew beards, businesses decorated their premises. With temperatures still dipping into the minus-30s, people flocked to the frozen river for dogsled races that brought mushers in from the bush to compete for fun, fame and a poke of gold.

The Sourdough Rendezvous generated hundreds of thousands of dollars each year, and it was an essential element of a concerted campaign by the new Yukon

WP&YR employee Roy Minter—flanked by Yukon tourism booster Bud Fisher at left and an unidentified official—was a keen promoter of tourism for Whitehorse and the Yukon.

Tourism Bureau, City Council, the Chamber of Commerce, White Pass, and other businesses and service clubs to generate interest in the city. New visitor facilities were created and existing ones expanded, including the Robert Service Campground beside the Whitehorse Rapids, RV parks, the relocation and restoration of the ss *Klondike* at Rotary Park, the Chadburn Lake picnic area, the expansion of MacBride Museum, new hotels and restaurants, and Miles Canyon boat tours.

Since the gold rush was a major theme for the city's budding tourism industry, there was serious concern when Edmonton named its annual exhibition "Klondike Days." Polite protest turned to outrage as the Alberta capital continued to exploit the name. The Yukon fought back, with White Pass & Yukon Route employee Roy Minter leading the charge from Whitehorse, joining with Dawsonites to form the Klondike Defence Force. Dances, rallies and parades raised money for a cross-country media campaign. MP Erik Nielsen—by now known as "Yukon Erik"—spiced up debate in the House of Commons by defending the true home of the Klondike.[15] The *cause célèbre* reached a crescendo when Edmonton proposed a Klondike Pavilion for Expo 67. Yukon defenders appeared before the National Centennial Commission in Ottawa, and the idea was quashed. Availing itself of federal funding, the Territory mounted a modest exhibit at the fair in Montreal, showcasing Yukon gold and the spectacular beauty and adventure of the North.

Centennial year celebrations back home kept Whitehorse hopping with special art exhibits, parades, dances, concerts, visits from dignitaries and major building projects. The new MacBride Museum building and the new city hall transformed the block formerly occupied by the Territorial Agent's offices. Bobby Gimby came to town, leading school kids in singing the infectious "Ca-na-da" song. The Klondike Voyageurs Club joined a national canoe pageant to retrace fur trade routes, wearing beaded tunics made by artists at the Indian Co-op Store.[16]

Whitehorse was always hungry for entertainment and good at creating its own fun. From the town's inception, citizens whooped it up at masquerade balls,

summer picnics, parades and community dances. In the 1960s and 1970s, the downtown bar scene was especially wild and woolly. Patrons could cruise from one bar to another, beer in hand, and kick it up to the music of Al Oster, the Canucks, Hank Karr, the Northernaires and Joe Loutchan, or party all night at Mimi's.

The social and cultural whirlwind continued throughout the 1970s. The Frantic Follies troupe—founded by brothers Jim and Lyall Murdoch, who grew up in New Westminster, B.C., and moved to Whitehorse in the late 1960s—capitalized on gold-rush themes to entertain the growing tourism market. A new regional library, opened in 1966, included a small gallery to showcase touring art from the south alongside the work of local artists. Both the Yukon Indian Craft Shop and the YuKraft store sold the work of local craftspeople, and the Yukon Arts Council was formed in 1971 by artists, arts enthusiasts and music teachers. New heritage organizations promoted and preserved history and culture.

A Whitehorse YWCA opened in 1971, offering recreation facilities and short-term housing for young workers, plus a coordinator to spearhead social events. Dozens of sports teams, clubs and associations advertised their programs at the Y's community information fairs, an amazing array considering that the city's population was just 14,000. As always, opportunities abounded to enjoy boating,

Staff member Barbro Baker showing crafts to Governor General Roland Michener at the Yukon Indian Craft Store, ca. 1975.

fishing, hiking and all manner of outdoor activities close by in pristine wilderness settings. Whitehorse residents were increasingly united in pursuit of a good northern life.[17]

SPORTS AND RECREATION 1960S & 1970S

In November 1963, the almost forgotten NSAA—the community's social, entertainment and sporting heart for the first 40 years of its existence—passed into oblivion with the passage of an ordinance by the Yukon Council. It wasn't the only sport group to disappear. Even the rivalries that fed the popularity of most sports had vanished. With the closing of the Canadian Army and RCAF bases in the mid-1960s, "Up the Hill" was gone, and being "the Town" didn't mean as much—all the teams were now "the Town." Under a different name (the Young People's Club), the former YPA sponsored a hockey team in 1964, but when the season ended, so did the group.

The Yukon Ski Runners and the Roundel Ski Club merged in 1960 to form the Whitehorse Ski Club. The group closed the Roundel Ski Hill and opened a larger ski area on Haeckel Hill, but the club ran deficits every year until 1964, when August and Olive Pociwauschek, owners of the local sporting goods store, assumed management of the hill. The couple returned the hill to the club in

1968 after they failed to turn a profit. Haeckel Hill closed in the 1970s and the Whitehorse Ski Club dissolved.

In 1968, the Territorial Experimental Ski Training (TEST) program—pioneered by Father Jean-Marie Mouchet in Old Crow—arrived in Whitehorse. Dave and Irene Brekke ran the program out of Takhini Elementary School, on a three-kilometre (two-mile) trail cut behind the school. Cross-country skiers used that trail for four years to hold local and regional sprint races, with longer races following old logging roads, survey lines and walking trails around the city. As the 1972 Arctic Winter Games approached, the Whitehorse Cross-Country Ski Club constructed a ski stadium with timing and warming shacks, west of Valleyview. They redeveloped existing trails from the former Roundel Ski Hill and cut additional trails around Mount McIntyre, with fourteen kilometres (nine miles) illuminated at night by large street lamps. It was the longest lit cross-country trail system in North America at that time.

Night skiing under the lights at Mount McIntyre, 1979.

When the first loosely organized soccer league in Whitehorse was formed, in the 1950s, it was a disaster. A number of former European First Division and other international players had immigrated to Canada after World War II, settling in Whitehorse. They were keen participants in the new Whitehorse Soccer League. Because coaches selected their teams with an eye to national origin more than to skill, the games were often marred by animosities carried over from past European conflicts.

Konrad Domes, a former player and coach from Germany, believed soccer should provide a venue in which differences were set aside and the game could heal broken individuals, cultures and societies. He asked businessman Howard Firth to sponsor a soccer team, with Domes as coach and the players selected by skill, with no more than two players of the same nationality playing at any time.

Konrad Domes (at right) and the 1960 Firth Canucks changed the face of soccer in Whitehorse and turned it into the fastest-growing sport in the city.

Fighting and gratuitous violence would not be tolerated. Domes suggested the name "Firth Canucks" to drive home the point. Firth agreed, and soccer moved from being on the athletic fringe to becoming the fastest-growing sport in the city.

The annual Yukon Sourdough Rendezvous had many attractions, but at its heart were the dogsled races. Mushers personified the true spirit of the festival—a bunch of northerners who came to town for a good time at the end of the long winter and raced for the sheer joy of it. Going down to the Yukon River for the start of the races became a tradition. Vehicles and people would pack onto the ice until many worried whether it could support all the weight. Hundreds more braved the early morning cold to stand along the riverbanks, cheering as the teams started at three-minute intervals. There was nothing professional about the mushers or the races they ran. However, the Yukon Dog Mushers Association (YDMA) formed in 1963 to organize the races. It incorporated as a society in 1974.

The Rendezvous races starred many colourful characters whose exploits, both on and off the trail, made them northern sport legends. Wilfred "Iron Man" Charlie won five Carling Trophies as Rendezvous dog mushing champion in the 1960s and 1970s. Charlie was wildly popular with the crowds because he didn't ride his sled but ran alongside or behind it for the entire 24 kilometres (15 miles). He earned the nickname "Iron Man" in 1969, when he won the Rendezvous snowshoe race just two hours after finishing the dogsled race.

Two-time world sprint champion Nick Molofy of Edmonton won the hearts of fans in 1973. Molofy was winning the race until fellow competitor Wilfred Charlie lost his dog team on the trail. When the runaway dogs caught up to Molofy, he stopped to control them and waited for Charlie to catch up. The decision to hold the team cost Molofy the championship—which was won by Charlie.

Musher Bob English once drove his team through the door of the Edgewater Hotel pub and across the room, scattering tables, chairs and patrons in every direction. Stopping the team beside the bar, he tilted a keg of beer into his sled, gave "gee" and "haw" commands to turn the dogs around and went out the same way he'd come in.

There were tragic stories too. Babe Southwick entered the Rendezvous dogsled races
in 1965. The popular 40-year-old pulled the
number eight starting position at the musher's banquet on Thursday night and ran a
respectable fifth on Friday morning. That
night, Southwick died of a heart attack. At the
start gate the next morning, mushers wearing black armbands wept as they observed a
minute of silence in her memory. The YDMA
withdrew the number eight, never to be worn again. Moved by what he had witnessed, *Edmonton Journal* editor Andrew Snaddon donated the Babe Southwick
Trophy for the fastest single lap by any team over the three days of racing, the
most popular award in the Rendezvous races to this day.

Alex Van Bibber, wearing bib
number 9, with family and friends
on the Yukon River in Whitehorse
as part of the dogsled races, 1969.

In the early 1970s, the Warriors, the first all-aboriginal team since the Baptist Indian Mission School team of the 1950s, played in the Whitehorse Senior
Hockey League. It was the first time a sports team had been defined by race
alone. Previously, the limited number of players of all backgrounds had imposed
integration. "Nobody cared about what race they were," recalls Howard Firth Jr.,
who played in the league for years. "If they wanted to play and could, then they
got the same kind of ice time as everyone else." According to Randy Merkel, one
of the Warriors' "young guns" who grew up playing road hockey on the streets
of Whitehorse, "First Nation people like sports, and they especially like hockey.
We've always been lucky enough to live in a place where ... for sure, some native
people were discriminated against ... but I'm First Nation and I never got
treated differently from any other kid. Especially in hockey—on the ice I never
had to face any racism."

The Warriors gave young aboriginal players the opportunity to play with
experienced veterans from the south, like Phil Fontaine, who moved to Whitehorse to work as regional director for the Department of Indian and Northern
Affairs and later would become National Chief of the Assembly of First Nations.
When the Warriors folded in 1973, the Yukon Indian Hockey Association (YIHA)
formed to promote aboriginal hockey.

Active since the mid-1970s, the YIHA still hosts the annual Yukon Native
Hockey Tournament in Whitehorse, raising funds for summer skill-develop-
ment programs for aboriginal youth and trips for senior and minor teams to

BENNY SHEARDOWN WAYNE HOGANSON WAYNE KINLEY JOHN BIRDINGHAM JACKIE SIMPSON P. ALLEN RAY HALL DAVID ALLEN HOWIE FIRTH

Yukon's Arctic Winter Games gold medal–winning hockey team celebrates in Jim Light Arena, 1972.

outside tournaments, including the Canadian First Nations championship. In addition to appealing to former professional players who come to lace up their skates, the weekend event attracts crowds reminiscent of early days in Whitehorse, when hockey was the only show in town. "The fans are so dedicated . . . so loyal," says Randy Merkel. "First Nations communities love it when their kids are in it. A lot of them have a son, a husband, a cousin or a nephew on the team. They can identify with the team."

In 1968, the first Polar Games were held in Whitehorse. Initially these were competitive games, with the winners earning medals and ribbons in multiple disciplines. In 1975, the focus changed to include a variety of non-competitive sports, to encourage participation by elementary school children. The Polar Games are still going, and every year between 700 and 1,000 students from 21 schools around the Yukon participate.

Some sports in Whitehorse retained a rustic look even as they grew in importance. Track athletes preparing for the 1969 Canada Summer Games in Halifax trained in their bare feet, running around a 200-metre (650-foot) loop marked with chalk in a grassy field across from Christ the King School in Riverdale. The first time any of the runners saw proper track shoes was the day they received

their uniforms before departing for the Games. The Whitehorse Marathon began in 1977 as a 42-kilometre (26-mile) race from the RCAF Rec Centre to the Takhini Hot Springs Road and back down Two Mile Hill to Rotary Park. Runners had to cross the intersection at Second Avenue and Main Street, one of only two intersections in town with traffic lights. If they didn't catch a green, they had to stop and wait for the light to change, and then sprint the last kilometre to the finish line.

The Don Twa rink, including L-R: Lionel Stokes, Kip Boyd, Chuck Haines, Don Twa, ca. 1970s. The Twa rink made history as the first northern team to play in the Canadian Men's Curling Association annual Brier, gaining acclaim by finishing second in the 1975 championship event.

As sports organizations matured in Whitehorse, the sports multiplex question resurfaced, with bitter debate over new facilities during the 1978 municipal election campaign. The Civic Centre arena—renamed Jim Light Arena in 1970, after a former Whitehorse Alderman—was aging, as were the ball field, the swimming pool and the curling rink. The Whitehorse Lions Club and local children sold buttons at 25 cents each to fund the construction of a roof over the pool, built by volunteers in 1972. But the building was still not insulated and could only be used in summer. A 1979 proposal for a Whitehorse Family Recreation Centre in Takhini included a gymnasium, racquetball courts, a ten-sheet curling rink, a 2,300-seat hockey arena, a 375-seat theatre, a swimming pool, a banquet room and a licensed lounge. The $1.8-million price tag, along with controversy over whether the facility was needed, fuelled many heated discussions until a public plebiscite rejected the proposal.

ARTS AND CULTURE EXPLOSION

Whitehorse folks weren't just partiers; they had an appetite for the plays, concerts and festivals found in larger centres to the south. Throughout the 1960s and 1970s, the local arts scene blossomed, nourished by an influx of artists and new ideas. For more than twenty years, the Whitehorse Drama Club had provided a steady stream of productions delivered with enthusiasm and a pure love of theatre. Volunteer set designers, actors, directors and costumers came together to entertain audiences with classics such as *Night Must Fall* and *You Can't Take it With You,* and modern drama like Edward Albee's *Who's Afraid of Virginia Woolf?*

Lyle and Jim Murdoch's *Frantic Follies* entertained visitors and locals and provided dancers, actors and musicians with gainful employment every summer.

Between 1957 and 1971, the Whitehorse Concert Association brought classical, jazz and popular music to Whitehorse. The city was the last Canadian stop on the Alaska Music Trail, a touring circuit established in the 1940s by Russian pianist Maxim Shapiro.[18] Duncan Sinclair remembers the community's enthusiastic support for these concerts, with folks raiding their own living rooms for lamps and chairs to provide atmosphere onstage.[19]

In 1969, the Whitehorse Choral Society sponsored the first Yukon Music Festival, which brought in a professional adjudicator to assess, coach and coax the best from music students, school bands and community groups. The society also raised funds to provide scholarships for students interested in pursuing professional careers. Sponsorship of the event was soon taken on by the Whitehorse Rotary Club, under a new name: the Rotary Music Festival.[20]

The brutally cold night in the winter of 1972 that the Edmonton Symphony Orchestra performed in the F.H. Collins gym is still remembered by Whitehorse citizens. Government of Yukon Arts Administrator Laurel Parry, then a young fan, recalls the pile of coats and boots in the gym, the smell of wet wool and the buzz of excitement as the orchestra tuned. She wrote a review of the concert for a school assignment: "I think that the Symphony was quite good at first and then it got boring after a while. But I don't see how people could watch it for three hours! The conductor was quite good too."[21]

When the Whitehorse Concert Association disbanded in 1971, the newly formed Yukon Arts Council took over the presentation of its annual concert series. The council fundraised tirelessly and, in 1979, with a boost from the Whitehorse Recreation Board, purchased a seven-foot Chickering grand piano.

As more musicians migrated north in the boom years of the 1970s, the pool of musical talent grew. A homegrown music scene was beginning to take shape, while in the rest of Canada, folk festival fever moved from east to west. It was just a matter of time before it came north. Barry Redfern, recreation director for the town of Faro, and musician David Essig concocted a plan for the first Farrago Music Festival in 1975.[22] From there the dominoes fell. When Mel Orecklin, music lover and volunteer coordinator at the Winnipeg Folk Festival, moved to the Yukon in 1977 to work for the Department of Indian and Northern Affairs, he volunteered at the Farrago Festival for two years running. In between, he produced concerts and square dances in Whitehorse, including, in 1978, the Rendezvous concert that was the precursor to the Frostbite Music Festival, held annually in Whitehorse since 1979.

Orecklin and fellow producer Larry Saidman from Mayo formed the not-for-profit society Folk Music in the Yukon in order to be eligible to use the Whitehorse Recreation Centre, nicknamed the "Ice Palace" when the pipes burst one winter and several inches of water froze in the basement. The Whitehorse Drama Club came to Frostbite's aid with spotlights for the event, but finding an affordable sound system was more difficult. In 1979, Orecklin purchased a system, beginning the long festival tradition in which Yukon arts organizations became the owners and managers of moveable property—tents, dance floors, portable bars, sound systems, lights, cube vans—and then begged, borrowed or rented equipment from one another.

Among the musicians at Frostbite that first year were Farrago veterans Pied Pear and David Essig, along with Willie P. Bennett. The roster of local artists on the program represented some of the best-known names in Yukon music: John Steins, "Harmonica" George McConkey, Dave Haddock and Two

Audiences crowded into workshop rooms to hear musicians at the 1982 Frostbite Music Festival.

Rivers, featuring Manfred Janssen and Jim Vautour. With the advent of Frostbite, Whitehorse musicians, accustomed to playing in packed and noisy bars, finally had access to a concert venue.

Following fast on the heels of Frostbite, the Yukon Arts Council organized the first Spring Festival in Whitehorse in April 1979. The whole artistic community got involved, from painters and musicians to writers and Highland dancers, and every possible venue was pressed into service. The 1979 festival program was a snapshot of the cultural organizations in the city: the Yukon Art Society, the Whitehorse Public Library gallery, the Whitehorse Weavers and Spinners Guild, the Whitehorse Choral Society, the Whitehorse Music Teachers Association, the Yukon Crafts Society, the Yukon Indian Arts and Crafts Society and Winter Afternoon Productions, "a small photography club, little-known to Whitehorse." Events were held at Jeckell Junior High School, Riverdale Baptist Church, Kishwoot Hall in Whitehorse Indian Village, the Whitehorse Elementary School gym, Takhini Elementary School, the MacBride Museum and numerous other venues. Yukon Archives showed archival films, Folk Music in the Yukon presented a noon-hour concert every day in the lobby of the Yukon government building, various groups presented craft shows, the Whitehorse Drama Club mounted performances, and the Whitehorse Public Library hosted a writers' circle.

In 1980, the Whitehorse Public Library brought poets Susan Musgrave and David McFadden to town. Together with playwright John Lazarus, they hosted a gathering of Yukon writers, and the next day appeared as guest authors at the first Young Authors' Conference. From this small beginning, the Yukon Writers' Festival emerged.

In the summer of 1980, led by arts advocate and theatre-lover Chris Dray, the Guild Society was established to convert two former army buildings donated by the Porter Creek Citizens' Association into a studio arts centre for the performing and visual arts. As Dray recalls, "We decided that we needed to do something public to attract volunteers and donations, so we printed 300 T-shirts and mounted the Founders Festival on the final weekend that August. All the local bar bands came to play, various singer-songwriters and a few theatre types."[23] The first show produced at the Guild Hall was Conrad Boyce's one-man show, *Bohemian*, based on the life of Robert Service. In 1981, Guild Productions, with help from the Yukon territorial government's Recreation Branch, launched its first full season. At last, Whitehorse had a dedicated performing arts venue.

The other important turning point for Whitehorse in 1981 was a territory-wide consultation concerning Yukon communities' recreation needs, led by the Yukon Arts Council and Minister of Education and Recreation Meg McCall. Some crucial recommendations emerged, including the ideas that culture should be resourced and developed as a separate entity from sport, recreation and education, and that policy and programming should work hand in hand to develop the arts in the Yukon. With these recommendations and the building of the Guild Hall, the seeds were sown for the rich cultural life that would develop over the next three decades.[24]

Guild Hall volunteers on steps of the old Porter Creek community hall at the beginning of its transformation to theatre and gallery space, ca. 1982.

Amidst this cultural renaissance, Whitehorse aboriginal people gained their own gathering place. The proceeds of a trust fund established from the estate of Skookum Jim were used to construct a modest building on Third Avenue in 1962. Skookum Jim Hall, known affectionately as "Skookies," offered teen and adult dances, sewing classes, kids' traditional dance programs, and a meeting space for people to discuss the future. Renamed Skookum Jim Friendship Centre in 1967 after joining the national coalition of aboriginal centres, it was a rallying point for cultural and political revival.[26]

The Skookies staff and volunteers lobbied governments for action on issues critical to aboriginal families: affordable, safe housing; an end to poverty and discrimination; access to education and employment; the revitalization of traditional culture; the reclaiming of lands and rights lost since the gold rush and Alaska Highway upheavals. The centre organized a kindergarten at Kishwoot Hall in the village, with a van to pick up kids around town. Health clinics, community health workers, the Native Court Worker program and many other initiatives assisted Status and non-Status people.

Reaching out to the broader community, Skookies held a series of popular hootenannies, attracting capacity crowds at F.H. Collins gym to hear aboriginal performers and raise money for the centre's programs. The Skookies stew and bannock lunch became an annual Rendezvous tradition to which all were welcome. In 1973, the centre presented the first annual Skookum Jim Folklore Show, a showcase for local performers and a chance to honour a First Nations Elder with the Keish Award ("Keish" is the traditional name of Skookum Jim). Bob Charlie and the Klukshu Flats Boogie Band got the crowd moving on the dance floor in the F.H. Collins gym.

The centre was also the birthplace of many Yukon aboriginal organizations. The Klondike Indian Movement formed in the mid-1960s, drawing on advice from visiting aboriginal organizers. The Yukon Native Brotherhood (YNB) was established to represent Status Indians in 1968. People lacking Indian Act standing organized the Yukon Association of Non-Status Indians (YANSI). The Yukon Indian Women's Association was founded in 1974.[27]

As rural schools expanded, fewer aboriginal students came to Whitehorse. Accommodation for out-of-town aboriginal children was consolidated at Yukon Hall after Coudert Hall closed in the late 1960s. The federal government leased

the vacant building to aboriginal organizations, which had outgrown the space at Skookies. The new Yukon Indian Centre created fresh synergy for Elders, leaders and young graduates to launch more programs. The *Yukon Indian News*, Themah Day Care Centre, the Yukon Indian Resource Library, a Curriculum Department creating aboriginal content for Yukon schools, the Ye Sa To Communications Society, and YNB and YANSI leadership had accessed federal grants to create jobs for over 100 people by the mid-1970s. The centre vibrated with creative energy, commanding new attention for aboriginal issues.[28]

The Yukon land claims movement had built slowly through the decades following Jim Boss's 1902 letter. Yukon aboriginal people closely followed land claim developments in Alaska and southern Canada, and they denounced the alienation of traditional lands and resources. When federal Indian Affairs Minister Jean Chrétien visited Whitehorse in 1968, Angela Sidney and others voiced sharp criticisms of the Liberal government's infamous *White Paper on Indian Affairs*. These concerns magnified as Yukon's economic boom

Skookies reached out to the whole community with hugely popular hootenannies in the mid-1960s raising funds for their Kishwoot Hall kindergarten and after school study programs.

encroached on more traditional lands and waters, with no input and few benefits for aboriginal people.

In 1973, the Yukon Native Brotherhood published a landmark "statement of claims and grievances" entitled *Together Today for Our Children Tomorrow*. In this historic document, they demanded access to economic opportunities, education, land, money, hunting rights and other compensation in exchange for ceding traditional lands and resources to the Crown. Led by Elijah Smith, twelve Chiefs travelled to Ottawa to present their case to Prime Minister Pierre Trudeau. The legendary meeting of these charismatic leaders produced a federal commitment to negotiate a modern treaty with Yukon First Nations people. YNB and YANSI formed a new Council for Yukon Indians (CYI) to negotiate the claim on behalf of all their members. Asked how long the process would take, CYI negotiator Dave Joe predicted "about one year." That time frame expanded into three decades of debate, tough bargaining and uncertainty inside and outside the organization. Whitehorse was the central meeting place for CYI leaders, but the heart of the issues lay in diverse communities around the territory, posing dilemmas with no resolution in sight by the end of the 1970s.[29]

THE MILITARY DEPART

Despite some grumbling through the years, no one doubted the positive effect of uniformed personnel on the Whitehorse economy and social life. As Canada and its allies focussed attention on new strategies to counter long-range missile attacks and the threat of nuclear war, however, Canadian forces began consolidating in key command centres located south of 60. Everyone knew there would be changes in Whitehorse when the army left in 1964, followed by the air force in 1966. Fond farewells were exchanged at official handover ceremonies. Civilian employees of the federal Department of Public Works assumed responsibility for Alaska Highway maintenance, and Department of Transportation staff took over airport management and communications.[30]

In the end, the departure of the military generated positive opportunities, rather than the dire consequences predicted by some pundits. The closure of military PX stores expanded the scope for local suppliers, since new federal employees shopped alongside townspeople. By the 1970s, Ottawa had sold most of the housing in Takhini, Hillcrest and Valleyview, releasing hundreds of well-built homes to the public at modest prices. The city adjusted smoothly

to a civilian majority. Uniforms reappeared annually when military personnel from the south attended the Rendezvous Air Show and the summer cadet
camp. Otherwise, a few plaques, remnants of buildings, wartime street names
in Takhini and lingering memories among old-timers marked the era of military
predominance.

RESOURCES AND RICHES

There was little time to lament the military departures, given the resource and
construction boom overtaking Whitehorse in the mid-1960s. The long-standing
dearth of jobs and taxation revenues evaporated in the excitement of successive
announcements for new roads, buildings, mines and oil and gas exploration that
headlined the *Whitehorse Star* and a new rival paper, the *Yukon News*.

Over less than a decade, huge developments were launched to the north,
south, east and west of the city. When the Yukon Consolidated Gold Corporation
pulled out of Dawson City in 1966, local operators carried on mining. A large
asbestos mine opened at Clinton Creek, near Dawson, and another at Cassiar,
in northern B.C. United Keno Hill Mines operated at full strength in the Mayo

The new Whitehorse Copper Mine
required experienced underground
miners. With good wages and benefits it attracted French-speaking
workers from northern Ontario and
Quebec, bolstering the existing
community and laying foundations
for a growing francophone presence in the coming decades.

region. The Vangorda lead zinc deposits near Ross River produced a huge open-pit mine, a mill and a townsite at Faro in 1969. Oil and gas drilling occurred at Eagle Plains and in the southeast Yukon, near Watson Lake. A new dam built at Aishihik Lake generated power for Faro and Whitehorse. All this activity stimulated the construction of new towns, roads, schools and public buildings, along with increased demand for workers, equipment and services.

In Whitehorse, New Imperial Mines and Metals, incorporated by Yukon MP Aubrey Simmons in 1954 to explore the Whitehorse Copper Belt, had steadily expanded its holdings and activities through the 1950s and 1960s, always seeking the right combination of investors and activities to develop a big mine. In 1964, Sumitomo Metal Mining of Japan began investing heavily in the operation. Within a few years, the new consortium had constructed a mill and started open-pit mining. In 1971, a new underground mining operation started, financed by several large corporations and operating under the name Whitehorse Copper Mines. For the next decade, the mine would pump millions of dollars into the economy, creating more than 100 new jobs. At last Whitehorse had a strong industrial base to diversify and strengthen its economy.[31] Cash registers were ringing everywhere.[32]

The White Pass & Yukon Route expanded its integrated freight system to carry ore by truck from the Faro, Clinton Creek, Keno and Whitehorse mines. This cargo was transferred to railcars at Utah Landing, near McCrae, and then transported to ships at Skagway for delivery to markets around the world. By the mid-1970s, resource extraction and associated industries represented more than half of Yukon's GDP, with the Cyprus Anvil Mine at Faro reported to be contributing as much as 25 per cent. The strong dependence of Whitehorse and the entire territory on this sector became glaringly obvious when strikes and work stoppages shut down Faro and other mines on several occasions, resulting in layoffs at White Pass and numerous other businesses.[33]

During and after World War II, the number of unionized workers grew steadily throughout the territory as more tradespeople, miners and others were hired for the many new construction projects, mines, and businesses. In 1953, the United Brotherhood of Carpenters and Joiners built a small meeting hall on Strickland Street.[34] In later years, several other unions based in the south would organize locals to represent Yukon workers in industry and the public sector. In 1980, the Yukon Federation of Labour was formed to present a strong voice for all workers, growing to represent over 4,000 people.[35]

BIG GOVERNMENT, BIG STORES

Whitehorse aspired to become a modern city of the North with all the amenities of a southern centre. Unfortunately, the municipality fell prey to many of the pitfalls of urban development. The 1960s were ushered in with the clearance of the shipyards infrastructure along the waterfront, as well as all White Pass structures except the roundhouse, the depot and a few small dwellings. The area became something of a wasteland.

Hougen's built a new-steel framed department store on Main Street in 1961, across the street from the federal building. The Taylor & Drury Store's time came to an end as the desire for televisions and fashionable clothes outstripped the demand for trapping outfits and gold-panning supplies. Old-fashioned retail establishments gave way to larger, more up-to-date stores and businesses. New hotels went up on Fourth Avenue and the historic Whitehorse Inn was demolished to make way for a bank. Symbolic of the city's new growth and business, no fewer than five banks occupied Main Street by the end of the 1970s.

Burning of the *Casca* and the *Whitehorse*, 1974. The town watched helplessly as two of the last four sternwheelers of the once mighty BYN fleet went up in flames.

264   WHITEHORSE

The 1970s also saw the city's mercantile core spread beyond Main Street. The new Qwanlin Mall included a Woolworth's and the city's first national chain grocery store. Across Ogilvie Street, the Hudson's Bay Company, previously a small outlet, opened a department store that covered half a city block. On Second Avenue, the Qwanlin Cinema Centre brought a twin theatre to town. These were all simple, blocky flat-roofed buildings, distinguished by various decorative treatments and signage on the facades.

The big new Government of Yukon Administration Building, erected on the site of the old hospital, was thoroughly 1970s in its design. The building was meant to centralize all territorial government operations, but the bureaucracy had outgrown the space before the building was even completed. By the end of the decade, government offices were scattered throughout the downtown, into Marwell and up along the highway and airport area. Usually the government offices moved into available rental space.

As part of this expansion, the Marwell Industrial Area grew enormously. The works yard became home to the Yukon Government motor pool. Combined with the offices and shops of departments such as Parks and the Liquor Board, the compound covered several acres. The Department of Highways occupied the former Standard Oil refinery offices. A large city lot on the site became the temporary home for a number of historic buildings that had been cleared from the downtown area. Local heritage enthusiasts lobbied hard to preserve the structures that remained. The swampy area at the northern limits of town was reclaimed to house Beaver Lumber and a tire business, as well as a Sandman Hotel.

Residential construction, having pretty well filled the river flat, moved to Porter Creek and Crestview, while Riverdale continued to fill the usable land on the east side of the river. Although the new subdivision planned above Hillcrest failed to materialize, the growth of country residential subdivisions began in earnest with developments like Wolf Creek.

In 1976, the RCMP opened a new headquarters on Fourth Avenue, just north of Main Street, at the location it had occupied since 1900. After the war, Poole Construction had built a two-storey frame building that was a combination barracks and guardroom, but the police rapidly outgrew the structure, and many administrative positions ended up in federal building offices. In July 1974, Whitehorse became the headquarters of a new "M" Division, responsible for all Yukon policing. The old detachment building came down, and a state-of-the-art structure took its place.

FACING TOP Hudson's Bay Company department store at left and part of the Qwanlin Mall, ca. early 1980s.

FACING BOTTOM Qwanlin Cinema, one of the new wave of buildings erected in the 1980s.

THE AIRPORT EXPANDS 1961–1980

Around 1960, the Yukon's first homegrown helicopter company, Pat Callison's Klondike Helicopters, relocated from downtown Dawson City to a shop in Hangar A at the Whitehorse Airport. It was followed in 1967 by the Yukon's Trans North Turbo Air, another locally owned company, which began operations in the old Department of Transport fire hall on the west side of the airport. The former fire truck bays nicely accommodated early Bell 47 "bubble" helicopters.

Commercial activity on the west side of the airport continued to expand, with flight training companies, charter services and scheduled flights. New companies on the site included Tintina Air, Yukon Flying Service, Great Northern Airways, and Globe Air Services, which eventually became Air North.

PIPELINE MANIA

Yet another huge project came barrelling into the city after Justice Thomas Berger presented his *Mackenzie Valley Pipeline Inquiry Report* to the federal government in 1977. Berger recommended a 20-year moratorium on pipeline construction in the NWT, citing the need to settle aboriginal land claims and prepare northerners to benefit from industrial developments. In response, the Canadian government turned to the Alaska Highway corridor as a less controversial route for transporting American natural gas from Prudhoe Bay to southern markets.

Suddenly, Whitehorse and other communities along the highway were at the centre of attention. The Alaska Highway Pipeline Inquiry, chaired by Kenneth Lysyk and including local residents Edith Bohmer and Willard Phelps, was established to survey the views of residents, which came fast and furious, with many opposed and many in favour of the proposed pipeline. Municipal, territorial and federal officials scrambled to learn from the Alaskan experience with the Alyeska Pipeline project. What they heard was sobering and often downright scary. The skyrocketing prices for housing, food and services related to the Alyeska project had created opportunities for some, but ordinary citizens struggled to maintain homes and families. There were stories of children neglected while parents pursued big salaries on long shifts; excessive drinking and other social problems were cited. This cautionary tale created a sense of urgency for more controls on

the Yukon portion of the Alaska Highway Pipeline. City and territorial planners used federal funds to develop the McIntyre and Granger subdivisions, in anticipation of thousands of new residents. The anticipated influx of strangers—who would come and go within a few short years—sounded disturbingly familiar to aboriginal people. Their leaders issued ominous warnings about the consequences of proceeding with a pipeline before land claims had been settled.

As it turned out, the pipeline dream burst almost as suddenly as it had appeared, with the collapse of the overheated Asian economy. Whitehorse was left with cleared and vacant subdivisions, businesses quickly corrected overblown estimates of profit, and government downsized pipeline-planning initiatives. Many residents breathed a sigh of relief, knowing their community was not prepared for another onslaught of mega-projects.[36]

A GROWING CITY

Pipeline fever underscored the significant challenges still facing Whitehorse at the end of the 1970s. In 1964, the city had hired academics from Queen's University to develop a metropolitan plan for the new subdivisions springing up along the highway. Residents in those areas had no services and paid no taxes to the city, yet were part of the overall demand on downtown municipal infrastructure. City boundaries expanded over several years, until Whitehorse was one of the largest municipal areas in Canada, at 416.5 square kilometres (161 square miles).

The city's growing size—its population was topping 16,000—called for significant changes to the structure of the city government. City Council expanded to six elected members in 1973. Elected in 1975, Ione Christensen fulfilled her campaign promise to work as the city's first full-time mayor, finding that the tasks at hand more than filled a regular work week. In 1976, City Council developed the City of Whitehorse General Plan, along with a regular process for updating it.[37]

As the territory's capital city, Whitehorse had become more concerned with its public image, upgrading downtown streetscapes and the waterfront. Citizens identified projects to address the continuing gaps in services for families. A group of local women organized the Minibus Society to provide the first city-wide public transit in 1976, a service later taken over by the city.

ABOVE Opening of the first session of the Yukon Legislative Assembly in the new chambers at the recently completed Yukon Administration Building, 1975.

LEFT The new Yukon Administration Building located on the riverfront at the south end of town, 1975.

The Women's Minibus Society organized briefs, raised funds and in 1976, finally obtained permits to operate the first city-wide transit service in small buses famously known as "the green toasters."

Government activity grew on all levels, leading some to question whether bureaucracy would soon outstrip all other industries in town. The Yukon government moved its headquarters to an impressive administration building on the waterfront in 1976. Constitutional reforms slowly added to the autonomous powers of territorial legislators. In 1979, Erik Nielsen engineered a spectacular coup as a powerful cabinet minister during the short-lived minority government of Joe Clark, propelling Indian Affairs and Northern Development Minister Jake Epp to issue a letter reducing the Yukon Commissioner's role and transferring authority to elected members of a new territorial Executive Council. Yukon attained responsible government overnight, but many loose ends remained, in particular unresolved aboriginal rights. Land claim negotiations were proceeding very slowly, with little common ground between the Council for Yukon Indians and the Yukon government.[38] As the 1970s closed, debates over pipeline routes, land claims and governance fuelled new political rivalries, along with concerns about the social and environmental impacts of development. Whitehorse citizens had much to ponder while considering future directions for their city.

ELIJAH SMITH 1912–1991

Edward Elijah Smith, the son of Annie Ned and Paddy Smith, was born on July 12, 1912, at Champagne. He continued to live in the Yukon all his life, except for the six years he served in the Canadian Army overseas during World War II. He was best known for his role in leading the Yukon First Nations people to settle their land claims.

When Smith returned to the Yukon after the war, he saw the difficult conditions confronting his people. By the mid-1960s, Yukon First Nations had started to organize and speak out. During hearings on the federal *White Paper on Indian Affairs* in Whitehorse in 1968, Smith spoke of his people being treated "like squatters in their own country." He said that Yukon Indians wanted the government of Canada to ensure that his people would get a fair settlement for the use of their land by non-natives.

Elijah Smith was the founding president of the Yukon Native Brotherhood in 1968 and in 1973 was the founding chairperson of the Council for Yukon Indians, since renamed the Council of Yukon First Nations. He spoke persuasively of the need for unity among First Nations people long before his vision was widely accepted.

In 1973, Elijah Smith led a contingent of Yukon Chiefs to Ottawa to present Prime Minister Pierre Trudeau with their position paper, entitled *Together Today for Our Children Tomorrow*. At the core of their message was a clear statement articulated so often by Smith: "Without land, Indian people have no soul—no life, no identity—no purpose." The event marked the beginning of negotiations resulting in the Umbrella Final Agreement two decades later.

Smith later served as Yukon Regional Director for the Department of Indian Affairs. He was awarded an honorary Doctor of Laws degree and was named to the Order of Canada for his dedicated service to his people and his ability to settle grievances peaceably. Smith

Standing on the steps of Parliament, Elijah Smith (far right, front row) led a contingent of Yukon Chiefs to Ottawa in 1973 to present their statement of claims to Prime Minister Trudeau, which initiated the long process of settling Yukon land claims.

Gertie Tom worked as a broadcaster at CBC Yukon in the early 1960s hosting a radio show that featured greetings and news from aboriginal communities around the Yukon.

always encouraged young people to stay in school. He personally guided many First Nations youth to pursue law degrees and other skills so they could undertake instrumental roles in land claims negotiations.

Elijah Smith remained a prominent figure throughout the land claims process until his death in a tragic road accident in October 1991. To honour his memory, the federal building in Whitehorse is named for him, as is the Elijah Smith Elementary School. He has been described as a plain-spoken man of wisdom and dedication, with a modesty that made him approachable by anyone.[39]

GERTIE TOM 1927–

Gertie Tom was born in 1927 at Big Salmon on the Yukon River, living there until 1948 with her parents, Jim and Jessie Shorty, and her eight siblings. The family lived by hunting and gathering, trapping and working at wood camps. When the RCMP came to take the kids away to residential school, Gertie's mother told them to hide. Her dad told the policeman, "If you put me in jail, you've got to feed my nine kids." The policeman left without the kids, so Gertie never attended residential school.[40]

In her childhood, Tom learned many of the skills that would support her later in life. She learned to sew from her mother, who insisted that she undo and then redo any part that she got wrong—good practice in learning to do things properly. Like other local kids, she hunted squirrels and prepared the pelts, selling them for five cents apiece. From her mother she learned to speak Northern Tutchone, and her family spoke English at the wood camps and when trading for food. Their annual trips to Whitehorse for supplies gave Tom a detailed knowledge of the region, including place names in both languages.

When the steamboats stopped running, Tom's family moved to Whitehorse, where her dad found work. They lived on the Fish Lake Road, then at Whiskey

Flats. Tom learned to read and write at Charles Camsell Hospital in Edmonton, where she was a patient in the early 1950s. When she returned home, she worked at the Yukon Laundry for 50 cents an hour. After she married, Tom and her husband bought a home in the Shipyards area. In 1982, they purchased a home in Porter Creek, where she still lives.

Tom joined the Yukon Indian Advancement Association in the 1950s. Members organized dances and craft shows and prepared newspaper reports. Later, she attended Yukon Native Brotherhood meetings at Skookum Jim Hall. In 1962, Tom was an executive member of the Whiskey Flats Residents Association. The group circulated a petition and then met with the Mayor and the Yukon Commissioner to develop plans for moving squatters' homes instead of destroying them. As a result, Tom's mother was able to move her house to Kwanlin Dün First Nation land near Marsh Lake.

Tom started work at CFWH in October 1961, broadcasting a one-hour show every Saturday for four years. People sent in requests for birthday and anniversary greetings. Tom played popular music records, translating song titles into Northern Tutchone.

In 1964, Tom went to Hobbema, Alberta, to take courses in first aid, public health and communicable diseases. Back in Whitehorse, she worked for the federal government's Public Health Services, visiting people at home to talk about health issues, and speaking Northern Tutchone to older people to explain directions for medicines and treatments. She gave up smoking to encourage kids to quit.

In the 1960s and 1970s, Gertie sold her beaded hats and mitts at Rendezvous craft shows, often winning prizes for her work. When the Yukon Native Products parka factory started up, Tom sat on the management committee with other community representatives. The factory ran for many years, closing when market conditions changed.

Tom worked at the Yukon Native Language Centre from 1977 to 1993. The centre began in the Whitehorse Elementary School basement and moved to its new Yukon College location in the late 1980s. Tom was one of the centre's founders, together with John Ritter, Julie Cruikshank and Carol Pettigrew. Tom taught Ritter how to speak her language; he taught her to read and write Northern Tutchone. Tom was the first speaker to help develop the written language, producing two books: *Èkeyi: Gyò Cho Chú: My Country, Big Salmon River* and *Dùts'um Edhó Ts'ètsi Yū Dän K'í: How to Tan Hides in the Native Way.*

Long-time resident Lucille Hunter lost her home to fire in 1961 when she was in her eighties.

Today, Gertie Tom remains active in the community, sewing and selling her beadwork, contributing to language workshops at the centre and participating in cultural events. She has achieved legendary status as an extraordinary woman of many careers.

LUCILLE HUNTER 1878–1972

Lucille Hunter was one of a very few African-Americans who came to the Yukon during the gold rush, travelling up the Stikine Trail in the fall of 1897 with her husband, Charles. Both Hunters were originally from the United States. Nineteen-year-old Lucille was pregnant when they set out for the goldfields, and in December she had a daughter and named her Teslin, after the lake where she was born. The family continued to the Klondike, where they staked several claims on Bonanza Creek. The Hunters worked their claims together for years and later acquired silver claims in the Mayo district as well. After Charles died suddenly in 1939, Lucille walked to Mayo and back to do the required work to keep all the claims in good standing. By then she was also caring for her grandson, Buster, as her daughter had died some years earlier.

Lucille and Buster moved to Whitehorse in 1942, where she operated a laundry on Wood Street, with Buster making the deliveries around town. When Buster left for southern B.C. a few years later, Lucille stayed on alone in Whitehorse, moving to a tiny house on Strickland and Eighth Avenue. There, she often held court, visited by photographers and reporters, as her legendary past became known beyond the Yukon. Her eyesight deteriorated as she reached her eighties; neighbours and friends kept a constant lookout, always worried that her heavy cigarette-smoking would cause disaster in the house, which was filled with newspapers and other hazards. In 1961, firefighters rushed to her home and rescued her from flames that had engulfed the building. Her clothes were already on fire.

Friends looked after her in a small apartment for a few years afterwards. As she approached her ninetieth birthday, she moved to Whitehorse Hospital, where she continued to receive visitors. The Yukon Order of Pioneers gave her an honorary membership in 1970—an extraordinary distinction, usually reserved for men only—recognizing her perseverance as a miner and long-time resident of the Yukon. Lucille Hunter was 93 when she passed away in the hospital in 1972.[41]

ROLF HOUGEN 1928–

Rolf Hougen arrived in Whitehorse in 1944, at the age of 15. His parents had moved north from their B.C. farm to take over a store started by his older brother, who planned to enlist in the armed forces. The teenaged Rolf was already a hard worker, an experienced entrepreneur and a social organizer of boundless ambition and optimism. He was one of the founders of the influential Young People's Association, and as a talented amateur photographer, he went on to document the organization's many activities as well as other happenings in his adopted hometown.

Rolf and Margaret Hougen at the Yukon Sourdough Rendezvous, 1998.

After high school, Hougen built his family's small variety store into the Yukon's largest department store. Hougen's became known for its creative promotions, including fashion shows, a Mexican "fiesta" with an imported mariachi band, and most importantly, the Santa Train—an annual highlight in the life of every Whitehorse child. He branched out into other business ventures as well, including automobile dealerships, a finance company and various communication enterprises.

Hougen was instrumental in bringing television to Whitehorse with his support of the cable company WHTV. In 1969, he founded the city's first commercial radio station, CKRW, still a family-owned business. He and his associates moved onto the national stage with the founding of Cancom, which pioneered the concept of using satellite technology to deliver encrypted or "scrambled" television signals to remote areas all over Canada. This major enterprise required broadcast partners from across the country, months of negotiations, massive capital investment and the surmounting of many obstacles before it was finally launched in 1981. In delivering Canadian broadcast services to formerly neglected areas, Cancom was recognized as a force for cultural sovereignty and national unity. For his part in this accomplishment, Hougen was appointed Officer of the Order of Canada in 1987.

Rolf and Marg, his wife and partner in all his endeavours, have spent decades as volunteers, community-builders and champions of Yukon culture, history and heritage. Yukon Archives has been enriched by thousands of Hougen's photographs as well as the invaluable E.J. Hamacher photograph collection, which he salvaged and preserved. He led campaigns to save the *Casca* and the *Whitehorse* before the sternwheelers were lost to fire in 1974, and he worked to save the White Pass and Yukon Railway when it closed in the 1980s and was on the verge of being sold for scrap. Most recently, the Hougen family supported the Yukon Art Society's Arts Underground venture and the Hougen Heritage Gallery in the lower level of their former store.

The six Hougen children, all Whitehorse residents, were raised to share their parents' ethic of hard work, self-reliance and giving back to the community. Although they are retired, Rolf and Marg are still engaged with their various volunteer commitments and charitable activities, and with enjoying their family, which includes eighteen grandchildren.[42]

BOB AND RUSTY ERLAM 1916–2009 & 1920–

Rusty and Bob Erlam qualified in many people's minds as part of the Yukon's "Colourful Five Percent." In 1947, on a whim, they moved to Whitehorse with their two-year-old son, Paul. Housing was scarce, and initially they shared a two-bedroom shack with two other couples. They immediately embraced the frontier town's frenetic social scene, helping organize events and revelling in the can-do spirit of the North.

Bob was born in Edmonton, Alberta, and later moved to Calgary. In his early twenties, he joined the Canadian Army, serving as a dispatch rider in Sicily, mainland Italy and North Africa during World War II. Largely self-taught, he could fix anything. In Whitehorse, he worked as a handyman and operator at the Yukon Electrical Company and at the army diesel power plant. Patricia Doreen "Rusty" Metson was a Winnipeg-born redhead with verve and wit to match her husband's. She was an avid supporter of the Whitehorse Drama Club, appearing in numerous productions during the 1950s.

Bob and Rusty Erlam celebrating in Rendezvous style with champion musher Wilfred Charlie, ca. 1968.

The Erlams left the Yukon briefly in 1957, returning in 1960 ready for new adventures. Bob drew a cartoon lampooning a dispute between Yukon Electrical and a local resident, which he tacked to the door of the *Whitehorse Star*. Publisher Harry Boyle put it on the front page of the paper, launching Bob's journalism career. Both Erlams went to work for Boyle, taking over the operations in 1963, when the publisher went outside to law school. They bought the paper in 1967 and ran it with the help of a small and dedicated staff until 1977. Rusty Erlam was the writer of the family, working as staff reporter for many years. Son Paul took over for a brief period in 1977. The family sold a part-interest in the paper to two staff members, Jim Beebe and Jackie Pierce, in 1979. They sold their remaining interest to Pierce in 2002.

The *Star* was the perfect vehicle for Bob Erlam's many interests. He kept all the machinery of the paper running, often with imaginative use of duct tape. Erlam believed the role of a newspaper was to keep a critical eye on government, and he wrote occasional opinion pieces himself during the Yukon's feisty 1960s and 1970s. He was an avid photographer, never seen without a camera slung around his neck. Several of his images ran in national and international publications. He photographed virtually all the ordinary and many of the extraordinary people and events of the time—plane crashes and rescues, Robert Kennedy's ascent of the mountain named for his brother, elections, sports, arts and his ultimate passion, the dogsled races at Sourdough Rendezvous. Erlam often borrowed enough dogs to harness up a team himself; he loved to sprint behind the sled, and continued to do so right into his seventies. The Erlams were proud patrons of champion musher Wilfred Charlie, playfully changing the *Star*'s banner to read: "Sponsor of the fastest dog team in the Yukon."

The Erlams retired to southern B.C. in 1979, spending their later years travelling and visiting family and friends. Their visits to Whitehorse were always occasions for reminiscing about the city's wild past, and the Erlams contributed many a tall tale themselves. They were soulmates for 63 years until Bob passed away in 2009. Rusty still lives in southern B.C.[43]

WHITEHORSE MAYORS

1960–1979

THE DEMANDS ON City Council during the 1960s and 1970s were relentless—Whitehorse was booming and the municipal government had to keep pace. Huge infrastructure projects and new facilities had to be built to accommodate the rapidly expanding population within the city limits and the many suburban developments surrounding the core.

VIC WYLIE 1960–1961

Vic Wylie had served as Alderman for one term when he defeated three other candidates to become Mayor in 1960. From Newfoundland originally, and a lawyer by training, Wylie worked for the Yukon government in Dawson City as Legal Advisor, Assistant Commissioner and Administrator during the early 1950s, then moved to Whitehorse to practise law in 1952. He was appointed a justice of the peace and also served as a juvenile judge. A prominent Liberal, he had great energy and ambitions for the new capital city.

Initially Wylie proposed building a city hall and proper council chambers for meetings. He was soon mired in the difficult issues of the day—sewer and water, city boundary expansion and residential housing needs. Despite his concerted efforts to gain support for the plebiscite authorizing the city to purchase Lot 19 to provide land for squatters, voters rejected the idea. Wylie decided not to run again as Mayor, but he ran in the next federal election as a Liberal against Erik Nielsen, losing by 500 votes. He was rumoured to be among the top candidates to replace Gordon Cameron as Commissioner in 1966, but another former city Alderman, Jim Smith, was chosen instead.[44] Wylie continued to practise law in the city for several years, and then retired outside.

ED JACOBS 1962–1965

Ed Jacobs served as an Alderman for three years before he was acclaimed Mayor for two terms, from 1962 to 1965. Jacobs first arrived in Whitehorse in 1943, delivering airplane parts to Canadian Pacific Airlines as the first civilian to drive the Alaska Highway. A machinist by trade and an innovator extraordinaire, he was renowned for his ability to build and weld original machinery to suit

Mayor Vic Wylie (in light tan overcoat), taking oath of office with fellow council members in 1961.

any purpose. Besides his machine shop and welding business, Jacobs was a miner and an entrepreneur, setting up the first oxygen supply business in the city.

During Jacobs's first term, the city administration was revamped, with a manager hired to ensure Council had better support. Progress was made on many fronts as additional federal grants brought low-cost housing units, more residential lots and economic development. Federal centennial grants prompted planning for a city hall and numerous other projects.

After leaving office, Jacobs continued to develop his businesses, as well as contributing knowhow to community projects such as the pivoting mount for the DC-3 weather vane. In 2003, he was inducted into the Yukon Transportation Hall of Fame in recognition of his many accomplishments. He died in Whitehorse in 2007, aged 91, still a legend in the community.[45]

HOWARD FIRTH 1966–1968

Howard Firth had the distinction of being the only person to serve as Mayor of two capital cities in Canada, since he was Mayor of Dawson City before the capital moved to Whitehorse. Realizing that business opportunities in Dawson were evaporating, Firth moved his family and business to the new capital in 1954. It was a natural step for Firth to lend his business acumen to the fledgling city government as Alderman from 1962 to 1963. He ran as Mayor in 1966, serving two years in that office.

As Mayor, Firth oversaw several outstanding events in city history—the move of the SS *Klondike* to the new Rotary Park site, the opening of the first city hall and the expansion of city boundaries in the downtown core. At the time, Whitehorse had no meeting place sufficiently elegant for entertaining visiting dignitaries, so the Mayor's duties included hosting official functions with his wife, Nancy, at their home. Princess Alexandra was one of their many distinguished guests when she visited the city in 1967. Howard Firth left office in 1968 to spend more time on family and business interests. He retired in the city and died in 1977.[46]

ABOVE LEFT Whitehorse still lacked basic organization in the '60s. Mayor Ed Jacobs and Fireman Bill Horback proudly display house numbers established in 1964 to assist firefighters responding to emergencies.

ABOVE RIGHT Mayor Howard Firth opening the new City Hall, July 1, 1967.

BERT WYBREW 1969–1973

Bert Wybrew served as an Alderman for one year before being elected Mayor in 1969. A former car salesman, he arrived in the Yukon in the 1950s, working at various jobs, including manager of the bowling lanes in the Whitehorse Inn basement. Wybrew's true claim to fame, however, is as one of the pioneer radio and television broadcasters in Whitehorse, bringing perseverance and ingenuity to that fledgling field. Rolf Hougen employed Wybrew for many years as manager and broadcaster at CKRW and WHTV, recognizing his innate talents and commitment to the task.

During his years as Mayor, Wybrew participated in a number of stellar events, including the first Arctic Winter Games, in 1970. He also experienced controversy during his time in office, when five Aldermen resigned from Council in 1973 in a dispute with the Yukon Commissioner and the Executive Committee over a financial deal the Council had made to purchase some downtown lots. Territorial officials asserted that the city had exceeded its spending authority in making the purchase; the Aldermen disagreed and resigned in protest over the perceived territorial interference in municipal affairs. Under the Municipal Act, the Yukon Commissioner had the authority to appoint an Administrator to run the city until new elections could be held. Commissioner Smith did just that. In the elections that followed, Wybrew was re-elected as Mayor, along with some of the former Aldermen and several newcomers. Wybrew only served until December 1973 and did not run in the next election. He later retired to Vancouver, where he died in 2004.[47]

TOP Mayor Bert Wybrew at a sport event, ca. 1970.

BOTTOM Mayor Paul Lucier, ca. 1974.

PAUL LUCIER 1974–1975

Paul Lucier initially served as an Alderman from 1964 to 1965. He ran unsuccessfully for Mayor in 1966, and then returned as Alderman from 1970 to 1973. He was elected Mayor in 1974, serving one term before he was appointed the Yukon's first Senator.

Lucier came north as a nineteen-year-old from LaSalle, a francophone community near Windsor, Ontario. He worked on the ss *Klondike* in the final years of sternwheeler transport on the Yukon, then as a fireman, an ambulance driver, a mechanic and a businessman. He and his first wife, Annette, were active members of the congregation at Sacred Heart Cathedral and in the Yukon Family Services Association, fostering many children in their home for over a decade. Lucier was an avid outdoorsman, a boxing coach and a supporter of many community events.

As Mayor, Lucier led the Council through the beginning stages of the City of Whitehorse General Plan. He remained active in Yukon politics all his life, in particular supporting the settlement of land claims with aboriginal people. He served in the Senate until his death in 1999.[48]

IONE CHRISTENSEN 1976–1979

Mayor Ione Christensen, seen here when she was sworn in as Yukon Commissioner in 1979, was the first mayor to serve full time in the office.

Ione Christensen had never run for election before she became the Mayor of Whitehorse in 1975. Christensen had chaired the city planning board and she had also served as a justice of the peace and juvenile court judge for several years, giving her a good sense of administrative process as well as the many social issues confronting the city. She and her Council approved the City of Whitehorse General Plan in 1976, creating a firm foundation for future city budgets and projects. She won re-election and served part of a second term from 1977 to 1978.

Born in the Peace River area and moving with her parents G.I. and Martha Cameron to live at Fort Selkirk as a small child in the 1930s, Christensen became well known in Whitehorse and throughout the Yukon. Her maternal grandparents had lived in Dawson City, where her grandfather was actively involved in the raucous politics of his day. She was an obvious choice for Yukon Commissioner and was appointed in 1979; but when the federal government changed the terms of reference for the job to more closely resemble those of a Lieutenant Governor, Christensen was not interested in continuing in the position. She resigned and ran for the Liberals in the 1980 federal election, losing narrowly to Erik Nielsen. She worked in various positions, chaired several committees and was a director on the Petro-Canada Board before being appointed to the Senate in 2000. Although she retired in 2007, she remains active in numerous community organizations and is the chair of the Whitehorse History Book Society.[49]

9

NOTHING IS AS CERTAIN AS CHANGE

1980–2000

FACING Rita Chretien holds the crowd spellbound at the Yukon International Storytelling Festival at Rotary Park, ca. 1990.

ALTHOUGH YUKON RESIDENTS were very familiar with booms and busts, no one was prepared for the enormity or speed of the mining markets collapse in the 1980s. Recession in Asia and worldwide slowdowns caused a huge decrease in the demand for Yukon minerals, which carried high labour and transport costs. All the big mines shut down, along with several communities. Reductions followed in both business and government. Some people relocated to the capital to look for work rather than leaving the territory. Whitehorse faced enormous challenges in managing its huge municipal area with the rising costs and demand for services.

These realities required creative thinking about the future. Gone were overblown predictions of mega-pipelines, refineries and smelters. Tourism and government were the remaining economic drivers, hardly a sustainable recipe for stability or growth. But adversity led to ingenuity, and many small entrepreneurs seized the occasion to invent new livelihoods. Fresh attention was focussed on heritage, the environment, education and arts and culture.

Winds of change blew through the political landscape too. Altered perspectives brought a resolution to aboriginal land claims, along with the devolution of more federal powers to territorial and First Nations governments. Aboriginal participation in governance was enshrined in the Canadian Constitution, and Whitehorse and other municipalities explored more collaborative approaches to community issues with First Nations. Tourism grew, with niche markets celebrating the unique cultures and the spectacular landscape of the Yukon. When mining returned as a strong economic force, balanced this time by a broad-based regard for the environment, the people of Whitehorse were embracing an expanding multicultural identity with enthusiasm, savouring new world beats, tastes and vibes.[1]

CAPITAL DEVELOPMENT

The 1980s opened with mixed messages of caution and optimism. The *Whitehorse Star* suggested that a land claims settlement would be good for the economy. Mayor Don Branigan and others promoted sports, health and education initiatives, warning that the big mines, including Whitehorse Copper, were running out of ore.[2]

In 1981, Flo Whyard was elected Mayor. Whyard was well prepared to lead the city with her background as both a journalist and a former MLA and territorial cabinet minister, plus her zest for getting work done. She would need every skill in her arsenal, along with her contacts among territorial and federal political leaders, to tackle what lay ahead. Within a few short months, all of the major mines in the territory had shut down, followed by the closing of the White Pass Rail Division in 1982—dire times indeed.

Jobs were critical to retaining the city's population and sustaining local businesses. The Mayor and Councillors identified capital investments that could generate work. The Liberals were back in power in Ottawa, so former Mayors Paul Lucier, now Yukon's Senator, and Ione Christensen were important allies in accessing federal ministers. MP Erik Nielsen kept up the pressure for aid from the opposition benches.

Federal funding jump-started several projects to upgrade existing facilities and build new infrastructure. The Lions Pool received a complete makeover, including a new water treatment plant and change rooms, and extended its seasonal operations. The City acquired more administrative space with the renovation of the old Cassiar Building on Fourth Avenue and a later expansion of the city hall.

Don Branigan returned to the Mayor's office in 1984, going on to serve several terms. The City of Whitehorse General Plan was updated to set out a comprehensive vision for future development. New streetlights, repaving, sidewalk-widening and landscaping rejuvenated downtown streets. Project Main Street focussed attention on the business centre, combining heritage values and contemporary design for a vibrant new look. The waterfront was identified as a scenic historic anchor for the city's evolving trails and parkland,

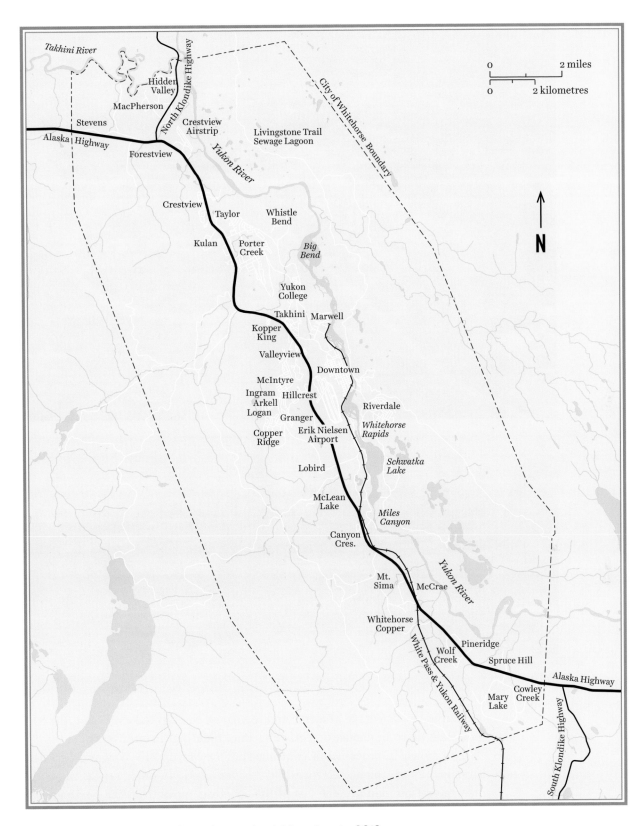

City of Whitehorse, current boundary and neighbourhoods, 2012

enhanced by projects to preserve and repurpose the White Pass Depot, the Old Fire Hall, the Roundhouse and other heritage buildings in later years.

Downtown improvements continued under Mayor Bill Weigand between 1991 and 1994. During Mayor Kathy Watson's time in office (1994–2000), a new relocation plan saw the last of the squatters move from the north end of town with financial compensation and options for alternative lots. While Ernie Bourassa held the Mayor's job, from 2000 to 2005, the city redeveloped the area

FACING TOP Hidden Valley, one of
the rural residential subdivisions,
seen from the air, 2010.

FACING BOTTOM Kwanlin Dün
First Nation Health Centre.

as Shipyards Park. It was designed for recreational use and public events, complete with a winter sliding hill that acquired the nickname "Ernie's Mountain."[3]

LIVING ON THE WILD SIDE

Residential developments in Whitehorse kept pace with downtown improvements. Riverdale, Porter Creek and Crestview filled with new homes through the 1980s and 1990s. Rural residential areas at Mary Lake, Canyon Crescent and MacPherson accommodated homeowners wanting minimal services and larger lots on which to garden or keep horses or dog teams. Beyond the city limits, settlement grew exponentially, stretching south to Marsh Lake, Tagish and Carcross, north to Lake Laberge, and west to Mendenhall, accommodating thousands of people. Those areas gradually developed their own fire protection, waste management and social amenities, as well as many small enterprises, thus contributing to regional prosperity.[4]

The economic slowdown in the early 1980s created the space and determination to resolve long-standing issues at the old Whitehorse Indian Village. Over 100 families still lived there in substandard conditions, surrounded by industrial activity and pollution. Chief Johnnie Smith and his Band Councillors worked with federal, territorial and municipal officials to develop the McIntyre subdivision as the new home of Kwanlin Dün First Nation (KDFN). Surveyed originally for the anticipated influx of pipeline workers in the 1970s, the subdivision had never been fully serviced. Completion of infrastructure and 50 modern houses allowed people to start moving from the old village in 1988. More homes, plus the KDFN administration building, the Nakwata Ku Potlatch House, the Nats'ekhi Health Centre and the Ashea Daycare Centre, added to the circle of community services in later years.[5]

The adjacent Granger, Logan, Arkell and Copper Ridge subdivisions grew in the 1990s to become the largest population segment within the city. In 1992, Elijah Smith Elementary School opened to serve KDFN and nearby families, followed by École Émilie-Tremblay, for French first-language students, in 1995. Traffic lights, sidewalks, bicycle paths and roundabouts contributed to the suburban ambience, but residents were reminded of the neighbouring wilderness when bears, moose, deer, coyotes and wolves occasionally strolled down their streets, or wildfires crept too close for comfort.

TOP Students and teachers celebrate *en français* at École Émilie-Tremblay located in Logan subdivision.

RIGHT A bear searches for snacks by overturning garbage bins in Granger subdivision, ca. 2010.

Despite the initial gloom of the 1980s, or perhaps because of it, people were brimful of ideas and ambitions. Political parties competed for votes with sophisticated platforms that incorporated many local initiatives. The Yukon Progressive Conservative Party (YPC) was firmly entrenched under territorial Government Leader Chris Pearson from 1978 to 1985. During the same period, the territorial Liberals won seats and the New Democratic Party (NDP) gained steadily at the polls. In 1985, the new YPC leader, Willard Phelps, called a spring election but lost to the NDP.

Tony Penikett led the new government, which included several First Nations cabinet members. This political change underscored significant demographic shifts throughout the territory, and especially in Whitehorse. The city's population of 20,000 included more than 2,000 civil servants in municipal, territorial, federal and First Nations positions. The NDP promoted ideas that appealed to a broad cross-section of newcomers and indigenous residents, including economic diversification, devolution and decentralization, with top priority given to the settlement of land claims.

Despite their political differences, Premier Penikett worked with Erik Nielsen, Deputy Prime Minister in the new Mulroney Progressive Conservative government, to reopen the Faro mine. Funds were secured for year-round maintenance of the Klondike Highway in order to truck ore to Skagway. Nielsen also shepherded plans for a modern airport terminal and a new federal building through Ottawa channels, transforming two more city landmarks.[6]

In 1986, the NDP government embarked on a unique project called Yukon 2000, inviting representatives from all communities to a year-long dialogue on the future. First Nations leaders, tourism operators, miners, trappers, artists, homemakers, health care workers, environmentalists, heritage volunteers, union leaders and civic officials worked together to generate ideas. There were many divergent views, but key points of agreement coalesced in the final reports: a desire for equitable opportunities across communities; a new emphasis on arts and culture; a renewed respect for wilderness, heritage and the environment; a recognition of the economic value of hunting and gathering; and support for agricultural activities, more advanced education programs and new technology infrastructure. Whitehorse stood to gain significantly, with funding subsequently awarded for several major projects. The Yukon 2000 report

Northern books on display at
Mac's Fireweed Books.

also identified rural community development as essential for sustaining a healthy economic base throughout the territory.[7]

A commitment to diversity and sustainability linked residents around the territory. Whitehorse was home to activist organizations such as the Yukon Conservation Society, the Canadian Parks and Wilderness Society and the Yukon Historical and Museums Association. First Nations leaders, long-time residents and newcomers joined together to promote long-range thinking about preserving environmental and heritage resources. It was a time of tremendous vitality in the volunteer sector, with many projects accomplished through concerted cooperative action.

The Yukon Historical and Museums Association worked with Mayor Whyard on heritage developments. The city purchased several lots on Third Avenue from the Finning company, with help from director Rolf Hougen, and the association restored the heritage buildings there with federal and territorial funding. Named LePage Park after pioneer woodcutter Aimé "Happy" LePage, the site provided a new downtown venue for storytelling, music and other cultural events. The society developed walking tours and produced a booklet on the heritage buildings of Whitehorse. A new society formed to develop the old rec centre into the new Yukon Transportation Museum, showcasing the territory's aviation history as well as other modes of transportation. Next door to that, the Yukon government developed the Beringia Centre, with exhibits on Yukon's paleontological and archaeological treasures.[8]

The Yukon Conservation Society (YCS) organized guided hikes along Miles Canyon, highlighting the flora and fauna of the area. YCS undertook numerous studies and campaigns to raise awareness about fragile northern ecosystems, promoting the establishment of a comprehensive protected areas strategy for the Yukon.[9]

Writers produced books of poetry, prose and history, while several small publishing houses and graphic designers brought a unique northern flavour to print sources. *The Lost Whole Moose Catalogue*, first produced in 1979 as a blend of serious and tongue-in-cheek guidance for Yukon living, was followed by second and third volumes featuring humorous and informational pieces by local authors. Some key organizers of the catalogue, including Max Fraser, Alison Reid, Mike Rice, Arnold Hedstrom, Wynne Krangle and Peter Long, established Lost Moose Publishing, operating out of their homes to produce Yukon titles including *The Kohklux Map*, *Law of the Yukon*, and *Yukon Quest: The 1,000-Mile Dog Sled Race through the Yukon and Alaska*. With financial backing from local businesses, Jim Robb published his first volume of *The Colourful Five Per Cent*, billed as a collection of stories about Yukon's most interesting characters—"read in all the better cabins in the Yukon." As the digital age progressed, websites flourished to send Whitehorse stories and images global.[10]

CAPTURING THE SPIRIT

The performing and visual arts in Whitehorse grew steadily in quality, quantity and diversity from the 1990s on. Arts supporters lobbied hard, and politicians and public servants responded with policies and resources for the development of cultural infrastructure. As the arts community grew stronger, the inventory of skilled technicians, arts administrators, producers and artistic directors increased. The opening of the brand-new Yukon Arts Centre in 1992 fulfilled the community's long-held dream of a first-rate performance hall and paved the way for an exciting new era in the performing arts.

By the late 1990s, the Yukon offered visiting artists the intimacy of a small community and a remote location combined with excellent presenting conditions: an artist's dream. The situation was similar for local artists. Community support also gave local artists the space and time to develop, with many sustaining at least a part-time career. Yukon artists developed a distinct voice that captured the essence of what it meant to live here. Other citizens threw themselves into the cultural melee as volunteers, board members and loyal audience members.

Storytelling had become a prominent part of the local scene. For many years, the Yukon International Storytelling Festival was the highlight of the Whitehorse summer. The festival got its start in 1988 as the Northern Storytelling Festival, founded by Tagish Elder Angela Sidney, storyteller Louise Profeit-LeBlanc and Anne Tayler, who was the executive director of the Yukon Arts

Council at the time. With land claims and self-government negotiations underway, an atmosphere of hope, pride and cultural renewal grew among Yukon First Nations people, and the storytelling festival captured that excitement. Any Elder who wanted to tell a story was welcomed onstage, and 5,000 people turned out to listen. "The involvement of the community, and their pride in their storytelling, was palpable," recalls Michele Emslie, producer of the inaugural festival.[11]

In the early years, the festival's focus was storytelling from the circumpolar North. There were some growing pains. Elders who had told stories only to small gatherings had to adjust to a stage, a microphone and a festival schedule that

Women of all ages create a button blanket at the Commissioner's Potlatch, ca. 1998.

couldn't accommodate stories that took hours to tell. Audiences had to learn the cultural context and develop new listening skills. In 1992, the festival was renamed the Yukon International Storytelling Festival and expanded to include countries beyond the circumpolar world, adding more dancing, theatre and music-accompanied storytelling to its program. By 1994, observed anthropologist Julie Cruikshank, Elders had grown comfortable with the festival context and were able to address two audiences: community members who had heard the stories before and "were present as knowledgeable and critical listeners… attentive to nuance," and audiences hearing the stories for the first time.[12] When 70-kilometre-an-hour (40-mile-an-hour) winds forced the relocation of the festival from Rotary Park to Yukon College that year, audience, artists and organizers rallied to move the whole shebang in less than two hours.

The waterfront continued to be a favourite cultural venue. In 1998, Yukon Commissioner Judy Gingell, a respected member of Kwanlin Dün First Nation, inaugurated the first Commissioner's Potlatch in Rotary Park on National Aboriginal Day—June 21. For a night and a day, the park was filled with drummers, artists, storytellers, dancers and First Nations citizens demonstrating traditional skills. The festivities ended with a community feast in the early evening, in generous Yukon First Nations style, setting a tradition for the potlatch for the next several years. Although its name changed to the Gathering of Traditions Potlatch when Gingell's tenure as Commissioner ended in 2000, the purpose of the celebration remained the same. The last potlatch was held in 2005, but the thread of continuity remained in the Skookum Jim Folklore Show (35 years old and counting), the Blue Feather Festival, the National Aboriginal Day celebrations, and events produced by the Society of Yukon Artists of Native Ancestry.[13]

Eric Epstein and Arlin McFarlane in a promotional photo for *Talley's Folly*, produced by Separate Reality Theatre Society.

ONSTAGE AND BEHIND THE CAMERA

In the mid to late 1980s, two professional theatre groups arrived on the scene in Whitehorse: Arlin McFarlane and Eric Epstein's Imaginary Force, later called Separate Reality, and Beth Mulloy and Sheila Langston's Nakai Players. For several years, these two companies produced plays and other events that toured the territory. In 1990, recognizing they would be stronger as a united force, they merged to become Nakai Theatre Ensemble, with a mandate to "develop a northern cultural expression through the literary and performing arts."[14]

From the start, Nakai focussed on encouraging northern playwrights. Its annual 24-hour playwriting contest was so successful that by the mid-1990s, Nakai's filing cabinets were stuffed with scripts. In 1996, artistic director Philip Adams produced New Theatre North, Nakai's first theatre festival, featuring readings, workshops and full productions in a format that served to both demystify and celebrate theatre.

In the early 2000s, artistic director Michael Clark introduced the annual Nakai Theatre/Comedy/Arts Festival and Nakai for Kids, bringing in comics such as Brent Butt, Ron James and Don Burnstick. When artistic director David Skelton took over in 2007, the comedy festival morphed into the present-day Pivot Festival, emphasizing experimental work by local and visiting artists.

Nakai's Homegrown Festival continued to show-case new work by local playwrights. In 2012, Peter Jickling's play *Syphilis: A Love Story*, first performed at the Homegrown Festival, travelled to the Edmonton Fringe Festival, where it was a major hit.

There had been previous iterations of a film society in Whitehorse when the Yukon Film Society (YFS) incorporated in 1984 to provide an alternative to the mainstream work shown in the commercial theatres. When a friend alerted YFS programmer Andrew Connors in 2000 that the Whitehorse Public Library was de-accessioning a large collection of old films, including many National Film Board productions, he scooped the discarded material and two years later packaged archival and new Yukon films into a touring show called Picturing the Yukon, which became an annual event in Whitehorse and outlying communities.

In the 1990s and early 2000s, the Yukon was a hot destination for filmmakers and commercial agencies seeking wilderness and snow. The government established the Yukon Film Commission to encourage visiting productions and foster the local industry. The new Northern Film and Video Industry Association provided one-stop shopping for crews and equipment. Digital technology made filmmaking cheaper and more accessible, and YFS and the Dawson-based Klondike Institute of Art and Culture offered filmmaking workshops.

As the film industry grew, so did the number of local artists making films. In the late 1990s, YFS brought the Moving Pictures: Canadian Films on Tour festival to Whitehorse. From there it was a short step to the first Available Light Film Festival, featuring local and visiting films and filmmakers, including Zacharias Kunuk, who introduced his film *Atanarjuat: The Fast Runner*. By 2008, the festival had moved to the Yukon Arts Centre, a financial gamble that paid off. In 2012, more than 4,000 tickets to the festival were sold.

YFS celebrated the tenth anniversary of the Available Light Film Festival in 2012.

In the winter of 1980–81, the Yukon government contributed $900,000 towards the construction of the Mount McIntyre ski chalet for the FIS World Cup Final to be held that March. Service clubs raised another $300,000, and 400 volunteers worked alongside professional tradesmen in every aspect of construction.

The Whitehorse Cross-Country Ski Club struggled to operate the chalet, and by 1984, closure seemed imminent. The deterioration of the city's curling rinks solved the problem. The Takhini Curling Club, based at Takhini Recreation Centre, and the Whitehorse Club, playing in the Civic Centre, both needed to replace their aging facilities. In 1983, accepting the need to amalgamate, they started developing solutions. The new Mount McIntyre Recreation Association opened an eight-sheet curling facility at the south end of the chalet in January 1986.

Subsequent demolition of the Whitehorse Curling Club building left only the Lions Pool on the former Civic Centre site after the Jim Light Arena closed in 1984. The new Takhini Arena at the top of Two Mile Hill seated 1,500 people. The Civic Centre pool closed in October 2002, when a new Whitehorse Lions Aquatic Centre opened on Hamilton Boulevard, across the highway from Takhini Arena to the Mount McIntyre chalet, the first phase of a new sports multiplex, culminating in the Canada Games Centre.

Softball Yukon members tired of playing on the crushed granite fields at F.H. Collins and started planning in 1978 for a dedicated softball complex with grass fields. They identified a site on Range Road near Takhini Elementary School. Whitehorse won the right to host the 1983 Western Canadian Senior B Men's Fast Pitch Championship, on condition the complex was playable before the ceremonial first pitch—and it was. Since then the facility has hosted 34 western and national Canadian championships, plus two world championships in 2008 and 2012.

The Yukon Quest Sled Dog Race, run over 1,576 kilometres (985 miles) through the northern wilderness in the cold heart of winter, traces historical mail runs, traditional trading routes, active trapping trails and long-abandoned roads across three mountain ranges and along frozen rivers and creeks through two gold-rush mining areas between Fairbanks and Whitehorse. The start alternates between the two cities, with Whitehorse hosting in odd-numbered years.

Canada Games Centre.

The Quest is the longest non-motorized race on earth, 40 kilometres (25 miles) longer than its better-known Alaskan cousin, the Iditarod.

Over 30 years, almost 400 dog mushers and more than 5,500 dogs have completed the race. In 1984, Whitehorse musher Lorrina Mitchell was the first woman to finish the Quest. In 1995, she was the first and only woman to serve as race marshal. That year, Frank Turner became the first Whitehorse musher to win the Quest, setting a record for the Whitehorse-to-Fairbanks direction at ten days, sixteen hours and twenty minutes—a record that stood for eleven years. Hans Gatt of Whitehorse was the first three-time champion, coming first in 2002, 2003 and 2004. Alaska's Lance Mackey is the only musher to have won both the Quest and Iditarod in the same year, accomplishing that feat in both 2008 and 2009.[15]

A HOME FOR *LA FRANCOPHONIE*

The 1980s and 1990s were a time of contentious debates over identity throughout Canada as Quebec reconsidered its place in the country. Those currents rippled through the Yukon too. In 1982, Whitehorse resident Daniel St. Jean appealed convictions for two speeding tickets on the grounds that the

The Centre de la francophonie in Whitehorse, ca. 1998.

documents were printed only in English. St. Jean believed he was entitled to legal proceedings in his first language by the Canadian Charter of Rights and Freedoms, arguing the territory was still legally under federal jurisdiction.

A complicated series of court rulings, appeals and proposed federal legislation to impose Canada's two official languages on the territory resulted in frustration on all sides. Many residents were puzzled by this development, with some vehemently opposed to the Territory being designated bilingual and others concerned about the status of aboriginal languages, but many understood the desire and the historic rights of francophone Canadians to operate in their language no matter where they lived. Finally a landmark agreement in 1988 led the Yukon government to pass an act guaranteeing the right to use English, French, or a Yukon aboriginal language in the Legislative Assembly, the publication of legislation in English and French, the right to use English or French in Yukon courts and to obtain services in French from government. The federal government in turn provided millions of dollars to the Territory to extend the recognition of aboriginal languages and French, and the provision of French language services.[16]

Stimulated by these events, the Association franco-yukonnaise (L'afy) organized in 1982 to protect and promote language, identity and culture. L'afy initially operated out of two small houses on Strickland Street, developing services for Whitehorse and rural residents that included *L'Aurore Boréale* newspaper, events with local and visiting artists, Les EssentiElles women's group, employment services, literacy programs, children's activities and much more. In 2001, L'afy opened a new Centre de la francophonie with great jubilation, establishing a permanent home for the community after more than a century of contributions to the Yukon.[17]

YUKON COLLEGE

By far the most ambitious project launched in the 1980s was a new community college on the bluffs above the city. The Yukon Vocational and Technical Training Centre had achieved enormous success over two decades at its Riverdale campus, adding university courses and teacher training in the late 1970s. In 1983, the Yukon government passed the College Act, under which the institution was renamed Yukon College and a framework was established for post-secondary education with a network of community campuses. Planning began for a new Whitehorse campus, budgeted at more than $30-million.

Construction proceeded over three years on state-of-the-art industrial shops for the mechanical, electrical and building trades, along with first aid and mine and workplace safety programs. Another wing for expanded arts and science programs allowed students to complete two years of study and then transfer to outside universities. Culinary arts, practical nursing, homecare, developmental studies, administrative and computer science programs added more options. A library supported all the programs, and residences were built for single students and those with families. The Yukon Native Language Centre relocated from Whitehorse Elementary School to a space purpose-built for the study of Yukon aboriginal languages.

Tagish Elder Angela Sidney led the official opening ceremonies for the college in October

Southern Tutchone workshop at Yukon Native Language Centre. Elders Irene MacIntosh Smith and Marge Jackson, first and second from left, ca. 2005.

THE STORY OF AYAMDIGUT

Elders George Dawson, Annie Ned and Angela Sidney participated in official opening ceremonies for the new Ayamdigut Campus of Yukon College in 1988. In background are Yukon MP Audrey McLaughlin, Father Jean-Paul Tanguay, unidentified woman and Commissioner Ken McKinnon.

ANGELA SIDNEY was asked to give the new Yukon College campus a First Nation name. She chose a Tlingit phrase: "Ay am da goot," translated as "She got up and went," which was shortened into the name "Ayamdigut." The name referred to the move of the college from its former downtown location up to the bluffs overlooking Whitehorse.

At the official opening, Sidney performed a prized Deisheetaan song, originally sung by Kaax̱'achgóok, a Coastal Tlingit hunter. Long ago, Kaax̱'achgóok became lost in a storm while seal-hunting with his nephews on the ocean. The party's canoes washed up onshore far from home; the men spent a whole winter surviving on an unknown island. When the sun returned in spring, Kaax̱'achgóok used sticks to chart its course in the sand in order to gain his bearings and plot a route to take them home. His kin were overjoyed at the return of their relatives, for whom they had already held a potlatch, believing them to have perished at sea. In return, Kaax̱'achgóok gave a potlatch and sang the songs he had made up during the long, lonely winter. One song told how "the sun came up and saved people," and how Kaax̱'achgóok "gave up hope and then I dreamed I was home." Sidney explained her choice of song for the occasion: "The reason I sang this song is because that Yukon College is going to be like a Sun for these students. Instead of going to Vancouver, or Victoria, they are going to be able to stay here and go to school here. We're not going to lose our kids anymore."[18]

1988. She bestowed the name Ayamdigut on the new campus, joining Elders George Dawson and Annie Ned to sing and drum for hundreds of well-wishers. Yukon Education Minister Piers McDonald acknowledged the significance of the new college, saying it would allow Yukon students to study close to the vital supports of home and community while gaining skills to participate in developing the Yukon's future.[19]

The college's site, Yukon Place, quickly became a cultural hot spot for the city, enhanced by the new Yukon Archives and the Yukon Arts Centre in 1990. Its large multi-purpose gym, with a capacity to hold 900 people, was a major addition to the city's recreational facilities.[20]

SETTLING LAND CLAIMS

Nothing signified change in the Yukon more profoundly than the settlement of aboriginal land claims. Difficult negotiations throughout the 1980s followed leadership changes in First Nations, federal and territorial governments. Council for Yukon Indians Chair Harry Allen and recent law graduates Dave Joe and Mike Smith worked with various federal and territorial negotiators to craft an Agreement in Principle (AIP) in 1984, but it was rejected by some First Nations communities over concerns about self-government and other issues.

In 1985, negotiators started over to address these concerns. The result was an Umbrella Final Agreement (UFA) signed in 1990 by CYI Chair Mike Smith, Premier Tony Penikett and DIAND Minister Pierre Cadieux.[21] The UFA served as a framework for model final and self-government agreements finalized in 1991, which established basic rights and authority for all self-governing Yukon First Nations. In May 1993, CYI Chair Judy Gingell signed the completed UFA at a public ceremony in Whitehorse, along with the Chiefs of Champagne and Aishihik, Na-cho Nyak Dun, Teslin Tlingit Council and Vuntut Gwitchin First Nations, the first four to ratify their final and self-government agreements. Yukon First Nations celebrated along with thousands of other residents. Together, Yukon citizens had made history with the first comprehensive modern treaties negotiated in Canada.[22]

Many difficult issues faced the First Nations still working on their agreements, especially the Kwanlin Dün First Nation (KDFN) and the Ta'an Kwäch'än Council (TKC). Their traditional lands and resources were located in the densely populated and developed urban areas of the Whitehorse valley, and the two

CYI Chair Judy Gingell celebrates the signing of the Umbrella Final Agreement on May 29, 1993 with Government Leader John Osta-shek (left), INAC Minister Tom Siddon (right), and Na-Cho Nyak Dun Chief Robert Hager (seated).

groups also had to reach agreement on recognition of the TKC as a new First Nation representing Lake Laberge families. The Ta'an Kwäch'än wished to affirm their separate identity after being arbitrarily amalgamated into the Whitehorse Indian Band by the Canadian government in 1956.

The CYI recognized the TKC as a separate nation in 1987. The federal government followed suit in 1998. For the next four years, negotiators led by Hereditary Chief Glen Grady and Council Chair John Burdek worked to achieve the TKC Final Agreement. It was signed in 2002, covering lands and financial compensation. In accordance with its constitution, the TKC is governed by a general assembly, board of directors, Elders council, youth council and judicial council, each with defined roles and responsibilities. Citizens elect a Chief and Deputy Chief every three years.

Today, the TKC owns and operates an administration building in Whitehorse, with cultural facilities at Helen's Fish Camp, on the west bank of Upper Laberge. The First Nation invests in various enterprises to generate capital from its original settlement monies. Its different departments address members' health and social needs, as well as overseeing research and the commemoration of heritage sites, events and important people. The TKC also sponsors a dance group, language lessons, a sewing circle and culture camps to promote and pass on the traditional knowledge of Elders to future generations.[23]

Kwanlin Dün First Nation reached its final agreements in 2005. KDFN has the largest, most diverse membership of any Yukon First Nation; many of its citizens originated in other communities but have long-standing affiliations

ABOVE Signing ceremony for the Ta'an Kwäch'än Council (TKC) Final Agreement, 2002. L-R TKC Chair John Burdek, INAC Minister Robert Nault, TKC Hereditary Chief Glen Grady, Yukon Premier Pat Duncan, with TKC Elder Kathleen Jones seated in back and drummer Linda Harvey at right.

LEFT INAC Minister Andy Scott, Chief Mike Smith and Premier Dennis Fentie at signing of KDFN Final Agreement, 2005.

with the former Whitehorse Indian Band. The final agreement recognizes the First Nation's ancient association with the Yukon River, along with the special circumstances arising from the location of the Yukon's capital and economic centre on traditional lands. In addition to settlement money and lands, the agreement covered protection for heritage sites, construction of a cultural centre on the Whitehorse waterfront, and Special Management Areas at Kusawa Park and the Lewes Marsh Habitat Protection Area.

The new government is structured to respect KDFN culture and to deliver appropriate programs for the health, wellness and prosperity of the people. A Chief and seven Councillors serve as elected leaders, supported by the Elders council, youth council and judicial council, with program and administrative support delivered by various departments.

At the official signing ceremony for the agreements, KDFN Chief Mike Smith acknowledged the huge changes in the transition from band status under the Indian Act to self-governing First Nation: "[Our] people have made the choice to take responsibility for our future. We look forward at this time to pass on our legacy to future generations. We are marking a new beginning for our people in economic prosperity, cultural strength and our rights under the law, which will be accepted and respected by other governments."[24]

CARING FOR PEOPLE OF ALL AGES

For decades, most non-native Yukoners had retired outside to escape the high costs and the cold climate. By the 1980s, though, more retirees were electing to stay in Whitehorse, where they had raised their families, made friends and enjoyed the comfortable ambience of a small city. Affordable, safe housing was a critical concern, as Macaulay Lodge and various seniors' apartments and housing units built in the 1960s and 1970s were full to overflowing. Seniors lobbied successfully for the construction of Closeleigh Manor, a downtown apartment building next to the waterfront, which opened in 1987.

Seniors had organized the Golden Age Society in 1976 and the Yukon Council on Aging in 1978 to lobby for improved services, access to facilities, and recognition of the contributions made by Elders and Seniors. Initially, a small house on Wood Street served as headquarters, with space for games, social events and meetings. In 1997, the Golden Age Society received a grant from the territorial government to purchase space in the new Sport Yukon building on the site of the former Jim Light Arena, where it hosts potluck suppers, card games, health clinics and other activities for a keen and active group of several hundred Seniors and Elders, mostly from Whitehorse. The Yukon Council on Aging rents a small adjacent office from the society; members produce a newsletter and organize initiatives to address ongoing issues related to aging in the Yukon.

As land claims negotiations progressed in the 1980s, the federal and territorial governments negotiated the devolution of more programs and responsibilities to the Yukon government. Health care had been a complicated issue for decades, especially when it came to funding and services for aboriginal people, though it had been resolved in part by the federal takeover of the hospital in the 1950s. By the late 1980s, the Yukon government was ready to resume responsibility for health care, and the federal government was anxious to make

Whitehorse has an active youth dance and urban arts scene. Breakdancers demonstrate their skills at a youth health workshop, Selkirk Street School, ca. 2010.

the transfer, but First Nations people wanted assurances that their needs would be met. Negotiations continued for several years, resulting in a phased process of redevelopment for the Whitehorse General Hospital (WGH), including specialized food and care services for aboriginal people, and a Healing Room open to all. For oversight of these programs, the position of Director of First Nations Health Programs was established.

The Hospital Act, passed in 1989, established the Yukon Hospital Corporation, with an arms-length board of trustees, including First Nations members and a First Nations health committee. The Thomson Centre for continuing care was built next to the hospital, opening in 1992. All WGH operations were transferred to the board in 1993, and multi-stage construction of new facilities began the following year, with all departments moved into new or renovated facilities by 1997. The new facility has over 350 staff, 49 in-patient beds, 10 bassinets for newborns, 10 surgical day care beds, an emergency department and several operating suites. In 2000, Copper Ridge Place opened in the newly developed subdivision on the west side of the Alaska Highway. Thomson Centre underwent extensive renovations to house a physiotherapy clinic and other therapeutic services.[25]

Before the 1980s, families with special-needs children were often compelled to move outside to access the appropriate supports. So, early in that decade, parents and local service clubs spearheaded a campaign to establish the Child Development Centre (CDC). From humble beginnings, the CDC grew to a full-fledged program funded by the Yukon government, operating out of the former Vocational School, which had been redeveloped as the Education Building in 1989. The CDC staff now includes physiotherapists, speech therapists and others

Volunteers stock shelves at the Whitehorse Food Bank.

helping children reach their full potential.[26]

Active programs for youth had been the focus of the Boys and Girls Club of Yukon since it was founded in an old warehouse on Third Avenue in the late 1970s. Today, it operates a large, bright facility in the former Pepsi bottling plant, complete with an indoor skateboard park and supported by significant contributions from many Whitehorse businesses. The Bringing Youth Towards Equality group (BYTE), established in the 1990s, gives older youth a voice on issues affecting them. BYTE sponsors an annual Battle of the Bands contest and, together with the Yukon government's Youth Directorate, organizes workshops for young people year round.[27]

Despite a growing economy, some Whitehorse people still experienced poverty and homelessness. Many new associations emerged to augment the decades-old support of service clubs. The Outreach Van was started as a partnership between several non-profit and First Nations groups, coordinated by Many Rivers (formerly the Yukon Family Services Association). The van travels the streets of downtown Whitehorse six nights a week, providing basic food, clothing and medical care to marginalized people. The United Way Society of the Yukon was founded in 1995 to raise funds for charitable causes. The Whitehorse Food Bank opened in 2008 to help people on low incomes. The Salvation Army has operated a men's shelter downtown for more than two decades.

A small women's transition home was established in Whitehorse in 1980 to assist women and children who were leaving abusive relationships. It was soon apparent that more space was desperately needed, and a larger facility opened downtown in 1992, named Kaushee's Place after the late Emma (Kaushee) Harris, a Tlingit mother of seven from Atlin who was one of the Yukon's first advocates for a safe home for women. The home is run by the Yukon Women's Transition Home Society, along with an apartment building which opened in 2013, named Betty's Haven after long-time staff member and Gwich'in Elder Betty Sjodin. Other programs are offered by the Victoria Faulkner Women's Centre, founded over 30 years ago to facilitate access to supports and services and provide a safe, welcoming meeting space. The centre was named for a legendary Yukon resident who served as secretary to eight Territorial Commissioners, first in Dawson and then in Whitehorse, and was a founding member of the Whitehorse Business and Professional Women's Association in the 1950s. The Whitehorse Aboriginal Women's Circle was founded as a non-profit society in 2003 to help aboriginal women meet new friends and access culturally appropriate education, health and justice services.[28]

The Fetal Alcohol Syndrome Society of the Yukon formed in the 1990s and is dedicated to the prevention of FASD and fostering an inclusive and supportive community. The Yukon Council on disABILITY organized in 1998 to offer specialized work opportunities and advocacy for persons living with disabilities. Blood Ties Four Directions was established in the 1990s to assist people dealing with AIDS and related issues. At their cosy facility on Hawkins Street, the Second Opinion Society developed programs for emotional wellness and provided education, information, support and advocacy on mental health issues and alternative healing. Many more groups contributed to the well-being of residents, with thousands of volunteers devoting time and energy to make Whitehorse a safe and caring community.[29]

THE WHITEHORSE AIRPORT TODAY

In 1984, the Canadian Pacific Airlines hangar on the east side of the airport fell victim to arson. All scheduled and charter air services now resided on the west side, where the three big wartime hangars had also disappeared, one by demolition and two by fire. A dozen smaller hangars, a modern control tower and a state-of-the-art air terminal building now dominate the landscape. From its own modern hangar, Alkan Air provides year-round up-to-date medevac services to the major centres outside. Several fixed-wing and helicopter charter companies continue to serve the bush-flying needs of mineral exploration companies, government departments and outfitters. The Yukon Forestry air tanker base, the RCMP Air Division, three aircraft maintenance shops and dozens of private aircraft complete the mosaic on the west side.

Through a series of name and owner changes since the 1970s, the former Canadian Pacific Airlines service has evolved into that of Air Canada. Dozens of other scheduled and charter air services have sprouted up over the years, only to fold their wings and disappear. Air North, a company born and bred at the

TOP Air North and Air Canada planes in front of Erik Nielsen International Airport, Whitehorse, ca. 2010.

BOTTOM On September 11, 2001, two Korean Air 747 planes were forced to land at Whitehorse after confusion in communications led to concerns that the planes may have been hijacked.

Whitehorse Airport, began as a flight-training school and single-plane charter service. In 2000, the Vuntut Gwitchin First Nation purchased a 49 per cent interest in the company, which later expanded to operate a daily jet service to points outside as well as to northern Yukon communities.

From the earliest flights in August 1920, the Whitehorse airfield had played a role on the world stage. On September 11, 2001, with the sudden shutdown of all United States airspace, two Korean Air Boeing 747 jumbo jets were diverted to Whitehorse, awaiting clearance to continue their journeys. In 1999, the German airline Condor began non-stop flights from Frankfurt direct to Whitehorse throughout the summer, carrying thousands of European tourists.

In the early 1990s, stewardship of the airport devolved from the federal Department of Transport to the Yukon government. In 2008, the government named the airport after veteran World War II bomber pilot Erik Nielsen, who by that time had served as the Yukon's MP for 29 years. Today a vibrant aviation industry continues to serve the Yukon.[30]

BUILDING FOR PERMANENCE

So many new facilities have been added to the Whitehorse landscape over the past three decades that newcomers and old timers alike are struck by the rich variety of recreational, cultural and lifestyle opportunities available in this small northern city. Governments at all levels have been generous in supporting both capital, and operations and maintenance costs.

LePage Park is a small downtown heritage enclave that preserves three historic homes. The buildings house volunteer organizations, and the park is the venue for the Arts in the Park programming through the summer months. The park is named in honour of the last family to live in the Donnenworth House. The LePages were well known for the string of wood camps they operated on the Yukon River. Their house was named after "Hobo Bill" Donnenworth, the original owner, who worked for White Pass. It is one of the few remaining buildings in Whitehorse that shows its origins as a tent, including the original canvas in the walls. It is now home to the Yukon Historical and Museums Association. The other two historic buildings are the Smith and Captain Martin Houses.

Heritage and cultural attractions have continued to grow over the past three decades, with expansions to the MacBride Museum in the 1980s and again in 2005, and upgraded exhibits at the Old Log Church, the Transportation

By 2012 events such as Canada Day celebrations had moved from Rotary Park to Shipyards Park, the old site of Moccasin Flats. The big-box stores of the Chilkoot Mall can be seen against the backdrop of the ancient and enduring clay cliffs.

Residents sort recyclables at Raven Recycling Centre, ca. 2010.

Museum and other heritage sites. In 2000, the Miles Canyon Historic Railway Society repurposed the old White Pass rails running along the waterfront to provide a scenic summertime trolley ride. The society also developed the Copperbelt Railway & Mining Museum, located on the Alaska Highway, and a small railway running through a nearby canyon. Improved interpretive signs and walkways along the riverfront, barrier-free trails and the new Frank Slim Building all contributed a modern look and feel to the downtown while showcasing the city's storied past and its beautiful natural setting.

Tourism was recognized increasingly as a Whitehorse economic mainstay. A new downtown Visitor Information Centre opened in 1996 near the Yukon River, housing a small theatre and exhibits. The YWCA building was redeveloped as a hotel in the 1980s, and the adjacent Lions Pool was refurbished as a convention centre after being decommissioned. Most downtown hotels have completed upgrades to meet rising visitor expectations. The Old Fire Hall on the waterfront offers a charming space for visual and performing arts. Attractions and other local businesses are promoted by the Whitehorse and Yukon Chambers of Commerce, the Yukon Convention Bureau, the Yukon Chamber of Mines, the Tourism Industry Association of the Yukon and the Yukon First Nations Tourism Association.

The Donnenworth and Smith
Houses flank the performance
stage at LePage Park, ca. 1990s.

The Yukon Justice Centre was completed in 1984 to house the courts, judges and Crown counsel offices as well as the Yukon Department of Justice. An imposing structure, it is clad in tile and features a four-storey atrium—rare features in the North. In 1985, it was renamed the Andrew A. Philipsen Law Centre, after the former Yukon Minister of Justice, who had died in a tragic accident after leaving office.

Formally named the Livingstone Trail Environmental Control Facility, the sewage lagoons went into operation in 1996. The system uses a combination of wind, natural sunlight and biological enzymes to break down sewage, which can sit in the lagoon for over a year before it is thoroughly decomposed.

The Elijah Smith Building was built in 1998 to replace the aging and cramped federal building and post office. Its completion marked the end of the central post office in Whitehorse; thereafter, postal service was handled through smaller outlets in retail facilities. The building retains one important feature of its predecessor: the mural by renowned artist Lilias Farley, which was removed from its original home and mounted in the Elijah Smith atrium in response to public concern that it might be destroyed.

Opened on January 20, 2011, the Public Safety Building at the top of Two Mile Hill provides an expanded capacity for the city's fire and emergency rescue services.

Starting in the late 1970s, Whitehorse became a regional retail hub, attracting shoppers from throughout the Yukon and well beyond. The opening of the

Dempster Highway to Inuvik in 1979 connected Northwest Territories residents along that corridor to the malls in the city. The Klondike Highway extension to Skagway opened year-round in 1986, bringing many people from coastal Alaska communities to Whitehorse stores, especially in times when the American dollar was worth more than the Canadian.

The growth in shopping malls and big-box stores stirred controversy in the late 1990s, when a large new development was proposed to the north of the downtown core. Many citizens rallied to support small enterprises, worried that big outside firms would destroy older local businesses. They denounced plans for the new Chilkoot Centre at City Council meetings, signed petitions asking politicians to stop the project and marched in protest at the site. Nevertheless, civic and territorial politicians decided to proceed with the multi-million-dollar development, believing it would contribute to long-term prosperity for the community. One of the last wetlands in town was levelled and drained to create space for a massive parking lot and clusters of mini-malls containing restaurants, specialty shops and several big-box stores. While some residents and visitors celebrated the proliferation of retail options, other citizens mourned the inevitable closures of numerous small businesses that followed.

Residents continue to discuss the future of city life, bringing environmental issues to the fore in every debate during municipal, territorial, First Nation and federal elections. The city opened a new landfill site in the mid-1970s and then reclaimed contaminated areas around its old Yukon River dumpsite. Despite substantial investments to develop the new dump, the growing economy and population were quickly generating more waste than the site could handle. Raven Recycling Society was started in 1989 by volunteers who presented compelling arguments for a rethink of waste management in the city. In 2009, City Council adopted comprehensive recycling initiatives to reduce landfill pollution, along with a sophisticated compost and garbage collection system.

By the time the new millennium dawned, the benefits of ingenuity and diversification were obvious, as demonstrated by a growing number of small and medium-sized businesses and by developments in the arts and cultural scene. Technology infrastructure was improving and expanding too, just in time for the next uptick in the economy. New mining prospects looked promising, with some pundits predicting a return to the prosperity of the 1960s and 1970s. Whitehorse residents had survived the worst of the economic downturns of the 1980s and the political uncertainties of the 1990s—it was time to move forward.

ANNIE AND JOHNNIE SMITH 1925- & 1922-2010

Johnnie Smith, the only son of Billy and Kitty Smith, was born in 1922 at the old village on the east shore of Marsh Lake, above the dam. His relatives included his uncle Tagish Charlie and his great-uncle Skookum Jim.

His father, Billy Smith, was raised in the Wheaton River area and later became a packer on the Chilkoot Trail; he also worked on the White Pass railroad. Billy was the first Kwanlin Dün Chief at the old Whitehorse Indian Village site along the Yukon River waterfront. Johnnie's mother, Kitty, was raised by Paddy Duncan at Shaw'ashe (Dalton Post) and became a renowned storyteller. Billy and Kitty lived at Carcross for much of their married life. When he was a young boy, Johnnie and his family moved to Teslin, where his father was gold mining, and returned to Whitehorse when he was fourteen. In those days, travel was by boat or on foot, using pack dogs in summer and sled dog teams in winter. Johnnie travelled extensively with his father, going as far as the Liard River country.

Johnnie married Annie Fred in the late 1940s. Her maternal grandfather, Chief Slim Jim, claimed traditional areas all around Marsh Lake. Her Tlingit father, Casey Fred, was from Angoon, and he had several cabins at the lake. During their early years together, Johnnie and Annie lived by trapping. They continued to trap and to raise their family on the land until the 1950s, when they moved to Whitehorse so that the children could go to school—Johnnie and Annie strongly believed in providing a broad education for their children, both on the land and in school.

Johnnie Smith served three terms as Kwanlin Dün Chief during the 1970s and 1980s. He was part of the delegation that delivered the historic land claim document *Together Today for Our Children Tomorrow* to Prime Minister Trudeau in 1973. He was also the architect of his First Nation's move from the Marwell Industrial Area to the McIntyre subdivision in the mid-1980s.

Johnnie Smith was a resilient and valued Elder who worked diligently to help Yukon First Nations people reclaim their culture. He believed that telling stories

Johnnie and Annie Smith cutting up a moose, ca. 1940s.

and teaching people about the land and his culture was very important work. He often shared his humorous side, which made his teachings memorable to a broad range of listeners. Together with Annie, he spent his final years mentoring children and youth, passing along traditions to be carried forward to future generations. Annie continues to harvest on the land with her family, to sew and to share her knowledge with the whole community.[31]

AUDREY McLAUGHLIN 1936–

Born in Dutton, Ontario, in 1936, Audrey McLaughlin studied by correspondence to earn her BA from the University of Western Ontario while she and her husband ran a mink farm near London. Later she worked as a teacher in Africa, then as a social worker in Toronto. She moved to Whitehorse in 1979 to work as a consultant. She was active in community groups in the city and was elected as Yukon's first NDP MP in a 1987 by-election. Known as an outspoken advocate for northern and women's issues, McLaughlin became national leader of the NDP in 1989 and served in that capacity until 1995. She resigned her House of Commons seat in 1997 to pursue international advocacy work, helping to organize the Grandmothers to Grandmothers Campaign for the Stephen Lewis Foundation, which assists families in Africa. McLaughlin has since served as president of Socialist International Women and as a special circumpolar affairs representative for the Yukon government. She was selected as an honorary pallbearer for Jack Layton's 2011 state funeral. Today, she remains active in various organizations from her home in Whitehorse.[32]

Yukon MP Audrey McLaughlin winning the leadership of the national New Democratic Party in Winnipeg, 1989.

Jeanne Beaudoin, long-time advocate for francophone culture in Whitehorse, 2007.

JEANNE BEAUDOIN 1958–

Jeanne Beaudoin was born in 1958 in Malartic, in northwestern Quebec. She came to the Yukon in 1982 to take a summer job as a tour guide for the Klondike historical sites in Dawson.

In 1984, Beaudoin started devoting her energy to the development of organizations, services and infrastructure for Yukon francophones. She worked as a volunteer host on the weekly francophone news and information program broadcast by CBC Radio throughout the Yukon. She also worked as a volunteer reporter for *L'Aurore Boréale.* She sat on the board of directors for the Association franco-yukonnaise, the Francophone Parents Society, the French daycare, the school council and the Francophone School Board. Beaudoin played a key role in the implementation of school governance for francophones, the creation of the Francophone School Board, and the revision of the Education Act. She was actively involved as well in the creation, development and construction of École Émilie-Tremblay, the French daycare, and the Centre de la francophonie.

Beaudoin has been recognized numerous times for her community involvement by the Association franco-yukonnaise, the Yukon government and Les EssentiElles. She received the Yukon Commissioner's Award in 1999 for her volunteer service. In 2012, Jeanne Beaudoin received the l'Ordre des francophones d'Amérique from the Quebec government's Conseil supérieur de la langue française (Superior Council of the French Language) for her involvement in maintaining and developing the French language in the Americas.[33]

WHITEHORSE MAYORS

1960–1979

WHITEHORSE MAYORS AND Councillors faced challenges on many fronts in the 1980s and 1990s as the Yukon economy seesawed up and down. An increasingly diverse and sophisticated population contributed to the growing opportunities for sustainable growth, but these changes generated rising expectations for new services and facilities—as well as a requirement for higher taxes to fund these amenities. Municipal politicians were on the front lines, responding to a rapidly changing socio-economic mosaic, collaborating with federal and First Nations colleagues, and meeting vital public needs for everyday living.

DON BRANIGAN 1979–1981; 1984–1991

Serving for more than a dozen years as Mayor, Don Branigan still holds the record for most terms in the office. He was Mayor from 1979 to 1981, and then again from 1984 to 1991. During that time, the city and the territory experienced severe economic upheavals, rebounding with massive infusions of federal and territorial funds. Branigan was a keen proponent of diversification as a means of insulating the city against the boom-bust cycles of the mining industry. He promoted health and recreation as well, believing that an active community is a healthy one.

Born in Alberta in 1933, Branigan graduated from the University of Alberta medical school in 1963, and then moved to the Yukon to begin his practice. He was often the centre of controversy for his practice of holistic and alternative therapies at his clinic in the Berrigan Cabins and at his pyramid healing centre in Atlin. As Mayor, Branigan suggested the novel approach of using a sonic blaster to treat sewage. He was a loyal friend and supporter to many First Nations people, who appreciated his concern and his respect for their traditional healing practices. A man of eclectic interests, he had business prospects in mining, real estate and numerous other ventures. He and his wife and children enjoyed Yukon outdoor life, especially at their ranch near Carcross. Branigan maintained a keen interest in community life up to the time of his death in 1999, at age 66.[34]

Dr. Don Branigan swearing oath of office as Mayor, 1979.

FLO WHYARD 1982–1983

Flo Whyard came to Whitehorse with her husband and family in 1955, just as the city was emerging from the post-war doldrums. Whyard had a journalism degree from the University of Western Ontario and had worked as a government information officer in Ottawa during the war. She plunged immediately into community activities, working as a freelance writer and broadcaster for CBC, then as editor of the *Whitehorse Star* for many years. Later she was a major contributor to the famed *Alaska Highway Milepost*. She and her husband, Jim, raised their three children in the city, enjoying all the excitements of the Yukon's vast outdoor spaces. An avid reader and student of history, Whyard became a close friend of Martha Louise Black, Yukon's first female MP, towards the end of Black's life, and produced an updated edition of Black's memoir, *My Ninety Years*.

Mayor Flo Whyard wearing her chain of office as mayor of Whitehorse.

Whyard entered territorial politics in the 1970s, serving as a member of the Yukon Legislative Assembly and on the Executive Committee. In 1982, she was elected Mayor of Whitehorse just as the economy tumbled and all major mines closed in the territory. Undaunted, Whyard worked with her Council, business leaders and her long-time friend, MP Erik Nielsen, to generate new economic opportunities in the city through federal and territorial programs.

Whyard lived a long and active life in the community and was recognized for her many contributions with an appointment to the Order of Canada and other honours. She died in Whitehorse in 2012, at the age of 95.[35]

BILL WEIGAND 1991–1994

Bill Weigand was born in 1928 at St. James, Manitoba, since absorbed into Winnipeg. After attending Britannia School, wartime opportunities beckoned. In 1943 he joined the civilian ground crew at the Commonwealth Air Training facility in Assiniboia, Saskatchewan. After the war he heard from a friend that the Canadian Army was hiring civilian fire fighters for the Northwest Highway System (NWHS) in the fast-growing town of Whitehorse. Eager to experience northern adventures, Weigand arrived in November 1946 to report for duty

Mayor Bill Weigand.

at Army Firehall No. 1, in one of the coldest winters on record. Temperatures plunged to minus-50 degrees Celsius (minus-60 Fahrenheit) and colder. With many homes heated with wood or oil stoves, the Army firehall was called often to supplement the volunteer town fire department. Weigand advanced through the firefighter ranks from 1946–65 becoming a fire inspector for NWHS, driving long rough miles on the Alaska Highway from Dawson Creek to Beaver Creek.

Meanwhile other interests blossomed and in 1965 he left the government. With his partner Mike Scott, he bought Murdoch's Gem Shop from George and Gladys Murdoch, building the business to include unique gifts and art, along with gold nugget jewelry designed by goldsmiths in the store, opening branches in Dawson City, Faro and Watson Lake. Those were exciting times as the Yukon was booming, with new mines, construction and tourism developments.

In 1968, Bill Weigand married Jerrine (Jeri) Buckler. Their blended family included six children. During the 1960s and 1970s, Bill and Jeri were active in many community organizations. Bill served as President of the Whitehorse Kiwanis Club and the Whitehorse Downtown Business Association, first Chair of the Yukon Liquor Board and Chair of the Yukon Utilities Board. After he sold his interest in Murdoch's he studied to become a realtor, joining son Darryl Weigand at RE/MAX in the 1990s.

In 1991, Bill Weigand was elected Mayor, his first foray into municipal politics. He brought many years of business acumen to the position and a strong desire to see city government move forward on sound planning principles. He and his Council faced huge issues and expenses, dealing with long-standing sewage treatment requirements, as well as upgrades to aging roads and other city infrastructure. Many projects were underway, the largest being the new sewage treatment centre and lagoons on the east side of the river. The Takhini subdivision was redeveloped to create infill in the former federal housing subdivision. Another issue was the location of the new Whitehorse Hospital, with Weigand and others promoting a new site above the town, in consideration of growing residential areas all along the Alaska Highway. In the end the hospital stayed at its Riverdale site.

A Yukon first, all senior political positions held by women. Commissioner Judy Gingell, MP Louise Hardy, Senator Ione Christensen, Mayor Kathy Watson and Premier Pat Duncan in 2000.

After Bill left office, he and Jeri were invited to do volunteer work in China for two years, assisting the municipal governments of Xining, Qinghai Province, and Beihai, Guangxi Province, as part of the Chinese government's Opening to the West policy. Through their work they promoted Yukon and Canadian ventures while learning about Chinese culture. They received several awards from the Chinese government for their contributions. In 2005, Bill and Jeri Weigand received the Commissioner's Award for Public Service. Upon their return to Canada in 1998, the Weigands left the Yukon after 50 years to settle in Vancouver. They retain close ties to family members and many friends in the Yukon.[36]

KATHY WATSON 1994–2000

Katherine Ann (née Shier) Watson was born in Saskatoon, Saskatchewan, in 1954 and grew up on a farm near Colonsay with her parents and four sisters. She attended school there until grade twelve. She moved to Whitehorse in 1976 on a mission of adventure and discovery, joining her sister Norma, who was already living here. She met and married Sam Watson, and together they started a small construction company. The Watsons had three children.

Kathy Watson volunteered in several community organizations and was elected as the first woman president of the Yukon Contractors Association. In 1991, she was elected to City Council. In the fall of 1994, she was elected Mayor; she was re-elected in 1997, serving until the fall of 2000, when she decided to pursue other interests and did not seek re-election. Her business background provided a solid foundation for tackling the many development issues arising during her term, as did her work as president of the Association of Yukon Communities and on the board of the Federation of Canadian Municipalities. Her focus as Mayor was on building economic opportunities in the city, taking advantage of Yukon anniversary celebrations—the Alaska Highway 50th, the Gold Rush 100th and others—to expand tourism infrastructure in the city. The early planning for the Canada Games Centre was underway, and difficult debates ensued over the location of a new sports complex. Major controversy also surrounded the development of new retail space north of downtown, with Watson and her Council deciding expansion was the right course for the city's future, against strong opposition from many citizens and some downtown businesses.

Watson moved to Edmonton after leaving the Mayor's post in 2000, where she has pursued a career in managing government relations as an advocate for non-profit organizations. She maintains close ties with family and friends in the north. As a former Yukoner, Watson still promotes Whitehorse as a great city for families and businesses, and continues to build links between Alberta and the Yukon.[37]

ERNIE BOURASSA 2000–2006

Ernie Bourassa was born in the old Whitehorse Hospital on Second Avenue in 1954. His parents met shortly after they arrived in Whitehorse in the early 1950s, where father Leo worked as a civilian for the Canadian Army on Alaska Highway maintenance and later as a rural ambulance supervisor for the Yukon government. Ernie's mother, Irma, was a teacher at the Lambert Street School, and later the librarian at Christ the King Elementary and Secondary Schools. Ernie Bourassa attended Christ the King as an elementary and high school student, finishing his senior grades at F.H. Collins. He pursued post-secondary studies at Royal Roads Military College, Simon Fraser University and the University of British Columbia, graduating with a Bachelor of Commerce degree in 1980. He returned to Whitehorse to work briefly for the Yukon Department of Finance, and then joined the Reed Stenhouse insurance brokers branch in Whitehorse, rising to the position of manager. In 1990, Bourassa became president and majority owner of Bourassa Richardson Insurance Brokers. Throughout these years, he was actively involved in many community organizations, serving on the boards of the Yukon Foundation, the Rendezvous Rotary Club, the Whitehorse Kiwanis Club and various sports groups.

As a long-time insurance agent and broker, Ernie Bourassa brought an in-depth knowledge of the city and a host of business contacts to the Mayor's position when he was elected in 2000. Waterfront development was a key focus during his two terms, with final steps taken to relocate the last squatters and to open up the Yukon River shoreline with walkways, heritage signposts and other attractions. The Millennium Trail linked the city to trails across Canada, bringing additional tourism interest and funds. Shipyards Park provided a new focus for community celebrations. Controversies provided anxious moments as well: a transit strike during the cold winter months of his first term, in 2000–01, created hardship for the public and difficult negotiations for the City. Later, a new anti-smoking by-law generated huge opposition from some residents and businesses, but was passed with support from a majority of citizens. Ernie Bourassa was keen to build new partnerships between the City, the Yukon government and First Nations governments, working on a variety of projects to enhance those opportunities, culminating in the opening of the Canada Games Centre and Athletes' Village, as well as the sale and transfer of waterfront lands to the Kwanlin Dün First Nation as part of a land claims settlement.

Mayor Ernie Bourassa.

After leaving civic politics, Bourassa served for a year as executive director of the Yukon Chamber of Commerce. Subsequently, he and his wife, Linda, moved to Kelowna to be close to their grandchildren. Today, he works part-time as a realtor in Whitehorse, spending winters with his family in B.C. and summers in the Yukon.[38]

BEV BUCKWAY 2006–2012

Bev Buckway was born at the old Whitehorse Hospital on Second Avenue in 1954. She attended early grades at Whitehorse Elementary School, and then moved with her parents to Beaver Creek, attending school there for several years while her father worked on the pipeline that ran between Fairbanks and Haines, Alaska. She went outside for one year to attend high school in Vancouver, then returned to Whitehorse to complete grades nine through twelve at F.H. Collins Secondary School.

Mayor Bev Buckway at the opening of the new Whistle Bend subdivision in 2011. This ambitious project is a partnership between the Yukon government and the City of Whitehorse.

After graduation, she studied agriculture at Fairview College and then went to barber school in Calgary, subsequently opening a barbershop at Grimshaw, in the Peace River country. After she had been in Alberta for five years, the Yukon called her home, and she returned to Whitehorse in 1979, owning and operating the Barbers II shop on Main Street for over two decades. She worked as executive director of the Yukon Council on DISABILITY from 2002 to 2003 and as manager of the Yukon Fish and Game Association from 2003 to 2004. She was active as a volunteer in numerous community organizations, including the Yukon Humane Society, the Crossroads addiction treatment centre, the Yukon Crisis Line, the Whitehorse Chamber of Commerce and the Whitehorse Rotary Club. An avid curler, she represented the Yukon at the Scott Tournament of Hearts; she also played volleyball at the Canada Winter Games and the Arctic Winter Games.

It was natural for Buckway to step into city politics after she sold her business in 2001. She was first elected as a Councillor in 2003, working to implement new policies on universal access and improved transit service. During her two terms as Mayor, Buckway led a concerted effort to develop more land for residential housing, unveiling the new Whistle Bend subdivision in 2012. She was a proud host as Whitehorse welcomed the athletes and spectators to the Canada Winter Games in 2007 and the Arctic Winter Games in 2012. She also served as president of the Association of Yukon Communities and served on the executive of the Federation of Canadian Municipalities, advocating for the Canadian government's implementation of the gas tax and long-term infrastructure plan for

the benefit of municipalities. The Canada Games Centre and the Public Safety Building were constructed during her terms in office.

Bev Buckway decided not to seek re-election in 2012. She returned to volunteer activities with Habitat for Humanity and the Vimy Heritage Housing Society while sitting on the Yukon Medical Council and pursuing a new career as a northern consultant. She received the Queen's Diamond Jubilee Medal in 2012 and the Hanseatic Award in 2013 for her work in municipal government and community development.[39]

DAN CURTIS 2012–

Current Whitehorse Mayor Dan Curtis was born and raised in Whitehorse, attending school here and then working for over twenty years as executive director of Skills Canada, an organization that supports technical and trades training for youth. In that capacity, he has travelled around the country and overseas promoting the Skills Canada program and its participants. He has also worked as a realtor and brings a broad knowledge of the community to the position of Mayor, his first elected office.[40]

Justice of the Peace and City Financial Services manager Valerie Anderson swears in new City Council. L–R: Valerie Anderson, Councillors Kirk Cameron, Mike Gladish, Betty Irwin, Mayor Dan Curtis, Councillors Jocelyn Curteanu, Dave Stockdale, John Streicker.

WHITEHORSE IN THE
NEW MILLENNIUM

HE SIGNING OF land claims agreements by the Ta'an Kwäch'än and Kwanlin Dün people ushered in a new era of confidence and collaboration between the First Nations, the City of Whitehorse, and the Yukon government. The exhilaration people felt at the signing ceremonies carried over to a series of spectacular events to mark the new millennium.

For years, local sports organizers had schemed about hosting the prestigious Canada Winter Games. Their dreams came true when Whitehorse won the bid for 2007. It was a rare opportunity to shine in the national spotlight, with thousands of athletes, performers, media and spectators converging on the city for two weeks of competition, cultural exchange and—best of all—celebration in true northern style. As the host city, Whitehorse had to build a world-class facility to accommodate pool, court and ice events. With federal, territorial and municipal funding, plus corporate sponsorship, the Canada Games Centre opened in 2005. At the time, it was the fourth-largest sports multiplex in Canada—a three-storey, 18,900-square-metre (203,000-square-foot) facility with three ice rinks, an indoor soccer field, a "flexihall," a fitness room, a physiotherapy clinic, meeting rooms, a running track and the Whitehorse Lions Aquatic Centre. As the largest single infrastructure project ever built in the city, it stands as a fitting testimonial to the dedication of sports enthusiasts, volunteers, business, government and community supporters over more than a century.[1]

This was the first time the Games were held north of 60. All fourteen Yukon First Nations joined together to host the Gathering of Northern Nations in a tent on the waterfront, showcasing Yukon First Nations culture and hospitality. The tent was warm and inviting, filled with the scent of spruce and smoky,

This rearing horse overlooks the city from the top of Two Mile Hill. It was created by Daphne Mennell together with welder Roger Poole using a variety of metal objects donated by the citizens of Whitehorse.

325

home-tanned hide. Artists and other community members demonstrated traditional arts and technology. Across the road, in another big tent, the Cultural Festival featured multicultural visual art, dance, theatre and music.[2]

Up the hill, Yukon College hosted the Athletes' Village. Two new residences, built for the Games, were later transformed into family units for students' and seniors' housing. With new attention focussed on the college and the North, more funds flowed in subsequent years to expand the Yukon Research Centre, supporting cold climate innovation, biodiversity monitoring, mine reclamation and other research programs to benefit northern residents. Yukon College began to plan for degree-granting status as Canada's foremost northern post-secondary institution.[3]

The talent and expertise developed in hosting the Canada Winter Games led to the next big dream for Yukon artists, performers and producers as the 2010 Vancouver Winter Olympics approached. The Yukon government sponsored a large cultural contingent to represent the territory at the Olympic and Paralympic ceremonies and performance venues. Katie Johnson and Charlene Alexander worked with the Council of Yukon First Nations to produce the Yukon First Nations 2010 troupe of artists, singers, dancers and drummers, who dazzled overflow crowds at the Aboriginal Pavilion and surrounding galleries.

Michele Emslie and Laurel Parry worked with non-aboriginal performers, who took the city by storm in venues from Whistler to GM Place and the myriad street venues.

Riding the wave of their Olympic successes, many performers found opportunities to extend their careers beyond the North. The Dakhká Khwáan Dancers travelled to Maori festivals in New Zealand the following year, while other performers toured in B.C. and beyond. In 2011, First Nations artists and performers launched the new Adäka Cultural Festival in tents on Front Street, with an art gallery and a gift shop in the Old Fire Hall. More than 8,000 people attended. In 2012, the festival moved to its new permanent home in the Kwanlin Dün Cultural Centre to present a vibrant program of traditional and contemporary events, with storytelling as just one of many offerings.[4]

A host of multicultural events blossomed in Whitehorse as the city continued to diversify, with new residents arriving from around the world. Whitehorse demographics had begun to change during and just after World War II, when many European immigrants came to rebuild their lives in a new land. Asian people arrived in increasing numbers in the following decades; some were Chinese and Japanese, attracted from Vancouver to work in restaurants and mine-catering businesses; others came from Vietnam as refugees in the late 1970s, and several South Asian families established businesses in the city. New residents from the Caribbean, Africa, South America and the Middle East have further diversified the city's culture in recent years.

The largest and fastest-growing group of newcomers originated in the Philippines, with a number of women arriving in the 1980s to work as nannies and caregivers. As the big new stores neared completion in 2000, managers struggled to find sufficient service staff. New immigration policies supplied

TOP Months of training and rehearsal culminate in high excitement onstage at the Yukon Arts Centre, just days before the Yukon First Nations 2010 contingents head to Vancouver to perform at the 2010 Olympics.

FACING BOTTOM Whitehorse thespian Al McLeod takes a flying leap during a performance of *Tales of a Lumberjack* by the Parka Ballet Company at the 2007 Canada Winter Games closing ceremonies.

the answer, with hundreds of Filipinos joining those who had arrived earlier. Today, the Filipino community has a newspaper, a grocery store and a strong social network. The Canadian-Filipino Association of the Yukon sponsors dances, Christmas parties, the Asian Heritage Festival and numerous services for its members. The savoury tastes of Filipino food, on offer at the association's annual Canada Day booth, quickly became a favourite of Whitehorse residents. The 2011 Census reported that Tagalog had the second-highest number of native speakers in Whitehorse among non-official languages.[5]

The 2012 municipal elections underscored the new cosmopolitan Whitehorse, with five candidates running for Mayor and eighteen for Council seats. There were First Nations, francophone, anglophone, South Asian and Filipino candidates. The new Council, led by Mayor Dan Curtis, included two women, with Filipina candidate Jocelyn Curteanu making history as the first woman of Southeast Asian ancestry elected as a Councillor.

Along with the benefits of all this development, residents must grapple with the many serious issues that arise from rapid growth. Affordable housing is still a major concern in Whitehorse, especially for young families. Housing prices are well beyond the means of many, and rental units are scarce. Many people are conscious of the irony in recent waterfront developments, as luxurious condos occupy the spaces where squatters once lived and from where they were displaced.[6] The Yukon Anti-Poverty Coalition, along with the Youth of Today Society, advocated for the establishment of a youth shelter, which was named Angel's Nest, after a young aboriginal woman who was murdered in the city. Those groups and many others offer support to people living without permanent shelter—a precarious situation in the extreme cold of a northern winter.

New condos on the waterfront, 2012.

Whitehorse continues to grow as a government town, with the Yukon taking over many former federal agencies to build a northern administration mirroring its provincial counterparts in roles and responsibilities, though still tied to federal authority under the Yukon Act. The Council for Yukon Indians adopted a new name as the Council of Yukon First Nations in 1995, and ten years later it moved to new offices on Second Avenue, where the leadership advocates on behalf of aboriginal people.[7] The City of Whitehorse is upgrading streets, sewer and water systems, along with developing residential capacity through rezoning, infill and new lots. Mayor Bev Buckway opened a massive new subdivision called Whistle Bend near Porter Creek in 2012, adding more than 100 new lots to the housing market.

Over the years, summers in Whitehorse and the region have grown busier; many new events—such as the Sunstroke Music Festival, started in 2005—offer jazz and contemporary electronica performances. In 2008, the Storytelling Festival was presented at the Yukon Arts Centre to an audience so small that some events had to be moved to the foyer; the board of directors decided it was time to take a breather and regroup.

The city's storied waterfront is the focus of ongoing development, with a mix of commercial, residential and public uses. Contemporary Whitehorse offers an amazing array of dining options. The "latte loop" stretches from Main Street to the malls and along the waterfront, with multiple trendy cafés serving delicious pastries, locally roasted coffees, exotic teas, and fusion foods combining tastes from around the world. Fine dining offers Mexican, Korean, Japanese, Chinese, Vietnamese, South Asian, Italian, French, and many other cuisines, sometimes featuring locally grown organic produce. Northern and ethnic culinary arts are

the focus of a new and growing tourism segment, providing opportunities for local chefs and businesses.

Ground was broken for the new Kwanlin Dün Cultural Centre on September 30, 2009. This landmark event marked the completion of land claims for the Kwanlin Dün people. The centre is designed to resemble a traditional longhouse and features conference rooms, an Elders' lounge, sacred space and an exhibition area. It also houses the new Whitehorse Public Library. Thousands joined the Kwanlin Dün people on the longest day in June 2012, when they came "back to the river," opening their spectacular new centre with a sacred fire and ancient songs, stories, drumming and dancing. The second annual Adäka Cultural Festival followed, along with the Sunstroke Festival, francophone celebrations, Canada Day, Discovery Day and Labour Day. All summer, the weekly Farmers' Market offered local produce, culminating in the Fall Harvest Fair.

As the winter of 2012–13 approached, a new symbol of peace arose beside the river, next to the landmark White Pass Depot. The Healing Totem—carved

by young artists at the Northern Cultural Expressions Society, led by master Tlingit carver Wayne Price, from Haines, Alaska—represents past struggles in residential schools, along with faith in recovery and reconciliation. Hundreds of residents and visitors from many nations joined the carvers to carry the immense pole step by slow step along Front Street to Main Street, their faces straining with the enormity of the burden. First Nations Elders, mothers, fathers and children, dressed in ceremonial regalia, came to honour the work of the carvers and to remember all those who were affected by residential school experiences. Thunderous drumming, tears, cheers and eagles soaring overhead accompanied the raising of the pole to its full magnificent height.[8]

A century after the gold rush created the town, and 60 years after municipal incorporation, Whitehorse had truly become a cosmopolitan city, celebrating its First Nations roots and welcoming the traditions of many newcomers—a peaceful home for all, a place where Wolf still visits on silent paws, and Raven soars above in clear blue skies.

FACING TOP First Nations people, non-aboriginal residents and visitors celebrated the official opening of Kwanlin Dün Cultural Centre on June 21, 2012. The fire pit and east-facing side of the building are viewed from across the river, with the centre's traditional Tlingit canoe and ceremonial paddle in the foreground.

FACING BOTTOM The Farmers' Market offers a wide variety of local produce every Thursday throughout the summer months in Shipyards Park.

ABOVE People of many nations carrying the Healing Pole to the Whitehorse waterfront, fall 2012.

Whitehorse in autumn, ca. 2006, looking northwest from the east bank of the river.

NOTES ON USAGE

GEOGRAPHY

The Yukon River at downtown Whitehorse flows from south (upriver) to north (downriver). Hence, many old-timers refer to going "down to Dawson" rather than "up north." Since the river twists and turns above and below the town, we found it easier to refer to riverside locations as "above" or "below" Whitehorse rather than pinpointing exact geographical directions. The town of Whitehorse was established on the west bank of the river. Since the original townsite was laid out as a simple grid, all streets run east-west, while avenues are aligned north-south.

Northerners tend to refer to every place south of the 60th parallel (the southern border of the northern territories) as "outside." So do we.

THE FIRST PEOPLES

We refer to the Yukon's first peoples as "aboriginal" or identify them by language group until Chapter 8, which covers the years 1961 to 1980. First Nations people began self-identifying as such during the land claims movement of the 1970s. The term "Indian" is used only in original names or quotes from other sources (for example, "Indian Agent," "Council for Yukon Indians").

WHITE HORSE/WHITEHORSE

The original name that newcomers gave to the hazardous waters below Miles Canyon was the White Horse Rapids. The settlement at the downriver end of Macaulay's tramway became known as White Horse Landing, after the rapids. The new townsite on the west side of the river was also named White Horse, but within a few years this had been condensed to Whitehorse. In an attempt to avoid confusion, we have referred to the first community as White Horse Landing and its replacement on the west side of the river as Whitehorse. It seems that once the town's name was condensed, so was the name of the rapids, which we call Whitehorse Rapids in the post-1900 period.

APPENDIX A

ABORIGINAL LEADERS IN THE WHITEHORSE AREA

FOR COUNTLESS generations, aboriginal people in the Whitehorse area lived according to their traditional ways, following leaders who demonstrated knowledge and skills in keeping their extended family safe and secure. Several groups of people, each with their own leaders, followed particular seasonal rounds at Tagish Lake, Marsh Lake, Lake Laberge and other areas, sometimes coming together briefly for summer celebrations or potlatches. Although the names of specific leaders are not identified, oral traditions indicate that women, as well as men, provided guidance to youth and kin through the passages of life and the time-tested ways of living in harmony with the land, animals, relatives and spirits around them.

As contact with non-aboriginal people expanded, new ideas of leadership developed, with the term "Chief" applied to the headmen most capable of dealing with traders, police and other government officials. Some men were acknowledged as Hereditary Chiefs because their older relatives had been leaders before them. The formal title of Chief was used after 1957, when the Whitehorse Indian Band was created by the federal government under provisions of the Indian Act. The new band governance amalgamated the aboriginal people of Marsh Lake, Lake Laberge and surrounding areas, with an elected Chief and council; however, it was some years before regular elections occurred. Leadership provisions changed again when the Ta'an Kwäch'än Council was created in 1987 to recognize the Lake Laberge people as a traditional group, designating the leader as Chair since the Council was not formally recognized as a band under the Indian Act. The signing of final agreements established the Ta'an Kwäch'än Council as a self-governing First Nation in 2000 and the Kwanlin Dün First Nation in 2005, with both groups deciding to use the term Chief for their elected leaders.

The following list is grouped in time periods denoting the changes in leadership through the years.

EARLY YEARS

Mundessa: Leader of Tàa'an Män (Lake Laberge) people in the late 1800s

Gunaatak' (Marsh Lake Jackie): Leader of the Marsh Lake people in the late 1800s

Kishwoot or Kashx̱óot (Jim Boss): Hereditary Chief and Leader of Tàa'an Män people from the 1890s to 1950

CHIEFS OF THE WHITEHORSE INDIAN BAND (AFTER 1957)

Billy Smith: 1957–1965
Scurvey Shorty: 1965–1967
Elijah Smith: 1967–1968
Andrew Clifford McLeod: 1968–1969
Johnnie E. Smith: 1969–1973; 1981–1988
Roy H. Sam: 1973–1981
Ann Smith: 1988–1990
Lena Johns: 1990–1996
Joe Jack: 1996–1999
Rick O'Brien: 1999–2002
Mike Smith: 2002–2005

CHIEFS OF THE KWANLIN DÜN FIRST NATION (AFTER 2005)

Mike Smith: 2005–2011
Rick O'Brien: 2011–

TA'AN KWÄCH'ÄN COUNCIL (1987–2002)

Glenn Grady: Hereditary Chief, 1987–
John Burdek: Chair, 1998–2002

CHIEFS OF THE TA'AN KWÄCH'ÄN COUNCIL (AS SELF-GOVERNING FIRST NATION AFTER 2002)

Ruth Massie: 2006–2009
Brenda Sam: 2009–2012
Kristina Kane: 2012–

APPENDIX B

WHITEHORSE MAYORS AND COUNCILLORS

MAYORS

H. Gordon Armstrong: 1950–1957
Gordon R. Cameron: 1958–1959
N.V.K. (Vic) Wylie: 1960–1961
E.J. (Ed) Jacobs: 1962–1965
Howard W. Firth: 1966–1968
A.J. (Bert) Wybrew: 1969–1973
J.W. Oliver (Administrator):
  July to September 1973*
Paul H. Lucier: 1974–1975
Ione J. Christensen: 1975–1979
Dr. D.W. (Don) Branigan: 1979–1981, 1984–1991
Florence E. Whyard: 1982–83
W.J. (Bill) Weigand: 1991–1994
Katherine Ann (Kathy) Watson: 1994–2000
Ernest J.R. (Ernie) Bourassa: 2000–2006
Beverly (Bev) Buckway: 2006–2012
Dan Curtis: 2012–

* On July 9, 1973, all five Aldermen resigned. This resulted in the appointment of an Administrator and an Advisory Committee, pursuant to the provisions of the municipal ordinance. September elections returned A.J. Wybrew to the Mayor's office.

COUNCILLORS

W.G. (Bill) Hamilton: 1950–1954
Sam McClimon: 1950–1951
James Norrington: 1950–1953
George Ryder: 1950
Ernest Lortie: 1951
T.G. Bain: 1952–1953
William L. (Bill) Drury: 1952–1957
Gordon R. Cameron: 1954–1957
O.P. Williams: 1954–1955
W. McLean: 1955
J.A. (Jim) Hanna: 1956–1958
J. Smith: 1956–1958
C.E. (Kip) Fisher: 1958
J.G. McCandless: 1958
N.V.K. (Vic) Wylie: 1958–1959
E.J. (Ed) Jacobs: 1959–1961
James W. Howatt: 1959–1960; 1962–1963;
  1971–1973
H.K. Law: 1959
C.J. Allen: 1960–1962
Norman S. Chamberlist: 1960–1961
William D. Taylor: 1960–1961
Howard W. Firth: 1962–1963
Jan A. Montgomery: 1962–1966; 1970–1971
K.E. Shortt: 1963
B.C. Daniels: 1964–1966
Paul H. Lucier: 1964–1965, 1971–1973
G.F. Smith: 1964–1965
S.W. Henke: 1966–1967; 1972–1973
R.J. (Jim) Light: 1966–1970
D.S. Collins: 1967
R.B. Cousins: 1967–1968
A.J. Wybrew: 1968
Jean E. Banks: 1968–1971
Kurt Koken: 1969–1971

Leo Van Vugt: 1968–1969

Arnold "Dutch" Vienott: 1971

Clive Boyd: 1972–1973

Alder Hunter: 1972–1973

John Watt: 1972–1975

R. Campbell Sr., Dr. A.R. Helm, P. O'Connor,
    D. Simpson: Advisory Committee,
    July–September 1973*

Chuck Hankins: 1973–1974

Pete Patrick: 1973–1975

Olive Pociwauschek: 1973–1975

Al Wright: 1973–1975

R. Cummings: 1974–1979

W. Palmer: 1974–1975

Douglas Bell: 1976–1977

S. Burns: 1976

O. Chippett: 1976–1979

Art Deer: 1976–1983; 1986–1991

Margaret Heath: 1976–1979

B. Pitzel: 1976–1977

Laurent Cyr: 1978–1979

Tony Penikett: 1978–1979

John Pierce: 1979–1983

Bert Law: 1980–1988

J. Linzey: 1980–1981

D. Sinclair: 1980–1981

Vern Toews: 1980–1986

Conrad Boyce: 1982–1983

Doug Gallup: 1982–1994

Truska Gorrell: 1984–1986

Marilyn King: 1984–1991

Dave Stockdale: 1984–

Gerry Thick: 1986–1991

Sue Edelman: 1988–1994

Duke Connelly: 1991–1994; 1997–2003

Ed Schulz: 1991–1994

Katherine Ann (Kathy) Watson: 1991–1994

Dan Boyd: 1994–1999

Barb Harris: 1994–2000

Katie Hayhurst: 1994–1997

Bernie Phillips: 1994–2000

Jared Storey: 1994–1997

Allan Jacobs: 1997–2000

Dave Austin: 2000–2012

Linda Casson: 2000–2003

Doug Graham: 2000–2011

Samson Hartland: 2000–2003

Beverly (Bev) Buckway: 2003–2005

Yvonne Harris: 2003–2004

Mel Stehelin: 2003–2005

Jan Stick: 2005–2009

Jeanine Myhre: 2006–2009

Florence Roberts: 2006–2009

Betty Irwin: 2009–

Ranj Pillai: 2009–2012

Kirk Cameron: 2011–

Jocelyn Curteau: 2012–

Mike Gladish: 2012–

John Streicker: 2012–

NOTES

CHAPTER 1

1. This phrase was coined by Yukon artist Jim Robb, who many believe is a Colourful Five Per Center himself.
2. Shirley Adamson, personal communication, July 9, 2013.
3. Julie Cruikshank, *Reading Voices: Dän Dhá Ts'edenintth'é—Oral and Written Interpretations of the Yukon's Past.* (Vancouver: Douglas & McIntyre, 1991), 16–17.
4. This section benefitted from consultation with Charlie Roots of the Geological Survey of Canada, 3 February 2013.
5. Cruikshank, 45.
6. Government of Yukon Department of Tourism and Culture website, "Łu Zil Män—Fish Lake: Uncovering the Past"; "Ta'an Kwächän—People of the Lake"; "From Trail to Tramway: The Archaeology of Canyon City" (see www.tc.gov.yk.ca).
7. Adamson, personal communication, July 9, 2013.
8. Chu Nii Kwan place name contributed by Shirley Adamson, personal communication, 9 July 2013; much of the information in this section derived from: Violet Storer, Frances Woolsey and Linda Johnson, *Ta'an Kwächän Council, Ta'an Kwächän Cultural History Project, Report and Transcriptions* (Whitehorse: Ta'an Kwächän Council, 1990).
9. Angela Sidney, *Haa Shagóon: Our Family History,* xi–xiii (various clan charts).
10. Yukon Archives: Bonar and Bessie Cooley, Tlingit and Haida Genealogy Chart.
11. Catharine McClellan, *Part of the Land, Part of the Water: A History of the Yukon Indians* (Vancouver: Douglas & McIntyre, 1987), 51–55.
12. Yukon Native Language Centre website, Culture & History, Dákeyi: "Southern Tutchone Place Names" (see www.ynlc.ca).

CHAPTER 2

1. Catharine McClellan, *Part of the Land, Part of the Water: A History of the Yukon Indians* (Vancouver: Douglas & McIntyre, 1987), 150–61.
2. Allen A. Wright, *Prelude to Bonanza: The Discovery and Exploration of the Yukon* (Sidney, B.C.: Gray's, 1976), 118–247.
3. Julie Cruikshank, *Do Glaciers Listen?* (Vancouver: UBC Press, 2005), 133.
4. Wright, 1–92.
5. Linda Johnson, *The Kandik Map* (Fairbanks: University of Alaska Press, 2009), 12.
6. Ibid., 134–42.
7. Ibid., 93–126.
8. François-Xavier Mercier, *Recollections of the Youkon: Memoires from the Years 1868–1885,* ed. Linda Finn Yarborough (Anchorage: Alaska Historical Society, 1986), 32.
9. *The Kohklux Map* (Whitehorse: Yukon Historical and Museums Association, 1995), map accompanying book.
10. Johnson, 135.
11. Wright, 134–36
12. Frederick Schwatka, "Report by Lieutenant Frederick Schwatka," in *Compilation of Narratives of Explorations in Alaska,* (U.S. Senate Committee on Military Affairs, 1900), 302.
13. Ibid.
14. Ibid.
15. Ibid., 293–301.
16. George Dawson, *Report on Exploration in the Yukon District, 1887* (Ottawa: Queen's Printer, 1887).
17. Ibid., 143.
18. Ibid., 161.
19. William Ogilvie, "Down the Yukon and Up the Mackenzie," *Canadian Magazine,* December 1898, 531.
20. Dawson, 183.
21. William Pierce, *Thirteen Years of Travel and Exploration in Alaska, 1877–1889* (Lawrence, Kansas: Journal Publishing Company, 1890), 50–68.
22. Dawson, 203.
23. Title borrowed from Allen A. Wright's *Prelude to Bonanza.*
24. J. Bernard Moore, *Skagway in Days Primeval* (Skagway, Alaska: Lynn Canal Publishing, 1997), 50–68.
25. Ibid., 44.
26. Ibid.
27. *The Moore Homestead.* U.S. National Parks Service pamphlet, ca. 2006; see www.nps.gov/klgo.
28. Violet Storer, Frances Woolsey and Linda Johnson, *Ta'an Kwächän Cultural History Project, 1989: Research Report* (Whitehorse: Ta'an Kwäch'än Council, 1990), 45–47.

CHAPTER 3

1. *Seattle Post-Intelligencer*, 17 July 1897; *San Francisco Call*, 18 July 1897.
2. Julie Cruikshank, *Reading Voices: Dän Dhá Ts'edenintth'é—Oral and Written Interpretations of the Yukon's Past.* (Vancouver: Douglas & McIntyre, 1991), 129–35.
3. Report of Supt. S.B. Steele, NWMP Annual Report, 1898, 22.
4. At the request of the Elders who told this story, the two Whitehorse-area First Nations, the City of Whitehorse and the Yukon government worked together in 2009 to erect a bronze plaque near the rapids to commemorate these and other deaths in the perilous rapids.
5. Roy Minter, *The White Pass: Gateway to the Klondike* (Toronto: McClelland & Stewart, 1987), 320.
6. Samuel B. Steele, *Forty Years in Canada* (Winnipeg: Russell Lang, 1915), 311–12.
7. Ibid.
8. Helene Dobrowolsky, *Law of the Yukon* (Whitehorse: Lost Moose Publishing, 1995), 42–43.
9. Linda Johnson, *At the Heart of Gold: The Yukon Commissioner's Office, 1898–2010* (Whitehorse: Legislative Assembly of Yukon, 2012), 5; *Dictionary of Canadian Biography Online*, s.v. James Morrow Walsh (see http://biographi.ca).
10. John Joe, quoted in Rob McCandless, *Yukon Wildlife: A Social History* (Edmonton: University of Alberta Press, 1985), 162.
11. Minter, 320.
12. Yukon Archives, YRG I, Series I, vol. 13, f. 2788.
13. NWMP Annual Report, 1898, 18.
14. Dobrowolsky, *Law of the Yukon,* 45.
15. Helene Dobrowolsky, *Canyon City Interpretation Plan & Interpreter's Manual.* With Brenda Carson, Wendy Wood & Gunter Glaeser. Prepared for Heritage Branch, Yukon Government, 1995.
16. Laurent Cyr interview in Helene Dobrowolsky et al., Canyon City Oral History Project, 1995; *Empreinte: la présence francophone au Yukon (1825–1950)* (Whitehorse: Association franco-yukonnaise, 1997), 12–13.
17. Patrick Martin, unpublished memoirs; Helene Dobrowolsky, *Patrick Martin, Master Mariner: Travelling Exhibit Project, Planning Report* (prepared for MacBride Museum Society, 2002).
18. Canada, www.pc.gc/Jim Boss news release and backgrounder, 14 July 2010.

CHAPTER 4

1. Harry Graham, *Across Canada to the Klondyke* (Toronto: Methuen, 1984), 66–67.

2. Roy Minter, *The White Pass: Gateway to the Klondike* (Toronto: McClelland & Stewart, 1987), 60–65; Gordon Bennett, *Yukon Transportation: A History* (Ottawa: Minister of Supply and Services Canada, 1978), 62.
3. *White Horse Star*, 24 April 1901; Yukon Archives Plan 8406, H.G. Dickson, D.L.S., Plan of Yards and Right of Way of the British Yukon M.T. & T. Co.'s Railway and Adjacent Property on the West Bank of Lewes or Fifty Mile River below White Horse Rapids, Yukon District, 28 October 1899.
4. *White Horse Tribune*, 21 July 1900.
5. *Daily Klondike Nugget*, 6 August 1900.
6. Samuel H. Graves, *On the White Pass Payroll* (Chicago: Lakeside Press, 1908), 141.
7. Helene Dobrowolsky and Rob Ingram, *Edge of the River, Heart of the City* (Whitehorse: Lost Moose Publishing, 1994), 14–15; Bennett, *Yukon Transportation*, 62–69.
8. The force underwent a few name changes over the years, becoming the Royal Northwest Mounted Police in 1904 and the Royal Canadian Mounted Police in 1919.
9. Helene Dobrowolsky, *Law of the Yukon* (Whitehorse: Lost Moose Publishing, 1995), 70–73; Yukon Archives, YRG I, GOV 1623, f. 2789, Whitehorse Townsite, 1899–1901.
10. Dobrowolsky, *Law of the Yukon*, 70–73, 94–98; NWMP Annual Reports, 1901 and 1902; Helene Dobrowolsky, "Yukon Workers Fatality Database," unpublished table compiled for Yukon Workers' Compensation.
11. Helene Dobrowolsky and Rob Ingram, *A History of the Whitehorse Copper Belt* (prepared for MacBride Museum and Indian and Northern Affairs Canada, 1993), 13, 15.
12. Ibid., 2–3; *White Horse Tribune*, 21 July 1900.
13. Ibid., 2–15; *Whitehorse Tribune*, 21 July 1900.
14. "Report of Insp. F.J.A. Demers, White Horse," RNWMP Annual Report, 1905; *Whitehorse Star*, 18 October 1905.
15. "Report of Insp. J.A. MacDonald, Whitehorse," RNWMP Annual Report, 1911.
16. Julie Cruikshank, *Reading Voices* (Douglas & McIntyre, 1991), 113.
17. "The Gold Rush That Never Was," MacBride Sourdough Stories, *Yukon News*, 9 September 2009.
18. *Whitehorse Star*, 19 February 1906; Murray Lundberg, *Fractured Veins and Broken Dreams* (Whitehorse: Pathfinder, 1996), 62–68.
19. Yukon Archives, YRG I, Series 5, vol. 11, f. 664; Series 5, vol. 7, f. 562; *Whitehorse Star*, 8 June and 2 November 1906.
20. The two main sources for this section are Murray Lundberg's *Fractured Veins and Broken Dreams* and the *Montana Mountain Research & Inventory Project* (1995), a report prepared by Midnight Arts for the Government of Yukon Heritage Branch.

21. Michael Gates, "Livingstone Creek Marked the Start of a Stellar Political Career," *Yukon News*, 16 September 2011; *Whitehorse Star*, 16 January 1901; H.S. Bostock and E.J. Lees, *Memoir 217: Laberge Map-Area, Yukon* (Ottawa: Department of Mines and Technical Surveys, 1938).

22. Yukon Archives, YRG I, GOV 1620, f. 1699, Municipal Matter—Whitehorse, 1900–02; YRG I, GOV 1623, f. 2817, Post Office, Whitehorse, 1901–1927.

23. Linda Johnson, *With the People Who Live Here, The History of the Yukon Legislative Assembly 1909–1961* (Whitehorse: Legislative Assembly of Yukon, 2009), 1-61.

24. *Whitehorse Star*, 90th anniversary edition, 16 June 1990; Archives Canada, Scharschmidt fonds, Administrative History/Biographical Sketch (see www.archivescanada.ca).

25. *Whitehorse Star*, 24 May 1912; Helene Dobrowolsky, *Environmental Assessment for the Whitehorse Riverfront Planning Project* (prepared for Gartner Lee Limited, October 1998), 10.

26. Dobrowolsky, *Law of the Yukon*, 39; Dianne Green, *In Direct Touch with the Wide World* (Whitehorse: Northwestel, 1992), 10–14; Bill Miller, *Wires in the Wilderness* (Surrey, B.C.: Heritage House, 2004), 21–38; Yukon Historical and Museums Association, *Whitehorse Heritage Buildings*, 12.

27. Helene Dobrowolsky and Rob Ingram, *A Structural History of the White Pass and Yukon Railway Depot, Whitehorse, and Associated Structures* (prepared for the Government of Yukon Heritage Branch, 1998), 10–11, 48–50.

28. Helene Dobrowolsky, *The Church in Yukon: A Thematic Study* (prepared for the Government of Yukon Heritage Branch, 1990), 33; Father Jean-Paul Tanguay interview by Helene Dobrowolsky, November 1989; Archives Canada, Our Lady of Victory Roman Catholic Mission fonds, Administrative History/Biographical Sketch (see www.archivescanada.ca).

29. Archives Canada, First Presbyterian Church fonds, Administrative History/Biographical Sketch (see www.archivescanada.ca).

30. Marjorie E. Almstrom, *A Century of Schooling: Education in the Yukon 1861-1961*, (Whitehorse, 1990), 115-118.

31. Dobrowolsky, *Law of the Yukon*, 40; (R)NWMP Annual Reports, 1899–1910; *Empreinte: La présence francophone au Yukon (1825–1950)* (Whitehorse: Association franco-yukonnaise, 1997), 244.

32. Athol Retallack, "C.D. Taylor," *Northern Miner*, December 1969.

33. *Whitehorse Heritage Buildings* (Whitehorse: Yukon Historical and Museums Association, 1983), 14–15; Yukon Archives Search File, Taylor & Drury; *Whitehorse Star*, 31 July 1974.

34. Miller, *Wires in the Wilderness*, 23–26; Association franco-yukonnaise, *Empreinte*, 292–93; *Whitehorse Star*, 6 February 1901; Dobrowolsky, *The Church in Yukon*, 33.

35. Julie Cruikshank, *Life Lived Like a Story* (Vancouver: UBC Press, 1990), 204.

36. Dobrowolsky, *Law of the Yukon*, 116; Copperbelt Railway & Mining Museum website, "Famous Miners" (see www.yukon-rails.com).

37. Les McLaughlin, "Ephraim J. Hamacher: A CKRW Yukon Nugget," on the Hougen Group of Companies website (see www.hougengroup.com/yukonhistory/); Yukon Archives website, Archives Descriptive Database: "E.J. Hamacher Biographical Sketch" (see http://yukon.minisisinc.com/).

38. http://heritageyukon.ca/historical-buildings/chambers-house.

39. "R.W. Service: Bard of the Yukon," *Whitehorse Star*, 90th anniversary edition, 16 June 1990, 29.

CHAPTER 5

1. RNWMP Annual Report, 1914, 224.

2. Gordon Bennett, *Yukon Transportation: A History* (Ottawa: Minister of Supply and Services Canada, 1978), 99–103.

3. Yukon Archives Search File, Biographies, Robert Lowe.

4. *Whitehorse Star*, 11 October 1912.

5. Yukon Archives, YRG I, GOV 1658, f. 30485: Indian Reserve, Whitehorse, 1916–19; Kwanlin Dün First Nation website, "About Kwanlin Dün" (see www.kwanlindun.com); Yukon Archives, Anglican Church of Canada, *Northern Lights*, November 1916.

6. A good overview of the fox-farming industry in the Yukon is found in Robert McCandless, *Yukon Wildlife: A Social History* (Edmonton: University of Alberta Press, 1985), 111–14.

7. *Weekly Star*, 28 March 1924 and 27 November 1925; Yukon Historical and Museums Association, with Midnight Arts and North Words Consulting, *Whitehorse Riverfront Heritage Resources* (report prepared for the City of Whitehorse, 1998), 33, 46.

8. WP&YR: *The White Pass and Yukon Route: Scenic Railway of the World* (Seattle: Century Printing, 1900).

9. The White Pass and Yukon Route, British Yukon Navigation Company, Ltd., Superintendent's Annual Report of Operation, 1920–35 YA, COR 722 and 723 (hereafter referenced as "WP&YR, SAR").

10. Linda Johnson, *At the Heart of Gold: The Yukon Commissioner's Office, 1898–2010* (Whitehorse: Legislative Assembly of Yukon, 2012), 43-49.

11. Yukon Bureau of Statistics; Bennett, *Yukon Transportation*, 94–97; Johnson, *With the People Who Live Here: A History of the Yukon Legislature, 1909–1961* (Whitehorse: Legislative Assembly of Yukon, 2009), 131–32.

12. Helene Dobrowolsky and Rob Ingram, *A History of the Whitehorse Copper Belt* (prepared for the MacBride Museum and Indian and Northern Affairs Canada, 1993), 10–12.

13. The *Weekly Star* stated that 100 White Pass employees were aboard the *Sophia*; according to Coates and Morrison (see endnote 14), it was 87 employees and dependents.

14. Ken Coates and Bill Morrison, *The Sinking of the Princess Sophia: Taking the North Down with Her* (Toronto: Oxford University Press, 1990); *The Weekly Star*, 1 November 1918; WP&YR, SAR, 1918.

15. John Scott interview by Helene Dobrowolsky, Yukon Historical and Museums Association Whitehorse Waterfront Study, 17 September 1992.

16. WP&YR, SAR, 1917.

17. Scott interview; Helene Dobrowolsky and Rob Ingram, *Edge of the River, Heart of the City* (Whitehorse: Lost Moose Publishing, 1994), 18–23.

18. Yukon River Aural History Project notes and index—interviews with various people who lived and worked on the Yukon River, conducted by Cal Waddington for Parks Canada, 1978 (notes and index prepared by Helene Dobrowolsky, 1981); Scott interview; WP&YR, SAR, 1904–18, 1927–34.

19. WP&YR, SAR, 1911.

20. Bennett, *Yukon Transportation*, 106–114; Stan Cohen, *Yukon River Steamboats: A Pictorial History* (Missoula, Montana: Pictorial Histories, 1982), 89–104.

21. The BYN tried using coal for some of its boats, but this was not a successful experiment, and the boilers were soon converted back to wood. Midnight Arts and Boreal Research Associates, *Inland Water Transportation System Research Project* (report prepared for Parks Canada, 1997).

22. WP&YR, SAR, 1923–25.

23. Violet Storer, Frances Woolsey and Linda Johnson, *Ta'an Kwäch'än Council, Ta'an Kwäch'än Cultural History Project, Report and Transcriptions* (Whitehorse: Ta'an Kwäch'än Council, 1990).

24. Dobrowolsky and Ingram, *A History of the Whitehorse Copper Belt*, 13–14; Copperbelt Railway & Mining Museum website, "Famous Miners" (see www.yukonrails.com); *Dawson Daily News*, 11 September 1907.

25. Les McLaughlin, "Phelps: A CKRW Yukon Nugget," on the Hougen Group of Companies website (see www.hougengroup.com/yukonhistory).

26. Ronald Keith, *Bush Pilot with a Briefcase* (Toronto: Doubleday Canada, 1972), 169–70.

27. Dobrowolsky, Yukon River Aural History Project notes and index; W.R. Hamilton, *The Yukon Story* (Vancouver: Mitchell Press, 1964), 93, 102–4; Obituaries from the End of the Trail website, "Herbert Wheeler" (see http://alaskaobits.org).

28. Jim Robb, "Buzzsaw Jimmy," in *The Colourful Five Per Cent*, vol. 1, no. 1 (Whitehorse: Touchstone Studios and The Colourful Five Per Cent Company, 1984), 13.

29. *Whitehorse Heritage Buildings*, 71.

30. W.D. MacBride, *All My Rivers Flowed West* (Whitehorse: Beringian Books, 1991), v.

31. Ibid., 94; MacBride Museum of Yukon History website (www.macbridemuseum.com).

32. "Top Businessman T.C. Richards wore many hats," *Yukon News*, 14 July 2010; Bennett, *Yukon Transportation*, 103; Yukon Archives Search File, Biographies, T.C. Richards; *Whitehorse Star*, 12 June 1998; The Yukon Register of Historic Places: T.C. Richards Building (see http://register.yukonhistoricplaces.ca); Jim Robb, "T.C. Richards," *The Colourful Five Per Cent*, vol. 1, no. 1, 11.

33. *Whitehorse Heritage Buildings* (Whitehorse: Yukon Historical and Museums Association, 1983), 56–57; Jane Gaffin, "John Olaf Erickson: Prospector and Hotelier" (see www.yukonprospectors.ca).

34. *Whitehorse Heritage Buildings*, 19.

35. Dobrowolsky and Ingram, *Edge of the River, Heart of the City*, 28–29.

36. Yukon Archives, Ryder Family fonds, Marny Ryder, *Ryder Wood Camps, 1907–1965, Whitehorse Area* (paper written for Yukon College course CUIT 396, 1987).

37. Les McLaughlin, "T.C. Richards (and the Whitehorse Inn): A CKRW Yukon Nugget," on the Hougen Group of Companies website (see www.hougengroup.com/yukonhistory).

38. "Top Businessman T.C. Richards wore many hats," *Yukon News*, 14 July 2010; Bennett, *Yukon Transportation*, 103; Yukon Archives Search File, Biographies, T.C. Richards; *Whitehorse Star*, 12 June 1998; The Yukon Register of Historic Places: T.C. Richards Building (see http://register.yukonhistoricplaces.ca); Jim Robb, "T.C. Richards," *The Colourful Five Per Cent*, vol. 1, no. 1, 11.

CHAPTER 6

1. Gudrun Sparling interview by Cathy M. Hoen, 18 December 1990, Whitehorse 50th Anniversary Society Oral History Project.

2. Indeed, a small Japanese force occupied two of the Aleutian Islands in June 1942 and managed to withstand a much larger American force for nearly a year.

3. Personal communications, Doug Bell (7 March 2013) and Bob Cameron (11 March 2013).

4. *Whitehorse Star*, 20 February 1942. Much of this chapter draws on material from the following report: Helene Dobrowolsky, *The Impact of Alaska Highway Construction on Whitehorse*, prepared for the Whitehorse 50th Anniversary Society, January 1991.

5. Fred Rust, *The Eighteenth Engineers Regiment (Combat) in Yukon Territory, April 1942–Jan. 1943* (typescript, n.d.), 4.

6. Ibid., 2.

7. *Whitehorse Star*, 8, 15, 22 May 1942.

8. Arthur Molans, *A Record of the Work and Activities of Company E 18th Engineers during the Construction of the Alaska Military Highway, April 2nd, 1942–January 11th, 1943* (typescript, 23 December 1943), 5.

9. Sparling interview.

10. John Schmidt, "Gwen Holmes Meets the Great Quong," in *This Was No Фухип Picnic* (Hanna, Alberta: Gorman & Gorman, 1991), 260–63.

11. Ibid., 265, 268–69.

12. *Whitehorse Star*, 12 December 1941; Gudrun Sparling, personal communication, February 2013; MacBride Museum artifact 1992.5.7, a piece of Regina Hotel stationary autographed by Joe Louis and Ruby Goldstein, dated 28 May 1945.

13. Gordon Bennett, *Yukon Transportation: A History* (Ottawa: Minister of Supply and Services, 1978), 134.

14. Yukon Archives, Map H909: Location of property sites used for military and construction purposes, February 22, 1944.

15. *Whitehorse Star*, 15 May 1942.

16. Yukon Archives, Map H909.

17. Arthur Molans, *Work and Activities of Company E 18th Engineers,* 61.

18. Sparling interview.

19. *Whitehorse Star,* 11 June 1937 and 17 April 1942; Babe Richards interview by Helene Dobrowolsky, 7 January 1991.

20. Quoted in Barry Broadfoot, *Six War Years: 1939–1945* (Toronto: Doubleday Canada, 1974), 216.

21. Fred Blaker interview by David Porter, 10 December 1990, Whitehorse 50th Anniversary Society Oral History Project.

22. George Peterson, "Whitehorse Boom Due to Highway 'Gold,'" from a collection of Peterson's columns reprinted from the *Minneapolis Star Journal* and *Sunday Tribune*, n.d. (ca. summer 1943); Lloyd Ryder interview by Cathy M. Hoehn, December 1990; Richards interview (January 1991).

23 Sparling interview.

24. Gudrun Sparling, personal communication, 24 October 1990.

25. Gertrude Baskine, *Hitch-Hiking the Alaska Highway* (Toronto: Macmillan Canada, 1944), 113.

26. Rust, 7.

27. *Whitehorse Star*, 19 June 1942.

28. Father Jean-Paul Tanguay, personal communication, 10 December 1990.

29. Peterson, "Morning Profiles Along the Alaska Highway," collected columns, n.d.

30. Lucy Wren interview by Violet Storer, Ray Marnoch and Diane Smith, 30 June 1993, Kwanlin Dün First Nation Cultural History Project.

31. Julie Cruikshank, *Life Lived Like a Story* (Vancouver: UBC Press, 1990), 326.

32. Julie Cruikshank, "The Gravel Magnet: Some Social Impacts of the Alaska Highway on Yukon Indians," in K.S. Coates, ed., *The Alaska Highway: Papers of the 40th Anniversary Symposium* (Vancouver: UBC Press, 1985).

33. Richards interview (January 1991).

34. Ken Coates and William Morrison, *Land of the Midnight Sun* (Edmonton: Hurtig, 1988), 235.

35. Gudrun Sparling, personal conversation, 10 January 1991.

36. Ryder interview.

37. *Whitehorse Star*, 24 July and 21 August 1942.

38. Schmidt, *This Was No Фухип Picnic*, 269–70.

39. Babe Richards interview by Helene Dobrowolsky, 1990.

40. Ibid.

41. Peterson, "Rumors and Dust Main Ingredients of the Road," collected columns, n.d.

42. Coates, 248.

43. *Whitehorse Star*, 28 September 1945; Dianne Green, *In Direct Touch with the Wide World* (Whitehorse: Northwestel, 1992), 28–29.

44. *Whitehorse Star*, 26 June 1942; Yukon Archives, Finnie Family fonds, 81/21.

45. Richards interview (January 1991).

46. *Whitehorse Star*, 4 September and 9 October 1942.

47. *Whitehorse Star*, 2 October 1942.

48. Gertrude Baskine, *Hitchhiking the Alaska Highway.* Toronto: Macmillan Canada, 1944.

49. Horace E. Moore, *All Year Round Guide to the Yukon,* prepared for the Kiwanis Club of Whitehorse by the *Whitehorse Star*, 1946.

50. Richards interview (January 1991).

51. Peterson, "Whitehorse Boom Due to Highway 'Gold,'" collected columns, n.d.

52. Ryder interview.

53. Les McLaughlin, "Les Cook: A CKRW Yukon Nugget," on the Hougen Group of Companies website (see www.hougengroup.com/yukonhistory).

54. Rob Ingram, Quong family interviews for "James Quong: Photographer," Yukon Archives exhibits, 2010.

55. Donna Marie Dillman, *Donuts and Silver Dollars: The Life of Captain Frank Slim* (master's thesis, Simon Fraser University, 2008); personal communications, Virginia and Joe Lindsay, 25 February and 4 March 2003; Yukon Transportation Museum release *1997 Transportation Pioneer of the Year, Frank Slim* (1997).

CHAPTER 7

1. *Whitehorse Star,* 5 April 1946.

2. Ibid., various issues, April–May, 1946.

3. Dianne Green, *In Direct Touch with the Wide World* (Whitehorse: Northwestel, 1992), 44–46, 85–87; Helene Dobrowolsky, *The Hougen Family in the Yukon, a Pictorial History: 1906–2011* (Whitehorse: Hougen Family, 2012), 138.

4. Linda Johnson, *At the Heart of Gold: The Yukon Commissioner's Office, 1898–2010* (Whitehorse: Legislative Assembly of Yukon, 2012), Introduction and Chapter 2; Parliament of Canada website, "Canadian Ministry" (see http://parl.gc.ca/membersofparliament).

5. Department of Northern Affairs and Natural Resources (and predecessor and successor departmental titles), Annual Report, 1945–1960.

6. Linda Johnson, *With the People Who Live Here: A History of the Yukon Legislature, 1909–1961* (Whitehorse: Legislative Assembly of Yukon, 2009).

7. *Whitehorse Star*, 21 November 1947 and various issues, 1948–52.

8. Ibid.

9. Ibid., 13 June 1947 and various issues, 1948–55.

10. Johnson, *With the People Who Live Here*, Chapters 7 and 8.

11. *Whitehorse Star*, various issues, 1948–55.

12. Johnson, *At the Heart of Gold*, Introduction and Chapter 2.

13. *Whitehorse Star*, various issues, 1945–50.

14. Ibid., 8 and 14 February, 1945.

15. W. Bro. Dennis M. Eve, "Freemasonry in the Yukon Territory," Grand Lodge of British Columbia and the Yukon website (see http://freemasonry.bcy.ca).

16. *Whitehorse Star*, 20 February 1953 and various issues, 1952–53.

17. Ibid.

18. John Firth, "Whitehorse Sports and Recreation," Report for Whitehorse History Book Society, 2012.

19. *Whitehorse Star*, 26 April 1946, various issues through May 1946 and 28 June 1946.

20. Johnson, *At the Heart of Gold*, Introduction.

21. *Whitehorse Star*, 26 May 1950.

22. Ibid., 30 June, 23 July, 4 August and 9 September 1950.

23. Ibid., 6 October 1950.

24. Ibid., 2 March 1951.

25. Ibid., 16 November 1951.

26. Johnson, *With the People Who Live Here*, 274–89.

27. Johnson, *At the Heart of Gold*, 111.

28. *Whitehorse Star*, 6 July 1951 and various issues, 1951–52.

29. Ibid., 29 May 1953.

30. Ibid., 6 June 1953.

31. Ibid., 14 July 1950.

32. Johnson, *At the Heart of Gold*, 60–64.

33. Yann Herry, *La francophonie: Une richesse nordique* (Whitehorse: Association franco-yukonnaise, 2003), 17; various issues of *Whitehorse Star*, 1946–50.

34. Johnson, *At the Heart of Gold*, 105–6.

35. Herry, *La francophonie*, 12–13, 18–19; Yann Herry and Renée Alford, personal communication to Linda Johnson, May 2013.

36. *Whitehorse Star*, various issues, 1953–60.

37. Johnson, *At the Heart of Gold*, 77.

38. Helene Dobrowolsky and Rob Ingram, *A Structural History of the White Pass and Yukon Railway Depot, Whitehorse, and Associated Structures* (prepared for the Government of Yukon Heritage Branch, 1998), 16–55.

39. Robert G. McCandless, *Yukon Wildlife: A Social History* (Edmonton: University of Alberta, 1985), 138

40. *Whitehorse Star*, various issues, 1956–60; Johnson, *With the People Who Live Here*, Chapter 7.

41. Herry, *La francophonie*, 18–19; *Empreinte: la présence francophone au Yukon (1825–1950)* (Whitehorse: Association franco-yukonnaise, 1997), 76–78.

42. Yukon Archives Search File, George Dawson.

43. Les McLaughlin, "Lilias Farley: A CKRW Yukon Nugget," on the Hougen Group of Companies website (see www.hougen-group.com/yukonhistory).

44. Georgianna Low, personal communication to Linda Johnson, December 2012.

45. *Whitehorse Star*, 4 June 1975.

46. Ibid., 18 October 2000.

47. *Whitehorse Star*, 8 September 1950.

48. Ibid., various issues, 1946–58; Les McLaughlin, "Mayor Gordon Armstrong: A CKRW Yukon Nugget," on the Hougen Group of Companies website (see www.hougengroup.com/yukonhistory).

49. Johnson, *At the Heart of Gold*, Chapter 1.

CHAPTER 8

1. Linda Johnson, *At the Heart of Gold: The Yukon Commissioner's Office, 1898–2010* (Whitehorse: Legislative Assembly of Yukon, 2012), Chapters 1 and 2.

2. *Whitehorse Star*, 5 October 1961.

3. Ibid., various issues, 1960–75.

4. Johnson, *At the Heart of Gold*, Chapters 1, 2, 5 and 6.

5. *Whitehorse Star*, various issues, 1960–85.

6. Ibid., 23 November 1964.

7. Jim Lotz, *The Squatters of Whitehorse, Yukon Territory* (Ottawa: Northern Affairs & Natural Resources, 1961), 37–68.

8. *Whitehorse Star*, 21 September 1961.

9. Ibid., various issues, 1960–63.

10. Ibid.

11. Ibid., various issues, 1960–90.

12. Ibid., various issues, 1960–63.

13. Ibid., various issues, 1962–70.

14. Yukon College Archives, Whitehorse Vocational Training School Yearbooks, *The Trade Wind*, 1963–66.

15. *Whitehorse Star*, 31 March, 4 April and 7 April 1966.

16. Ibid., various issues, 1965–67.

17. Ibid., various issues, 1970–80.

18. "North to the Future: Musical Reflections on Alaska's History" (see www.alaskamusic.net/40s-60s).

19. Duncan Sinclair, personal communication to Michele Genest, 2013.

20. Spring Festival 1979 brochure, 7; Government of Yukon file, Spring Festival 2.2.

21. Laurel Parry, personal communication to Michele Genest, 2013.

22. Wayne Potoroka, "Faro A Go-Go: Remembering the Farrago Music Festival," *Yukon North of Ordinary,* 5, no. 3 (fall 2011).

23. Chris Dray, personal communication to Michele Genest, 2013.

24. Yukon Arts Council, Proceedings of Seminar and Annual General Meeting November 27–29, 1981; Government of Yukon file, Reports & Studies (Culture) 2.1.3.

25. *Together Today for Our Children Tomorrow* (Whitehorse: Council for Yukon Indians, 1973).

26. *Whitehorse Star,* 2 February 1961.

27. Council of Yukon First Nations website, "Our History" (see www.cyfn.ca/ourhistory).

28. Frances Woolsey, personal communication to Linda Johnson, January 2013.

29. CFYN website, "Our History."

30. *Whitehorse Star,* 29 June 1964 and 29 August 1966.

31. Helene Dobrowolsky and Rob Ingram, *A History of the Whitehorse Copper Belt* (prepared for the MacBride Museum and Indian and Northern Affairs Canada, 1993), 18–22.

32. Johnson, *At the Heart of Gold,* Chapter 2.

33. *Whitehorse Star,* various issues, 1970–80.

34. Ibid, 6 February 1953.

35. Yukon Federation of Labour website (www.yukonfed.com); *Wikipedia,* s.v. Yukon Federation of Labour.

36. Johnson, *At the Heart of Gold,* Chapters 3 and 4.

37. Ibid.

38. Ibid.

39. Les McLaughlin, "Elijah Smith: A CKRW Yukon Nugget," on the Hougen Group of Companies website (see www.hougengroup.com/yukonhistory).

40. Gertie Tom, personal communication to Ingrid Johnson, 2013.

41. Hougen Group, "Yukon Nuggets."

42. Helene Dobrowolsky, *The Hougen Family in the Yukon, a Pictorial History: 1906–2011* (Whitehorse: Hougen Family, 2012), 191.

43. Jackie Pierce, personal communication to Linda Johnson, April 2012; Hougen Group "Yukon Nuggets."

44. *Whitehorse Star,* 7 January 1960, 28 January 1960 and 10 October 1961.

45. *Whitehorse Star,* 28 June 1962, 25 November 1965; *Yukon News,* 10 June 2007.

46. *Whitehorse Star,* various issues, 1950–90 and 18 October 2000.

47. Ibid., various issues, 1950–75; Hougen Group website, "Yukon Nuggets" (see www.hougengroup.com/yukonhistory).

48. *Whitehorse Star,* various issues, 1964–99; Hougen Group, "Yukon Nuggets"; Parliament of Canada website, Senator Biographies: "Paul Lucier" (see www.parl.gc.ca).

49. Johnson, *At the Heart of Gold,* Chapter 5.

CHAPTER 9

1. Linda Johnson, *At the Heart of Gold: The Yukon Commissioner's Office, 1898–2010* (Whitehorse: Legislative Assembly of Yukon, 2012), Chapters 5–7.

2. *Whitehorse Star,* various issues, 1979–81.

3. Ibid., various issues, 1980–2000.

4. Anna Hercz, *Residential Land Use Planning and Housing in Whitehorse, Yukon Territory: Public Involvement in the Land Development Process* (PhD thesis, McGill University, 1985).

5. *Kwanlin Dun Relocation* (Whitehorse: Indian & Inuit Affairs, 1985).

6. Johnson, *At the Heart of Gold,* Chapters 5–7.

7. *The Things That Matter: A Report of Yukoners' Views on the Future of Their Economy and Their Society* (Whitehorse: Yukon Government, 1987).

8. Proceedings of the Adäka Heritage Conference, October 27–29, 1999, Whitehorse, Yukon (Yukon Heritage Board).

9. See www.yukonconservation.org for a review of YCS history and issues.

10. Lost Moose Publishing is now owned by Harbour Publishing; see catalogue at www.harbourpublishing.com.

11. Michele Emslie, personal communication, 27 July 2012.

12. Julie Cruikshank, "Negotiating with Narrative: Establishing Cultural Identity at the Yukon International Storytelling Festival," *American Anthropologist* 99, no. 1 (March 1997), 56–69.

13. Brigitte D. Parker, "Second Commissioner's Potlatch a Success," *Raven's Eye* 3, no. 3 (1999) (see www.ammsa.com).

14. Media Release, 29 March 1990; collection of Arlin McFarlane.

15. John Firth, "Whitehorse Sports and Recreation," Report for Whitehorse History Book Society, 2012.

16. *Whitehorse Star,* various issues, 1980–85.

17. L'Association franco-yukonnaise, *anniversary booklet*; Steve Smyth, "Colonialism and Language in Canada's North: A Yukon Case Study," *Arctic,* vol. 49, no. 2 (June 1996), 155–161.

18. Yukon College Archives, Heritage Library, Mrs. Angela Sidney, *The Story of Kaax'achgook,* ca. 1992.

19. *Whitehorse Star,* various issues, October 1988.

20. Yukon College Archives, Heritage Library, various reports.

21. Council of Yukon First Nations website (www.cfyn.ca).

22. Johnson, *At the Heart of Gold,* Chapter 8.

23. Ta'an Kwäch'än Council website (www.taan.ca).

24. Kwanlin Dün First Nation website (www.kwalindun.com).

25. Yukon Hospital Corporation website (www.yukonhospitals.ca).

26. Child Development Centre website (www.cdcyukon.com).

27. BYTE website (http://yukonyouth.com).

28. Yukon Women's Transition Home website (http://yukontransitionhome.ca); Victoria Faulkner Women's Centre website (victoriafaulknerwomenscentre.blogspot.ca); Whitehorse Aboriginal Women's Circle website (www.wawc.ca).

29. Whitehorse Volunteer Bureau website (http://volunteeryukon.ca).

30. Bob Cameron, "Whitehorse Airport," Report for Whitehorse History Book Society, 2012.

31. Linda Johnson, *At the Heart of Gold: The Yukon Commissioner's Office, 1898–2010* (Whitehorse: Legislative Assembly of Yukon, 2012), 259-265.

32. *Wikipedia,* s.v. Audrey McLaughlin.

33. L'Association franco-yukonnaise, Jeanne Beaudoin biography, prepared for the Whitehorse History Book Society, April 2013.

34. *Whitehorse Star*, various issues, 1979–99.

35. Les McLaughlin, "Flo Whyard: A CKRW Yukon Nugget," on the Hougen Group of Companies website (see www.hougen-group.com/yukonhistory).

36. Bill Weigand, personal communication to Linda Johnson, May 2013.

37. Kathy Watson, personal communication to Linda Johnson, May 2013.

38. Ernie Bourassa, personal communication to Linda Johnson, May 2013.

39. Bev Buckway, personal communication to Linda Johnson, May 2013.

40. City of Whitehorse website (www.city.whitehorse.yk.ca).

EPILOGUE

1. John Firth, "Whitehorse Sports and Recreation," Report for Whitehorse History Book Society, 2012.

2. Michele Genest, "Whitehorse Arts and Culture," Report for the Whitehorse History Book Society, 2012.

3. Yukon College website (www.yukoncollege.yk.ca).

4. Genest, arts and culture manuscript.

5. Census 2010 report (see www.statcan.ca).

6. *Whitehorse Star*, various issues, 2000–12.

7. Council of Yukon First Nations website (www.cyfn.ca).

8. *Whitehorse Star*, various issues, October 2012.

PHOTOGRAPHIC CREDITS

The credits below match the order of the images as they appear on the pages indicated, reading from left to right, top to bottom.

p. ii: Alaska State Library P277-017-003; YA, James Y.C. Quong fonds, 2006/140 #1-5-1; YA, EJH (MRH), 2002/118 #253; YA, James Y.C. Quong fonds, 2006/140 #1-5-586; YA, James Y.C. Quong fonds, 1-5-743; detail from YA, John Scott fonds, 89/31 #10; Yukon International Storytelling Festival fonds; KDFN

p. x: KDFN, John Meikle photo

p. xii: YA, James Y.C. Quong fonds, 2006/140 #1-5-1

p. 2: Cameron Eckert

p. 3: KDFN

p. 4: William Ogilvie, William Ogilvie fonds, LAC 1974-442, C-074934

p. 5: Eric Leinberger

p. 6: MA

p. 7: KDFN, John Meikle photo

p. 8: Courtesy Jeff Bond, Yukon Geological Survey

p. 10: YG; Matrix Research Ltd.; YG; Matrix Research Ltd.

p. 12: BOTH: Cameron Eckert photo

p. 13: Ione Christensen coll.

p. 15: MA; MA; YG; KDFN

p. 17: YG

p. 18: YG

p. 20: Lerbekmo, J.F. , J.A. Westgate, D.G.W. Smith and G.H. Denton, 1975, "New Data on the Character and History of the White River Volcanic Eruption, Alaska," *Quaternary Studies,* edited by R.P. Suggate and M.M. Cresswell, p. 203-209. Royal Society of New Zealand. Wellington. As redrawn by Rob Ingram; Matrix Research Ltd.

p. 22: Ione Christensen coll.

p. 23: YG

p. 24: Alaska State Library P277-017-003

p. 28: Eric Leinberger

p. 33: Paul Kandik and François Mercier, Bancroft Library Map Collection G4370 1880 K3 Case XB

p. 36: YA, *Compilations,* 1900, sheet #3, opposite p. 303

p. 37: Alaska State Library P22-056

p. 38: George M. Dawson, LAC 1969-120NPC, PA-052792; George M. Dawson, LAC 1970-088, PA-052724

p. 39: William Ogilvie, William Ogilvie fonds, LAC 1946-072, C-074908

p. 41: YA 1897-067, Veazie Wilson, *Glimpses,* p. 18; p. 33

p. 45: YA 1897-067, Veazie Wilson, *Glimpses,* p. 29

p. 46: YA, EJH (MRH), 2002/118 #420

p. 48: YA, UW fonds, #1195

p. 49: YA, Dave Bohn coll. 83/102, #4

p. 50: YA, Larss & Duclos photographers, Jacqueline Greenbank coll. 89/12, #12; UW, PH Coll 373.5, UW 28675

p. 51: Eric Leinberger

p. 52: *Map-guide, Seattle to Dawson* (Humes, Lysons and Sallee, 1897)

p. 53: UW, PH Coll 274, Eric A. Hegg coll., Hegg 719A; E.J. Hamacher fonds, 85/75 #11

p. 54: YA, Eric Hegg fonds, #2583; #2695

p. 55: MMYH, #4114, H.C. Barley photo

p. 56: YA, Robert P. McLennan fonds, #6525

p. 57: YA, Emil Forrest fonds, 80/60 #6

p. 60: UW, PH Coll 519, Asahel Curtis Klondike-Alaska coll., Klondike 29087; UW, LAR216, La Roche 2035

p. 61: YA, H.C. Barley fonds, #5302

p. 62: YA, H.C. Barley fonds, #5320

p. 64: Canada Lands Survey Plan 8406; YA, H.C. Barley fonds, #5473

p. 65: YA, UW coll. #1334

p. 66: Dawson City Museum, 984.27.2.02

p. 67: YA, H.C. Barley fonds, #4666

p. 68: BOTH: Paul Cyr coll.

p. 69: YA, EJH (MRH), 2002/118 #759

p. 71: YA, EJH (MRH), 2002/118 #210

p. 72: YA, EJH (MRH), 2002/118 #91

p. 74: YA, EJH (MRH), 2002/118 #261

p. 75: YA, EJH (MRH), 2002/118 #231

p. 76: YA, Whitehorse Townsite, 1899-1901. GOV 1623, f. 2788

p. 77: YA, Anton Vogee fonds, #263

p. 79: YA, EJH (MRH), 2002/118 #45

p. 81: YA, EJH (MRH), 2002/118 #357; #366

p. 82: Glenbow Archives, NA-1663-23

p. 83: YA, H.C. Barley photo, MP-0000.2024.21 © McCord Museum; YA, EJH (MRH), 2002/118 #277; Provincial Archives of Alberta, B2097

p. 84: YA, EJH (MRH), 2002/118 #327

p. 85: YA, Helen Horback fonds, 2001/134 #44

p. 86: MMYH, 83/8 #11

p. 88: YA, EJH (MRH), 2002/118 #208

p. 89: UW, PH Coll 373.5, UW 3347, W.E. Priestly photo

p. 92: YA, EJH (MRH), 2002/118 #329

p. 95: YA, EJH (MRH), 2002/118 #807

p. 97: YA, Ernest Brown fonds, #865

p. 99: YA, EJH (MRH), 2002/118 #290

p. 100: YA, H.J. Woodside coll. #605; YA, EJH (MRH), 2002/118 #288

p. 101: MMYH, #5650

p. 103: YA, EJH (MRH), 2002/118 #257

p. 104: YA, EJH (MRH), 2002/118 #395; #1059; #363

p. 105: YA, Watson family fonds, 80/12 #5; YA, EJH (MRH), 2002/118 #287

p. 106: YA, EJH (MRH), 2002/118 #68; #265

p. 107: Roman Catholic Diocese of Whitehorse coll.; YA, EJH (MRH), 2002/118 #2193

p. 108: YA, EJH (MRH), 2002/118 #1067; #292

p. 110: YA, EJH (MRH), 2002/118 #253

p. 111: YA, EJH (MRH), 2002/118 #254; YA, William L. Drury fonds, 93/38 #1

p. 112: B.C. Archives, F-03352

p. 114: Judy Gingell coll.

p. 115: YA, E.J. Hamacher fonds, 78/29, #55

p. 116: YA, Harbottle family fonds, #6095

p. 117: YA, John Scott fonds, 89/31 #11

p. 118: YA, John Scott fonds, 89/31 #10

p. 121: YA, EJH (MRH), 2002/118 #397; #390

p. 122: YA, EJH (MRH), 2002/118 #268; #267

p. 124: YA, EJH (MRH), 2009/81 #923

p. 125: Mickey McCarthy photo; Lloyd Ryder photo

p. 126: YA, Rolf and Margaret Hougen fonds, 2009/81 #984

p. 127: YA, NAC coll. #398; Detail from YA, EJH (MRH), 2002/118 #22; #211

p. 129: Detail from YA, EJH (MRH), 2002/118 #649

p. 130: YA, Wilf and Dorothy Veysey fonds, 92/1R #80

p. 131: YA, Harbottle family fonds, #6159; YA, Laurie Todd fonds, #9016; YA, James Y.C. Quong fonds, 2006/140 #1-5-553

p. 132: YA, EJH (MRH), 2002/118 #1087; MMYH coll. #3864

p. 133: YA, EJH (MRH), 2002/118 #408

p. 134: Parks Canada, G.I. Cameron coll. #32

p. 136: MMYH coll. 83/08, #16

p. 137: Royal BC Museum, BC Archives E-00570

p. 139: YA, EJH (MRH), 2002/118 #7; #79

p. 140: YA, John Scott fonds, 89/31 #154; YA, EJH (MRH), 2002/118 #92

p. 141: YA, EJH (MRH), 2002/118 #897; James Y.C. Quong fonds, 2006/140, #1-5-14

p. 142: YA, James Y.C. Quong fonds, 2006/140, #1-5-20

p. 144: YA, EJH (MRH), 2002/118 #1112

p. 145: YA, EJH (MRH), 2002/118 #94

p. 146: Linda Johnson coll.; YA, Evelyn Brunlees fonds, 2001/139R, #14

p. 147: YA, Claude and Mary Tidd fonds, #7544; MMYH 1989.1.1.130

p. 148: YA, John Scott fonds, 89/31 #6

p. 149: YA, John Scott fonds, 89/31 #131

p. 150: YA, Rolf and Margaret Hougen fonds, 2008/81 #455

p. 151: MMYH 1989.1.201

p. 152: YA, Rolf and Marg Hougen fonds, 2009/81, #961; #494

p. 153: Gudrun Sparling coll.

p. 154: YA, Rolf and Margaret Hougen fonds, 82/346 #4156

p. 155: YA, H.C. Barley fonds, #5545

p. 156: YA, Rolf and Margaret Hougen fonds, 2009/81 #18

p. 157: YA, Ryder family fonds, 98/134, #23; YA, Finnie family fonds, 81/21 #38

p. 158: YA, Harry Pepper fonds, 89/59 #9

p. 160: YA, Robert Hays fonds, #5693

p. 161: YA, Robert Hays fonds, #5691; #5676

p. 162: YA, Finnie family fonds, 81/21, #444; YA, Lewis G. Billard fonds, 2000/49 #311

p. 165: YA, Florence Cust coll., 84/64 #36

p. 166: YA, Robert Hays fonds, #5689

p. 167: YA, Teresa Chanatry fonds, 99/68, #153; #69

p. 168: YA, Finnie family fonds, 81/21 #435; #456; YA, William Pathman fonds, 95/63 #56

p. 171: YA, Teresa Chanatry fonds, 99/68, #2

p. 172: YA, W. Al Turner coll. 87/102 #17; YA, W.C. Cameron fonds, 93/77 #83; YA, Paul Vergon coll. 82/18 #5

p. 173: YA, Finnie family fonds, 81/21 #449

p. 174: YA, Frank and Jeanne Harbottle fonds, #6203; YA, Teresa Chanatry fonds, 99/68, #9

p. 175: YA, Cliff Schroeder fonds, 93/1 #22; #12

p. 177: YA, Harry Pepper fonds, 89/59 #29; #40

p. 179: YA, Jim Wake fonds, 89/73 #76

p. 180: YA, Cliff Schroeder fonds, 93/1 #24

p. 181: James Y.C. Quong fonds, 2006/140 #1-11-302

p. 182: YA, Rolf and Margaret Hougen fonds, 82-346 #438; YA, James Y.C. Quong fonds, 2006/140 #1-5-462; YA, Rolf and Margaret Hougen fonds, 2010/91 #434; Ione Christensen coll.

p. 183: YA, Claude and Mary Tidd fonds, #8274

p. 185: YA, Finnie family fonds, 81/21 #37; G.I. Cameron coll.

p. 186: YA, Maggie's Museum 82/331 #44

p. 187: YA, Robert Ward fonds, #8767

p. 188: Quong family coll.; YA, James Y.C. Quong fonds, 2006/140 #2-5-11

p. 189: YA, John Scott fonds, 89/31 #23

p. 190: YA, James Y.C. Quong fonds, 1-5-743

p. 193: YA, James Y.C. Quong fonds, 1-5-342

p. 194: YA, WS fonds, 82/563 f.166 #19

p. 195: YA, Sybil Milligan fonds, 99/103 #42; #78

p. 196: YA, Rolf and Margaret Hougen fonds, 2009-81-282

p. 197: YA, James Y.C. Quong fonds, 1-5-581

p. 199: YA, James Y.C. Quong fonds, 1-11-467; 1-11-317; 1-5-123

p. 200: YA, James Y.C. Quong fonds, 1-11-364; YA, Rolf and Margaret Hougen fonds, 2010-91 #322

p. 201: Anna Hercz, "Residential Land Use Planning and Housing in Whitehorse, Yukon Territory" (PhD thesis, McGill University, 1985)

p. 202: Ione Christensen coll.; YA, Rolf and Margaret Hougen fonds, 82-346 #169; #467

p. 203: YA, Rolf and Margaret Hougen fonds, 82-346 #67

p. 204: YA, Rolf and Margaret Hougen fonds, 82-346#40

p. 206: YA, Rolf and Margaret Hougen fonds, 2009-81 #727

p. 208: YA, Rolf and Margaret Hougen fonds, 82-346 #93

p. 209: YA, Rolf and Margaret Hougen fonds, 82-346 #115

p. 210: YA, James Y.C. Quong fonds, 2-3-19

p. 211: YA, Rolf and Margaret Hougen fonds, 2009-81 #1008

p. 212: YA, WS fonds, 82/563 f.164 #7

p. 214: YA, James Y.C. Quong fonds, 1-11-403

p. 215: Medical Services Branch, LAC 1970-088 PA-052724

p. 217: YA, Rolf and Margaret Hougen fonds, 82-346 #361

p. 218: YA, James Y.C. Quong fonds, 2-3-24; 1-5-334; 2006/140, 3-7-323; YA, WS fonds, 82/563 f.166, #69

p. 220: YA, James Y.C. Quong fonds, 1-11-319; 3-5-47; YA, Rolf and Margaret Hougen fonds, 2010-91 #510; YA, James Y.C. Quong fonds, 2006/140 1-11-370

p. 221: YA, James Y.C. Quong fonds, 2006/140, 1-11-329

p. 222: YA, William Preston fonds, 85/78 #77; YA, Harrington fonds, 79/27 #105; YA, WS, 82/257, CS 696, W43-10

p. 223: BOTH: Robert Cameron coll.

p. 225: YA, WS fonds, 82/563 f.103 #27

p. 266: Ione Christensen coll.

p. 227: YA, WS fonds, 82/563 f.96 #85

p. 228: Richard Harrington fonds, 79/27 #370

p. 229: YA, Rolf and Margaret Hougen fonds, 2009-81 #727

p. 231: Ione Christensen coll.

p. 234: YA, Rolf and Margaret Hougen fonds, 2009-81 #541

p. 235: YA, Bob Cameron fonds, 2010/110 #282

p. 236: YA, James Y.C. Quong fonds, 3-7-150

p. 239: YA, WS fonds, 82/563 f.165, #36

p. 240: YA, WS fonds, 82/527, CS 224 H-37 item 9; CS 510 S-45 item 3; 82/563 f.165, #44

p. 242: YA, Rolf and Margaret Hougen fonds, 2009/81 #771

p. 243: Yukon College Archives Photo coll. item 008; YA, WS fonds, 82/527, CS 676 V-15 item 12

p. 245: YA, WS fonds, 82/563 f.110, #144; YA, Rolf and Margaret Hougen fonds, 2010/91 #212

p. 246: YA, WS fonds, 82/563 f.161 #12

p. 247: YA, WS fonds, 82/527, CS 303 G-18 item 3

p. 248: Ellis 2012-08-03

p. 249: 1981 FIS World Cup souvenir book, John Firth photo

p. 250: Firth family photo

p. 251: YA, Rolf and Margaret Hougen fonds, 2010/91 #128

p. 252: WS

p. 253: Lionel Stokes photo

p. 254: Lyle Murdoch photo

p. 256: WS, Frostbite 1982-1

p. 257: Peter Long photo

p. 259: YA, WS fonds, 82/527, CS 257 H-61 item 5

p. 261: YA, WS fonds, 82/563 f.167, #64

p. 263: YA, Rolf Hougen coll., 1-066

p. 264: YG; MA

p. 267: R.B. Cameron coll.; R.B. Cameron coll., Pat Callison photo

p. 269: YA, YG PA, 90/51, file 11, #508; #514

p. 270: City of Whitehorse, MiniBus001

p. 271: KDFN

p. 272: Yukon Native Language Centre, WS, Jan. 7, 1963

p. 274: YA, Richard Harrington fonds, 79/27 #277

p. 275: Rolf Hougen coll.

p. 277: YA, WS fonds, 82/563 f.111, #7

p. 278: YA, WS fonds, 82/527, CS 712 W-73 item 11

p. 279: YA, WS fonds 82/527, CS 261 h-63 item 3; YA, Rolf and Margaret Hougen fonds, 2009/81 #30

p. 280: YA, WS fonds 2009/81 #938; YA, YG PA, file #10, #361

p. 281: YA, CHP Christensen coll.

p. 282: Yukon International Storytelling Festival fonds

p. 285: Eric Leinberger

p. 286: City of Whitehorse Planning Dept.; KDFN

p. 288: YG PA I13-02-23dp; YG Env Bear

p. 290: YG PA G1-19-07-4dp

p. 292: YG; YG; YG file 2.3.2 "Yukon Artists," Mike Rice photo

p. 293: YG

p. 294: Mike Rice photo, personal coll. of Arlin McFarlane

p. 295: Poster by Guiniveve Lalena, coll. of Yukon Film Society

p. 297: WS

p. 298: Association franco-yukonnaise

p. 299: Yukon Native Language Centre

p. 300: Yukon College Archives

p. 302: Government of Canada

p. 303: Ta'an Kwächän; KDFN

p. 305: YG PA 110-5-08-36dp

p. 306: WS Food Bank Dec. 2010, 9056

p. 308: Robert Cameron coll.; WS

p. 309: YG

p. 310: YG PA G-1-15-03-47dp

p. 311: Bruce Barrett photo

p. 313: YA, CHP, Judy Gingell personal coll.

p. 314: Murray Mosher image 89K52

p. 315: Association franco-yukonnaise

p. 316: WS

p. 317: WS

p. 318: Weigand family coll.

p. 319: Aasman Design

p. 321: WS

p. 322: City of Whitehorse

p. 323: Christian Cunanan

p. 324: Louis Schilder

p. 326: Robin Armour; YG

p. 328: YG; Christian Cunanan

p. 329: Peter Long photo

p. 330: Peter Long photo; YG

p. 331: Heather Jones

p. 333: YG

SELECTED BIBLIOGRAPHY

Almstrom, Marjorie. *A Century of Schooling: Education of the Yukon, 1861–1961*. Whitehorse: Marjorie Almstrom, 1990.

Association franco-yukonnaise. *Empreinte: la présence francophone au Yukon (1825–1950)*. Whitehorse: Association franco-yukonnaise, 1997.

Baskine, Gertrude. *Hitchhiking the Alaska Highway*. Toronto: Macmillan Canada, 1944.

Bennett, Gordon. *Yukon Transportation: A History*. Ottawa: Minister of Supply and Services Canada, 1978.

Berton, Pierre. *Klondike: The Last Great Gold Rush, 1896–1899*. Toronto: McClelland & Stewart, 1972.

Cameron, R.B. *Yukon Wings*. Calgary: Frontenac House, 2012.

Coates, Kenneth, ed. *The Alaska Highway: Papers of the 40th Anniversary Symposium*. Vancouver: UBC Press, 1985.

Coates, Ken, and Bill Morrison. *The Sinking of the Princess Sophia: Taking the North Down with Her*. Toronto: Oxford University Press, 1990.

Cruikshank, Julie. *Reading Voices: Dän Dhá Ts'edenintth'é—Oral and Written Interpretations of the Yukon's Past*. Vancouver: Douglas & McIntyre, 1991.

Cruikshank, Julie, in collaboration with Angela Sidney, Kitty Smith and Annie Ned. *Life Lived Like a Story*. Vancouver: UBC Press, 1990.

Dawson, George M. *Report on an Exploration in the Yukon District, N.W.T. and Adjacent Northern Portion of British Columbia, 1887*. Whitehorse: Yukon Historical and Museums Association, 1987. First published 1889 by William Foster Brown.

Dobrowolsky, Helene. *The Hougen Family in the Yukon, a Pictorial History: 1906–2011*. Whitehorse: Hougen Family, 2012.

———. *Law of the Yukon*. Whitehorse: Lost Moose Publishing, 1996.

———. "Macaulay and Hepburn Tramways," in *Society for Industrial Archaeology Study Tour of the Yukon and Alaska*. Prepared for Parks Canada, 1990.

Dobrowolsky, Helene, and Rob Ingram. *Edge of the River, Heart of the City*. Whitehorse: Lost Moose Publishing, 1994.

———. *A History of the Whitehorse Copper Belt*. Report prepared for the MacBride Museum and Indian and Northern Affairs Canada, 1993.

———. *Listen to the Stories: A Pictorial History of the Kwanlin Dün, Our Land and People*. Whitehorse: Kwanlin Dün First Nation, 2013.

———. *A Structural History of the White Pass and Yukon Railway Depot, Whitehorse, and Associated Structures*. Report prepared for the Government of Yukon Heritage Branch, 1998.

Emmons, George Thornton. *The Tlingit Indians*. Edited with additions by Frederica De Laguna. Vancouver: Douglas & McIntyre, 1991.

Firth, John. *Yukon Quest: The 1,000-Mile Dog Sled Race through the Yukon and Alaska*. Whitehorse: Lost Moose Publishing, 1998.

Green, Dianne. *In Direct Touch with the Wide World*. Whitehorse: Northwestel, 1992.

Hammer, T.J., and Greg Hare. *From Trail to Tramway: The Archaeology of Canyon City*. Prepared for the Government of Yukon and Kwanlin Dün First Nation, with assistance from Yukon Energy Corporation, 1999.

Herry, Yann. *La francophonie: Une richesse nordique*. Whitehorse: L'Association franco-yukonnaise, 2004.

Johnson, Linda. *At the Heart of Gold: The Yukon Commissioner's Office, 1898–2010*. Whitehorse: Legislative Assembly of Yukon, 2012.

———. *The Kandik Map*. Fairbanks: University of Alaska Press, 2009.

———. *Ta'an Kwäch'än Cultural History Project*. Whitehorse: Ta'an Kwäch'än Council, 1989.

———. *With the People Who Live Here: A History of the Yukon Legislature, 1909–1961*. Whitehorse: Legislative Assembly of Yukon, 2009.

Lotz, Jim. *The Squatters of Whitehorse, Yukon Territory*. Ottawa: Department of Northern Affairs and National Resources, 1961.

MacBride, W.D. *All My Rivers Flowed West*. Whitehorse: Beringian Books, 1991.

McCandless, Robert. *Yukon Wildlife: A Social History*. Edmonton: University of Alberta Press, 1985.

McClellan, Catharine. *My Old People Say: An Ethnographic Survey of Southern Yukon Territory*, vols. 1 and 2. Ottawa: Canadian Museum of Civilization, 2001. First published 1975 by National Museum of Man.

———. *Part of the Land, Part of the Water*. Vancouver: Douglas & McIntyre, 1987.

Minter, Roy. *The White Pass: Gateway to the Klondike*. Toronto: McClelland & Stewart, 1987.

Robb, Jim. *The Colourful Five Per Cent*, vol. 1, no. 1. Whitehorse: Touchstone Studios and The Colourful Five Per Cent Company, 1984.

Robb, Jim, and Julie Cruikshank. *Their Own Yukon*. Whitehorse: Yukon Indian Cultural Education Society and Yukon Native Brotherhood, 1975.

Sidney, Angela. *Haa Shagóon: Our Family History*. Whitehorse: Yukon Native Language Centre, 1983.

Steele, Samuel B. *Forty Years in Canada*. Winnipeg: Russell Lang, 1915.

Twist, Susan. *A Guide to Who Lies Beneath Whitehorse Cemeteries*. Whitehorse: Old Log Church Museum, ca. 2000.

Whitehorse Star. Various issues, 1900–2012.

Wright, Allen A. *Prelude to Bonanza: The Discovery and Exploration of the Yukon*. Sidney, B.C.: Gray's, 1976.

Yukon Historical and Museums Association. *Whitehorse Heritage Buildings*. Whitehorse: Yukon Historical and Museums Association, 1983.

———. *The Kohklux Map*. Whitehorse: Yukon Historical and Museums Association, 1995.

The following reports, commissioned by the Whitehorse History Book Society in 2012, were essential to this book.

Bob Cameron, "Whitehorse Airport."

John Firth, "Whitehorse Sports and Recreation."

Michele Genest, "Whitehorse Arts and Culture."

Ty Heffner, "Whitehorse Area Archaeology and Life at Géis Tóo'e' and Tàa'an Män."

Rob Ingram, "Whitehorse Buildings and Infrastructure."

Marilyn Jensen and Ingrid Johnson, "Yukon First Nations People, Culture and History."

DONORS, PATRONS AND SPONSORS

PERSONAL DONORS

Andrea Bailey

Bev Buckway

Arthur K. Christensen

The Hon. Ione J. Christensen, CM

Ron and Kip Veale

CORPORATE DONORS

Air North, Yukon's Airline

Association franco-yukonnaise

Austring, Fendrick &
    Fairman—Lawyers

Hougen's Ltd., Marg and
    Rolf Hougen, OC

Kobayashi + Zedda Architects

Dr. Sally MacDonald

Macdonald & Company
    Lawyers

Mackay LLP

Northern Vision
    Development LP

Pelly Construction Ltd.

Scotiabank, Whitehorse

T. A. Firth & Son Insurance Ltd.

Total North

Whitehorse Motors Ltd.

Whitehorse Star

Yukon Chamber of Mines

GRANTS RECEIVED

City of Whitehorse, Heritage
    Reserve Fund

Government of Yukon,
    Department of Economic
    Development, Minister
    Currie Dixon, Community
    Development Fund

Government of Yukon,
    Department of Tourism
    and Culture, Minister Mike
    Nixon, Yukon Historic
    Resources Fund

The Yukon Foundation
    Contributions from the
    following funds: Heritage
    North, Hougen Family,
    Klondike Defence Force,
    Roy Minter, Northern Writers
    Circle, and John and
    Doris Stenbraten

WHITEHORSE HISTORY BOOK SOCIETY PATRONS

ALX Exploration Services

Dan Anton

David Skinner Ashley

Austring, Fendrick &
    Fairman—Lawyers

Tom, Tammy and Paul Banks

Jeremy Baumbach and
    Yvette Lepage

Colin Beairsto

Jean and Patricia Besier

Larry J. Bidlake

Bill and Helen Bowie

Gary and Susan Boyd

R. Hugh Bradley (in memoriam)

Michael and Alexis Brandt

Bernice Broder

Dianne A. Bruce

Gwen Byram

Karen Byram

Keith Byram

Jennifer Byram

Lori Byram

Faye Cable

In memory of G.I. and
    Martha Cameron

Kirk Cameron and Sons,
    Michael, Andrew and
    Mackenzie

N. Campbell and J. Walsh

Cardinal Contracting Ltd.

Bruce Chambers

Victor A. (Chappie) and
    Frances D. Chapman

Maria Chaput, Senator

Allan and Diane Chisholm

Paul C. Christensen and
    Michelle Christensen-Toews

Harrison Cameron
    Christensen-Brown

Minnie and James Clark

Donna Clayson (née Storing)

Bonar and Bess Cooley,
    Teslin, Y.T.

Shanon Cooper

Lois Craig

Curtis family

Frances Curtis
Judy and Paul Dabbs
Marjorie Derry
Helene Dobrowolsky, Rob
    Ingram and Joelle Ingram
Larry and Christine Doke
Peggy Duncan
Yvonne P. Ellingson
Greg and Mary Fekete
Tony and Hazel Fekete
Debra Fendrick
Reub and Rena Fendrick
Helen Fitzsimmons
Missy Follwell
Four Seasons Bed & Breakfast
    (Gregory Bryce)
Don and Muriel Frizzell
Michael and Kathy Gates
Tony Gonda
Doug Graham
W.C. Gryba
Keith Halliday and Stacy Lewis
Ellen Harris
J. Douglas Harris and
    Claire Tixhon-Harris
Verna (Taylor) Hart
Famille Herry-Saint Onge
Ronald and Helen Holway
Steven and Meg Horn
Jan Horton
Lorraine Hoyt
Senator Elizabeth Hubley
Erin and Lea Jacobs
Robert and Angela Jacobs
Niels and Laurie Jacobsen

Wanita Johnson
Donna-Lynne Jones
Millie Jones
Ken Kapty, CA
Diane (Bidlake) and Pat King
Lee Kirkpatrick and Jim Hajash
Tim and Jan Koepke
Lee and Arlene Kubica
Sally MacDonald
Simon Mason-Wood and
    Charly Kelly
Aileen McCorkell
Gordon and Ruth McIntyre
Norman McIntyre and
    Rhonda Holway-McIntyre
Tom and Mary Mickey
Bill Munro
David Neufeld and Joy Waters
Rick and Maureen Nielsen
Geert Jacobus Nijstad
Harry T. Nixon and
    Hazel A.M. Nixon
Jackie Pierce
Ranj and Delilah Pillai
Porsild-Davignon Family
Elizabeth (Lee) Pugh
Arla and Corky Repka
Bill Richardson
Ian and Silvia Robertson
Meredith and Elliot Rodger
C. Phyllis Rogers

Sandor's Clothing Ltd.
Paul, Kerri, Cassel and
    Hannah Scholz
Rhea and Roy Slade
Fred and Mary Lou Smith
Dorothy Sorensen
Irene Sova
Karen Sprenger
Ralph Sprenger
In memory of Doris Stenbraten
    (née McMurphy)
Jan Stick
Dave Stockdale
K.A. Enid Tait
Kim Tanner
In memory of C.D. (Charlie)
    and Betty Taylor
Joe Trerice
Richard Trimble and Ella
    LeGresley
Underhill Geomatics Ltd.
M.P. Velišček
Janet and Douglas Watson
Art Webster
William J. Weigand and
    Jerrine R. Weigand
White Pass & Yukon Route
    Railroad
In memory of Flo Whyard
Ron and Pat Wilson
Douglas Wing
Whitehorse Star
Teresa Wylie
Yukon College
Gordon Zalmers

CONTRIBUTING AUTHOR BIOGRAPHIES

BOB CAMERON—pilot, engineer and former operations manager of Trans North Turbo Air—recently published *Yukon Wings,* the definitive history of Yukon aviation. Cameron is a lifelong aficionado of the Yukon's early aircraft and flying personalities, and no one is more qualified to talk about the history of Whitehorse Airport and the various flying services.

JOHN FIRTH is the award-winning author of four books on Yukon history and people who use sport to change the world. A former sports reporter, he makes an eloquent case for sport as a community builder.

MICHELE GENEST has been involved in the Whitehorse cultural scene for many years, as a writer, performer, volunteer, arts administrator with the federal government and, most recently, a food columnist for *Yukon, North of Ordinary* magazine and author of *The Boreal Gourmet.* She drew on these experiences to write about our many innovative and successful cultural festivals.

TY HEFFNER has sixteen years of experience conducting archaeological impact assessments, inventory studies and research excavation projects throughout western Canada. Prior to co-founding Matrix Research, Ty worked for archaeological consulting firms and for government agencies including Yukon Heritage and Parks Canada. He drew upon his Yukon experience to help tell the story of early peoples in the southern Yukon.

ROB INGRAM has been researching, planning and interpreting Yukon's historic sites for over thirty years. He drew on his fascination and expertise with built heritage to trace the changing "City's Footprint." He also did double duty as our image wrangler and took on the challenging task of charting and organizing literally thousands of photos.

MARILYN JENSEN (YADULTIN) is Inland Tlingit of the Tagish Dakla'weidi Clan (Killerwhale Crest), from the Carcross/Tagish First Nation, and was raised in Whitehorse. She holds an MA in indigenous governance from the University of Victoria. She teaches First Nations governance courses at Yukon College. Marilyn is a founding member and leader of the Dakhká Khwáan Dancers group, which is revitalizing Inland Tlingit dance and drumming traditions.

INGRID JOHNSON is an Inland Tlingit woman born and raised in Teslin, Yukon. She attended the University of British Columbia, obtaining an MA in anthropology. Her research and teaching specialties include northern beadwork and clothing design, Yukon land claims and self government, education and community development.

INDEX

ice hockey, 96, *97,* 130, *131,* 171, 204–205, 248, 251
Ice Lake Road, 178
ice rink, 239
Iditarod, 297
Imaginary Force, *292, 294*
immigration, 327–328
Imperial Oil, 216
Imperial Order of the Daughters of the Empire, 198
incorporation, 97, 207–210, 331
Ind-A-Yanek (guide), 35–37
Indian Act, 258
Indian Affairs, *212*
Indian Affairs and Northern Development, 270
Indian Agent, 110, 126, 196–197
Indian Co-op store, 246
Indian Craft Store, 247, *248*
Indian Status, 189, 195, 227, 243, 258
Indigenous peoples. *see* aboriginal peoples; First Nations; *specific Nations and peoples*
infrastructure, 191, 239, 318, 322–323
Inland Tlingit peoples, 20, 146
Inuvik, Northwest Territories, 224
Irvine, Polly, 44
Irwin, Betty, *323*
Iseag (Aishihik) peoples, 90

Jackson, Marge, *299*
Jackson McDonnell Hall, 95
Jacobs, Ed, 229, 238, 278–279, *279*
Jacquot family, 216
James, Norman, *245*
James, Ron, 294
Janssen, Manfred, 256, *292*
Japanese nationals, 166
Jeckell, George, 192, 198, 208
Jeffries, Bill, 203
Jensen, Walter, 141
Jickling, Peter, 295
Jim, Annie (Łande), *45,* 70, 227
Jim, Ginnie, 189
Jim, Slim, 189, 313
Jim Light Arena, *202, 252,* 253, 296, 304
Joe, Dave, 260, 301
Joe, John, 62
Joe, Julia, *18*
Joe Joe Road House, *121*
Johns, Angela, 229, 230
Johns, Johnny, 129, 213, 216, 230
Johnson, Charles H., 155
Johnson, Katie, 326

Johnson's Crossing, *188*
Jones, Kathleen, *303*
Juneau, Alaska, 124–125

Káa Goox (Dawson Charlie), 48
Kaax'achgóok song, 300
Kàdùkikh (Kitty Smith), 2, 113–114, *114,* 177, 227, 313
Kandik, Paul, *33,* 34
Kandik map, *33,* 34
Kane, Lily, 177
Karr, Hank, 247
Kashxóot. *see* Jim Boss (Kashxóot)
Kaushee's Place, 306
Keenleyside, Hugh, 208
Keish "Skookum Jim." *see* Skookum Jim (Keish)
Keith, Ronald, 149
Kenny's Drive-In, 230
Keno vessel, *141,* 143, 189, *226,* 226–227
Keno mines, 262
Keobke, Bucky, 203
Kershaw, Annie, 117
King, Ross, 204
Kishwoot Hall, 258
Kiwanis Club, 184
Klondike: gold rush, 47–48, 69, 116, 176, 216; mining, 134, 148
Klondike Airways, 123, 124, 152
"Klondike Days," 246
Klondike Defence Force, 246
Klondike Helicopters, 266, *267*
Klondike Highway, 224, 289, 312
Klondike Indian Movement, 258
Klondike Institute of Art and Culture, 295
Klondike Nugget newspaper, 78
Klondike Pavilion (Expo 67), 246
Klondike vessel, 135, 143
Klondike vessel (second), *xii, 142,* 143, 217, *236,* 246, 279, 280
Klondike Voyageurs Club, 246
Klondyke Cafe, 184
Kloosulchuk (Minto) peoples, 90
Kluane country, 154
Kluane gold rush, 91, 116
Kluane vessel, 111
Kluchoo (Kloo Lake) peoples, 90
Klukshoo (Klukshu) peoples, 90
Klukwan Coastal Tlingit peoples, 146
Kodak picnic, *133*
Kohklux (Chilkat Chief). *see also* Shotridge: 29, 30
The Kohklux Map, 291
Kokrine, Gregory, *24*
Korean Air, *308*
Krangle, Wynne, 291
Kunuk, Zacharias, 295

Kusawa Park, 303
Kwädä dá ghàlan, 2, 8–12
Kwanlin Canyon. *see* Miles Canyon (Kwanlin)
Kwanlin Dün First Nation (KDFN): Cultural Centre, 327, 330, *330;* Filipino Christmas, *328;* Final Agreement, 2005, *303;* Gingell, Judy, 293; land claims, 301, 302–304, 325; in McIntyre subdivision, 287; Smith, Billy, 313; Smith, Irene MacIntosh, *292;* Smith, Johnnie, 313–314

Laberge, Michel, 32
Ladéroute, François-Xavier, 68
Ladue, Joseph, *24,* 32, 45
Lake Bennett, 52, 63
Lake Kluktassi, *36*
Lake Laberge: Tàa'an Män peoples, 44
Lake Laberge peoples. *see* Ta'an Kwäch'än peoples (Lake Laberge)
Lake Laberge (Tàa'an Män): aboriginal names, 32; Adamson, Irene, 44; archaeological findings, 8, *18;* boats, *50;* cabin rentals, 175–176; footpaths, 12; forming of, 6; map, *36, 51;* Marsh Lake Dam, 144; Mundessa, 19–20, 44, *45,* 70, 227; rendition, *8;* Slim, Frank, 189; Tàa'an män peoples, 13, 19–20; winter camp, 13
Lake Marsh (Marsh Lake, M'Clintock River) peoples, 90
Lake McIntyre, 6
Lake M'Clintock, 6, *8*
Lambert Street School, *108,* 108–109, 198, 211, 320
land claims, 71, 270, 271, 292, 301–304, 325, 330
Łande (Annie Jim), *45,* 70, 227
land reserves, 128, 239
land survey, 63–65, *64,* 77, 169
Langholtz, Frederick and Frances, 129
Langston, Sheila, 294
languages. *see also* linguistics: Athapaskan, 20–21; Chinook trade, 44; English, 32; francophone, 297–298, 328; Northern Tutchone, 20; Southern Tutchone, 2, 9, 12, 20–21, 189, 299; Tagalog, 328; Tagish, 39–42; training, 243
Larose, Al, *46*

Larose brothers, 93
laundry, 156, 183, 184
Laurier, Wilfrid, 59, 75–76
L'Aurore Boreale newspaper, 299, 315
Law of the Yukon (Dobrowolsky), 291
Layton, Jack, 314
Lebarge, Billy, 44–45, 88, *146,* 146–147
Lebarge, Jenny, *146,* 146–147
Lee, Harold and Lydia, 196
Lefebvre, Father Camille, 107–108
LePage, Aimé "Happy," 290
LePage Park, 70, 290, 309, *311*
LeRoyer, J.-A., 123
Lesage, Jean, 209
Lewes Marsh Habitat Protection Area, 303
Liberal Party of Canada, 238, 284, 289
library, 198, 239, 247, 259, 295, 330
Light, Jim, *240*
Lime Peak, 3
lingonberry *(Vaccinium vitis-idaea),* 15
linguistics, 20–21, 39, 189
Lions Pool, 284
liquor store, *173, 174, 183,* 184
literacy, 243
Livingstone, Hana, 148
Livingstone Creek, 92–93
Livingstone Trail Environmental Control Facility, 311
Lockheed airplane, *125*
Logan subdivision, 287, 288
log skyscrapers, 181, *181, 182*
Long, Peter, 291
Longest Days Festival, *328*
Loon vessel, 142, 170, 226
Lord Minto (Elliot-Murray-Kynynmound), 75
l'Ordre des francophones d'Amérique, 315
Lortie, Ernest and Doris, *209*
Lost Moose Publishing, 291
Lost Whole Moose Catalogue, 291
Lot 19, 242, 278
Lot 226 (Whitehorse Indian Reserve No. 8), 126–128, 213
Louis, Joe, 169
Loutchan, Joe, 247
Low, Doug Sr., 229
Low, Georgianna, 229–230
Lowe, Robert, 94, 97, 100–101, 123, *147,* 147–148
Lowe Street, 148
Lucier, Paul, 238, 239, *280,* 280–281, 284